펼쳐 보면 느껴집니다

단 한 줄도 배움의 공백이 생기지 않도록
문장 한 줄마다 20년이 넘는
해커스의 영어교육 노하우를 담았음을

덮고 나면 확신합니다

수많은 선생님의 목소리와
정확한 출제 데이터 분석으로 꽉 찬
교재 한 권이면 충분함을

해커스북 중·고등
HackersBook.com

WHY
HACKERS
GRAMMAR SMART?

Completely master English grammar

누구나 쉽게
이해할 수 있는

간결한 문법 설명

실생활에서 그대로
사용할 수 있는

유용한 표현과 예문

Smart Check → Practice →
Writing Exercise →
Chapter Test로 이어지는

단계별 문제 풀이

HACKERS
Grammar Smart

Starter

HACKERS
Grammar Smart

Level 1

HACKERS
Grammar Smart

Level 2

HACKERS
Grammar Smart

Level 3

Effectively prepare for middle school English exams

학교 시험 기출경향을
완벽 반영한 문제로

서술형 포함 내신 완벽 대비

풍부한 문제의 Workbook과
다양한 부가 학습 자료로

학습효과 Up Up!

Hackers Grammar Smart 시리즈를 검토해주신 선생님들

경기

강무정	광교EIE고려대학교어학원
강민정	김진성의 열정어학원
김민성	빨리강해지는학원
윤혜영	이루다영어수학학원
이창석	정현영어학원
이창헌	더블원영어학원
정필두	시흥배곧 정상어학원
조은혜	이든영수학원

최희정	SJ클쌤영어
탁은영	EiE고려대학교어학원 태전퍼스트캠퍼스
한지수	위드유어학원
홍영숙	솔로몬학원
황정민	한수위학원

부산

배미경	삼정아카데미학원
이미영	수영학원

서울

신봉철	강북세일학원
양세희	양세희수능영어학원
이현아	이은재어학원
채가희	대성세그루학원
최세아	씨앤씨학원

인천

송인택	변화와도전학원

해커스 어학연구소 자문위원단 3기

강원

박정선	잉글리쉬클럽
최현주	최샘영어

경기

강민정	김진성열정어학원
강상훈	평촌RTS학원
강지인	강지인영어학원
곽은영	나디아잉글리쉬어학원
권пер미	A&T+ 영어
김미아	김쌤영어학원
김설화	업라이트잉글리쉬
김성재	스윗스터디학원
김세훈	모두의학원
김수아	더스터디(The STUDY)
김영아	백송고등학교
김유경	벨트어학원
김유경	포시즌스어학원
김유동	이스턴영어학원
김지숙	위디벨럽학원
김지현	이지프레임영어학원
김해빈	해빛영어학원
김현지	지앤비영어학원
박가영	한민고등학교
박영서	스윗스터디학원
박은별	더킹영수학원
박재홍	록키어학원
성승민	SDH어학원 불당캠퍼스
신소연	Ashley English
오귀연	루나영어학원
유신애	에듀포커스학원
윤소정	ILP이화어학원
이동진	이룸학원
이상미	버밍엄영어교습소
이연경	명품M비욘드수학영어학원
이은수	광주세종학원
이지혜	리케이온
이진희	이엠원영수학원
이충기	영어나무
이효명	갈매리드앤톡영어독서학원
임한글	Apsun앞선영어학원
장광명	엠케이영어학원
전상호	평촌이지어학원
전성훈	훈선생영어학원
정선영	코어플러스영어학원
정준	고양외국어고등학교
조연아	카이트학원
채기림	고려대학교EIE영어학원
최지영	다른영어학원
최한나	석사영수전문
최희정	SJ클쌤영어학원
현지환	모두의학원
홍태경	공감국어영어전문학원

경남

강다원	더(the)오르다영어학원
라승희	아이작잉글리쉬
박주언	유니크학원
배송현	두잇영어교습소
안윤서	어썸영어학원
임진희	어썸영어학원

경북

권현민	삼성영어석적우방교실
김으뜸	EIE영어학원 옥계캠퍼스
배세왕	비케이영수전문고등관학원
유영선	아이비티어학원

광주

김유희	김유희영어학원
서희연	SDL영어수학학원
송수일	아이리드영어학원
오진우	SLT어학원수학원
정영철	정영철영어전문학원
최경옥	봉선중학교

대구

권익재	제이슨영어
김명일	독학인학원
김보곤	베스트영어
김연정	달서고등학교
김혜란	김혜란영어학원
문애주	프렌즈입시학원
박정근	공부의힘pnk학원
박희숙	열공열강영어수학학원
신동기	신통외국어학원
위영선	위영선영어학원
윤창원	공터영어학원 상인센터
이승현	학문당입시학원
이주현	이주현영어학원
이헌욱	이헌욱영어학원
장준현	장쌤독해종결영어학원
주현아	민쌤영어학원
최윤정	최강영어학원

대전

곽선영	위드유학원
김지운	더포스둔산학원
박미현	라시움영어대동학원
박세리	EM101학원

부산

김건희	레지나잉글리쉬 영어학원
김미나	위드중고등영어학원
박수진	정모클영어국어학원
박수진	지니잉글리쉬
박인숙	리더스영어전문학원
옥지윤	더센텀영어학원
윤진희	위니드영어전문교습소
이종혁	진수학원
정혜인	엠티엔영어학원
조정래	알파카의영어농장
주태양	솔라영어학원

서울

Erica Sull	하버드브레인영어학원
Jung Nick	이은재어학원
강고은	케이앤학원
강신아	교우학원
공현미	이은재어학원
권영진	경동고등학교
김나영	프라임클래스영어학원
김달수	대일외국어고등학교
김대니	채움학원
김문영	창문여자고등학교
김상백	강북세일학원
김연희	이은재어학원
김정은	강북뉴스터디학원
김혜경	대동세무고등학교
남혜원	함영원입시전문학원
노시은	케이앤학원
박선정	강북세일학원
박수진	이은재어학원
박지수	이플러스영수학원
서승희	함영원입시전문학원
신지웅	강북세일학원
양세희	양세희수능영어학원
우정용	제임스영어앤드학원
이박원	이박원어학원
이승혜	스텔라영어
이정욱	이은재어학원
이지연	중계케이트영어학원
임예찬	학습컨설턴트
장지희	고려대학교사범대학부속고등학교
정미라	미라정영어학원
조민규	조민규영어
채가희	대성세그루영수학원
허민	이은재어학원

울산

김기태	그라티아어학원
이민주	로이아카데미
홍영민	더이안영어전문학원

인천

강재민	스터디위드제이쌤
고현순	정상학원
권효진	Genie's English
김솔	전문과외
김정아	밀턴영어학원
서상천	최정서학원
이윤주	트리플원
최예화	영웅아카데미

전남

강희진	강희진영어학원
김두환	해남맨체스터영수학원
송승연	송승연영수학원
윤세광	비상구영어학원

전북

김길자	맨투맨학원
김미영	링크영어학원
김효성	연세입시학원
노빈나	노빈나영어전문학원
라성남	하포드어학원
박재훈	위니드수학지앤비영어학원
박향숙	STA영어전문학원
서종원	서종원영어학원
이상훈	나는학원
장지원	링컨더글라스학원
지근영	한솔영어수학학원
최성령	연세입시학원
최혜영	이든영어수학학원

제주

김랑	KLS어학원
박자은	KLS어학원

충남

김예지	더배움프라임영수학원
김철홍	청경학원
노태겸	최상위학원

충북

라은경	이화윤스영어교습소
신유정	비타민영어클리닉학원

HACKERS

GRAMMAR
SMART 1

LEVEL

HACKERS

Contents

Preview

명쾌한 설명과 실용적인 문장으로 Smart하게 학습 ————

---

① UNIT 02 | must, have to, should

1 must

❶ 의무(~해야 한다)
You **must** wear a seat belt.
We **must not** lie to our parents.
→ must not은 강한 금지(~하면 안 된다)를 나타낸다.

❷ 강한 추측(~임이 틀림없다)
That boy **must** be Oliver.
She **must** be very happy.
TIP 강한 추측을 나타내는 must의 부정은 cannot[can't](~일 리가 없다)를 쓴다.
That boy **cannot[can't]** be Oliver.

2 have to

의무(~해야 한다)를 나타내며, must와 바꿔 쓸 수 있다. 주어가 3인칭 단수일 때는 has to를 쓴다.
I **have to** meet my friend.
Cindy **has to** repair her laptop.
Does he **have to** go now?
You **don't have to** worry about me.
→ don't/doesn't have to는 불필요(~할 필요가 없다)를 나타낸다.

3 should

충고·의무(~해야 한다)를 나타낸다.
We **should** wake up early tomorrow.
You **should not[shouldn't]** forget this.

② Smart Check 다음 빈칸에 들어갈 가장 알맞은 것을 고르시오.

1 Her grandfather is sick. She _____ be sad.
① must ② have to ③ must not

2 Liam has many cups. He _____ buy more.
① has to ② don't have to ③ doesn't have to

3 My brother _____ clean his desk. It's dirty.
① must not ② should ③ doesn't have to

---

③ Practice Answers p.6

A 밑줄 친 부분의 의미를 <보기>에서 골라 그 기호를 쓰시오.

<보기> ⓐ ~해야 한다 ⓑ ~하면 안 된다 ⓒ ~임이 틀림없다 ⓓ ~할 필요가 없다

1 Eric should wear warm clothes. [ ]
2 You don't have to do the dishes now. [ ]
3 The students must not break the rules. [ ]
4 That woman has blond hair. She must be Alice. [ ]
5 Children shouldn't drink coffee. [ ]

B 다음 두 문장의 의미가 같도록 have to를 활용하여 문장을 완성하시오.

1 I must find my credit card. → I _____ my credit card.
2 Jason must study hard. → Jason _____ hard.
3 They must be quiet here. → They _____ quiet here.
4 She must tell the truth. → She _____ the truth.

C must not 또는 don't/doesn't have to와 괄호 안의 동사를 활용하여 문장을 완성하시오.

1 The milk smells strange. You _____ it. (drink)
2 The weather is nice. I _____ an umbrella. (bring)
3 She _____. The store is very close. (drive)
4 Mr. Smith _____ much. His bones are weak. (exercise)

D 우리말과 같도록 괄호 안의 말을 활용하여 빈칸에 쓰시오.

1 너는 나를 따라올 필요가 없다. (have to, follow)
= You _____ me.
2 Hall씨는 부엌에 있는 것이 틀림없다. (must, be)
= Ms. Hall _____ in the kitchen.
3 우리는 나쁜 말을 하면 안 된다. (must, say)
= We _____ bad words.
4 나의 할머니는 혼자 걸으시면 안 된다. (should, walk)
= My grandmother _____ alone.

④
warm 휑 따뜻한
clothes 명 옷
do the dishes 설거지를 하다
break a rule 규칙을 어기다
blond hair 금발 머리

find 통 찾다
quiet 휑 조용한
truth 명 사실

smell 통 ~한 냄새가 나다
strange 휑 이상한
close 휑 가까운
bone 명 뼈
weak 휑 약한
exercise 통 운동하다

follow 통 따르오다, 따라가다
kitchen 명 부엌
say 통 말하다
word 명 말, 단어
alone 휑 혼자

각 레벨에 딱 맞는
Essential Grammar Units

❶ Grammar Lesson
해당 레벨에서 익혀야 할 문법 개념을 명쾌한 설명과 실용적인 예문을 통해 정확하게 이해할 수 있습니다. TIP을 통해 내신 시험에서 출제되는 심화 문법까지 학습하여 고난도 문제에도 대비할 수 있습니다.

❸ Practice
다양한 유형의 풍부한 연습문제를 통해 문법 개념을 자연스럽게 이해할 수 있습니다.

❷ Smart Check
간단한 문제를 통해 위에서 배운 문법 개념을 잘 이해했는지 바로바로 확인할 수 있습니다.

❹ Vocabulary
연습문제에 쓰인 주요 어휘를 추가로 학습하여 어휘력까지 높일 수 있습니다.

*어휘 정리에 사용된 약호
몡 명사   통 동사   휑 형용사   쀼 부사   쩐 전치사   쩝 접속사

기초부터 실전까지 Perfect하게 완성

기초를 탄탄히 다지는
기초 문법

중학영문법을 이해하기 위해 꼭 알아야 하는 기초 문법이 정리되어 있어, 문법 실력이 부족한 학생들도 기초를 탄탄히 다지고 본학습을 시작할 수 있습니다.

쓰기 활동으로 문법을 체득하는
Writing Exercise

다양한 유형의 서술형 문제를 풀어보며 쓰기 연습을 충분히 할 수 있습니다. 이를 통해 서술형을 강조하는 최근 내신 평가 트렌드에 대비할 수 있습니다.

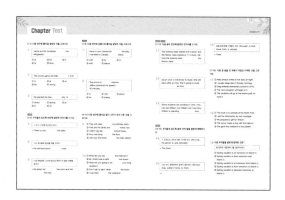

문제 풀이로 학습 내용을 확실히 점검하는
Chapter Test

전국 내신 기출문제 출제 유형을 기반으로 한 다양한 문제를 풀어보며 실제 시험에 대비할 수 있습니다. 서술형 주관식 문제 및 고난도 문제로 학습한 문법 개념에 대한 이해도를 점검할 수 있습니다.

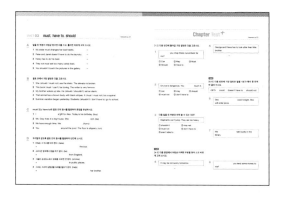

학습 효과를 더욱 높이는
Workbook

각 UNIT별, Chapter별로 풍부한 양의 추가 문제를 풀면서 본교재에서 익힌 문법 개념을 확실히 복습하고 부족한 부분은 보완할 수 있습니다.

해커스북 중·고등

www.HackersBook.com

기초 문법

영어 문법, 그 기초부터 알고 들어가자!

1 품사 | 영어 단어의 8가지 종류

영어 단어는 기능과 성격에 따라 **명사, 대명사, 동사, 형용사, 부사, 전치사, 접속사, 감탄사**로 분류할 수 있으며, 이를 품사라고 한다.

❶ 명사

명사는 사람, 사물, 장소, 개념 등의 이름을 나타내는 말로, 문장에서 **주어, 목적어, 보어**로 쓰인다.

Sam is in his room. <주어>

She doesn't eat **pineapples**. <목적어>

I am a **student**. <보어>

❷ 대명사

대명사는 **명사를 대신해서 쓰는 말**로, 문장에서 **주어, 목적어, 보어**로 쓰인다.

He is a writer. <주어>

I have three dogs. I love **them**. <목적어>

My umbrellas are **these**. <보어>

❸ 동사

동사는 사람, 동물, 사물 등의 **동작이나 상태를 나타내는 말**로, be동사, 일반동사, 조동사가 있다.

Dora **is** happy now.

The dolphins **swim** fast.

My father **can drive** a truck.

❹ 형용사

형용사는 **명사나 대명사의 형태, 성질, 상태 등을 나타내는 말**로, 문장에서 명사나 대명사를 꾸미는 **수식어**, 또는 주어나 목적어를 보충 설명하는 **보어**로 쓰인다.

She is a **tall** girl. <수식어>

The weather is **nice**. <보어>

⑤ 부사

부사는 동사, 형용사, 다른 부사, 또는 문장 전체를 꾸미는 말로, 문장에서 수식어로 쓰인다.

Brian sings well.

The cake is very delicious.

⑥ 전치사

전치사는 명사나 대명사 앞에서 장소나 시간 등을 나타내는 말이다.

The cat is sitting next to the box.

The class starts at 8:30.

⑦ 접속사

접속사는 단어와 단어, 구와 구, 절과 절을 연결해주는 말이다.

There are four apples and two pears in the fridge.

Ben was hungry, so he made a sandwich.

⑧ 감탄사

감탄사는 기쁨, 놀람, 슬픔과 같은 다양한 감정을 표현하는 말이다.

Oh, it's snowing outside.

Wow, the flower smells great.

Check-up 다음 단어들에 해당되는 품사를 쓰시오.

1 bright, funny, round [   ]   **5** Mr. Smith, computer, air [   ]

2 quickly, sometimes, very [   ]   **6** when, if, because [   ]

3 be, have, read [   ]   **7** in, for, after [   ]

4 Oh, Wow, Ouch [   ]   **8** you, that, her [   ]

정답 1 형용사 2 부사 3 동사 4 감탄사 5 명사 6 접속사 7 전치사 8 대명사

2 문장의 성분 | 영어 문장을 만드는 재료

영어 문장을 만드는 여러 가지 재료로 **주어, 동사, 목적어, 보어, 수식어**가 있으며, 이를 **문장의 성분**이라고 한다.

1 주어

주어는 **동작이나 상태의 주체가 되는 말**로, '누가, 무엇이'에 해당한다.

The Earth moves around the Sun.

Katie likes basketball.

2 동사

동사는 **주어의 동작이나 상태를 나타내는 말**로, '~하다, ~이다'에 해당한다.

Jason watched a movie last night.

The door is open.

3 목적어

목적어는 **동작의 대상이 되는 말**로, '~을/를, ~에게'에 해당한다.

I brushed my teeth.

Mom baked us cookies on Sunday.

4 보어

보어는 **주어나 목적어를 보충 설명하는 말**이다.

Those shoes are small. <주격 보어>

Mr. Evans made them quiet. <목적격 보어>

5 수식어

수식어는 **문장에 반드시 필요하지는 않지만 다양한 위치에서 여러 가지 의미를 더해주는 말**이다.

The red dress is expensive.

Laura and I will take a walk at the park.

Check-up 다음 밑줄 친 부분의 문장 성분을 쓰시오.

1 The weather was cold yesterday. [   ]
2 We can go to the mall.   [   ]
3 I ate dinner at 6.   [   ]
4 Jamie likes popcorns.   [   ]
5 The library was very large.   [   ]
6 You should wash your hands.   [   ]

정답 1 보어 2 주어 3 수식어 4 동사 5 수식어 6 목적어

3 구와 절 | 말 덩어리

두 개 이상의 단어가 모여 하나의 의미를 나타내는 말 덩어리를 **구**나 **절**이라고 한다.

❶ 구

구는 「주어 + 동사」를 포함하지 않은 두 개 이상의 단어가 모인 말 덩어리로, 문장에서 **명사, 형용사, 부사** 역할을 할 수 있다.

My favorite fruit is an orange.
　　명사구(주어)

The cup **on the table** is Jenny's.
　　　　형용사구

Eric is talking with a clerk **at the shop**.
　　　　　　　　　　　부사구

❷ 절

절은 「주어 + 동사」를 포함한 두 개 이상의 단어가 모인 말 덩어리로, 문장에서 **명사, 형용사, 부사** 역할을 할 수 있다.

I know **that you are right**.
　　명사절(목적어)

This is the house **which my parents bought**.
　　　　　　　　　형용사절

His pants got wet **because it rained heavily**.
　　　　　　　　　부사절

Check-up　다음 문장의 밑줄 친 부분이 구인지 절인지 쓰시오.

1 George wants to practice the piano. 　　　[　　　]

2 Lisa enjoys swimming in the sea. 　　　[　　　]

3 He heard that they moved to Seoul. 　　　[　　　]

4 I'll buy some milk when I go to the supermarket. 　[　　　]

5 The cloud in the sky looks like a sheep. 　　　[　　　]

6 Tina took a shower and brushed her hair. 　　　[　　　]

7 Let's go home after we meet Kevin. 　　　[　　　]

8 You can cut the paper with a pair of scissors. 　[　　　]

정답 1 구 2 구 3 절 4 절 5 구 6 구 7 절 8 구

Chapter

01

be동사

be동사는 주어의 상태를 나타내는 동사로,
나타내는 시점과 주어에 따라 형태가 달라진다.

UNIT 01 | be동사의 현재형과 과거형

1 **be동사**

주어의 상태를 나타내는 동사로, '~이다, ~(하)다, (~에) 있다'의 의미이다.

I **am** a singer.
Maria **is** smart.
They **are** in the living room.

---

2 **be동사의 현재형과 과거형**

❶ be동사의 현재형은 주어의 인칭과 수에 따라 형태가 달라지며, 주어가 인칭대명사인 경우 줄여 쓸 수 있다.

인칭	수	주어(인칭대명사)	be동사의 현재형	줄임말
1인칭	단수	I	**am**	I'm
	복수	We	**are**	We're
2인칭	단수·복수	You	**are**	You're
3인칭	단수	He / She / It	**is**	He's / She's / It's
	복수	They	**are**	They're

I **am** hungry. I**'m** thirsty, too.
They **are** my classmates. They**'re** in the classroom.

❷ am과 is의 과거형은 was이고, are의 과거형은 were이다.

Jason **was** sick.
We **were** at the beach yesterday.
→ 과거형은 yesterday, last night, an hour ago, in 1990 등의 과거를 나타내는 표현과 주로 함께 쓰인다.

---

3 **There + be동사**

「There + be동사」는 '~이 있(었)다'라는 의미로, 뒤에 오는 명사의 수에 따라 be동사의 형태가 달라진다.

There	+	is / was	+	셀 수 있는 명사의 단수형 또는 셀 수 없는 명사
		are / were		셀 수 있는 명사의 복수형

There is *a bird* on the branch.
There were *many flowers* in the vase.

Smart Check 다음 빈칸에 들어갈 알맞은 것을 고르시오.

1 Lydia _____ tall and strong.

① am   ② is   ③ are

Practice

Answers p.2

A 다음 문장의 밑줄 친 부분을 줄여 쓰시오.

1 I am nervous. → _____

2 She is a fashion designer. → _____

3 They are in the car. → _____

4 He is on the stage. → _____

5 You are handsome and gentle. → _____

nervous 형 긴장한
fashion designer 패션 디자이너
stage 명 무대
handsome 형 멋진, 잘생긴
gentle 형 친절한

B 괄호 안에서 알맞은 것을 고르시오.

1 I (am / is) at the baseball stadium.

2 We (is / are) volleyball fans.

3 There (is / are) a wallet on the street.

4 Bentley and William (was / were) quiet.

5 It (was / were) a bestseller in 2019.

baseball stadium 야구장
volleyball 명 배구
fan 명 팬, 선풍기
wallet 명 지갑
street 명 거리, 도로
quiet 형 조용한
bestseller 명 베스트셀러

C 다음 빈칸에 알맞은 be동사를 <보기>에서 한 번씩만 골라 쓰시오.

<보기>	is	are	was	were

1 He _____ a teenager last year.

2 Sandra _____ from Sydney.

3 They _____ tired yesterday.

4 There _____ four people on the bus now.

teenager 명 십대
tired 형 피곤한, 지친
people 명 사람들

D 우리말과 같도록 괄호 안의 말과 be동사를 활용하여 빈칸에 쓰시오.

1 Alex는 지난 크리스마스에 행복했다. (Alex)

= _____ _____ happy last Christmas.

2 그녀는 우리의 담임 선생님이시다. (she)

= _____ _____ our homeroom teacher.

3 팬케이크는 내가 가장 좋아하는 음식이다. (pancakes)

= _____ _____ my favorite food.

4 지붕 위에 고양이 세 마리가 있었다. (there, three cats)

= _____ _____ _____ _____ on the roof.

homeroom teacher 담임 선생님
favorite 형 가장 좋아하는
roof 명 지붕

UNIT 02 | be동사의 부정문과 의문문

1 be동사의 부정문

「주어 + be동사 + not」의 형태이며, 줄여 쓸 수 있다.

주어(인칭대명사)	be동사 + not	현재형의 줄임말	과거형의 줄임말
I	am/was not	I'm not	I wasn't
He		He's not / He isn't	He wasn't
She	is/was not	She's not / She isn't	She wasn't
It		It's not / It isn't	It wasn't
We		We're not / We aren't	We weren't
You	are/were not	You're not / You aren't	You weren't
They		They're not / They aren't	They weren't

I am not[**I'm not**] ten years old.
We were not[**We weren't**] at the café last night.

2 be동사의 의문문

❶ be동사 현재형의 의문문은 「Am/Are/Is + 주어 ~?」의 형태이며, 긍정의 대답은 「Yes, 주어 + am/are/is.」, 부정의 대답은 「No, 주어 + am/are/is + not.」의 형태이다.

인칭	수	be동사 현재형의 의문문	긍정의 대답	부정의 대답
1인칭	단수	Am I ~?	Yes, you are.	No, you aren't.
	복수	Are we ~?	Yes, we/you are.	No, we/you aren't.
2인칭	단수	Are you ~?	Yes, I am.	No, I'm not.
	복수	Are you ~?	Yes, we are.	No, we aren't.
3인칭	단수	Is he/she/it ~?	Yes, he/she/it is.	No, he/she/it isn't.
	복수	Are they ~?	Yes, they are.	No, they aren't.

A: **Are you** Korean?　　　B: **Yes, I am. / No, I'm not.**

❷ be동사 과거형의 의문문은 「Was/Were + 주어 ~?」의 형태이며, 긍정의 대답은 「Yes, 주어 + was/were.」, 부정의 대답은 「No, 주어 + was/were + not.」의 형태이다.

A: **Was she** late for school?　B: **Yes, she was. / No, she wasn't.**

Smart Check　다음 빈칸에 들어갈 알맞은 것을 고르시오.

1 We _____ sleepy.

① not were　　　　　　　② weren't　　　　　　　③ was not

Practice

Answers p.2

A 괄호 안에서 알맞은 것을 고르시오.

1 (Is / Are) it a lemon tree?

2 Turtles (isn't / aren't) fast on land.

3 (Are / Were) they tired last night?

4 I (am not / not am) sad now.

turtle 몡 거북
fast 혱 빠른
land 몡 육지, 땅
sad 혱 슬픈

B 다음 문장을 부정문으로 바꿔 쓰시오. (단, 줄임말로 쓰시오.)

1 We were at Disneyland.

→ _____ at Disneyland.

2 They are afraid of spiders.

→ _____ afraid of spiders.

3 It was a popular place in Korea.

→ _____ a popular place in Korea.

afraid of ~을 무서워하는
spider 몡 거미
popular 혱 유명한, 인기 있는
place 몡 장소

C 괄호 안의 말과 be동사를 활용하여 대화를 완성하시오.

1 A: Is the orange sour?

B: No, _____ _____. It is sweet. (it)

2 A: Was Ms. Baker a doctor?

B: Yes, _____ _____. (she)

3 A: _____ _____ from Hong Kong? (they)

B: No, they aren't. They are from Taiwan.

4 A: _____ _____ at the shopping mall? (you)

B: No, I wasn't. I was at the park.

sour 혱 신, 시큼한
sweet 혱 단, 달콤한
doctor 몡 의사
shopping mall 쇼핑몰
park 몡 공원

D 우리말과 같도록 괄호 안의 말과 be동사를 활용하여 빈칸에 쓰시오.

1 어제는 별들이 밝지 않았다. (the stars)

= _____ _____ _____ bright yesterday.

2 그는 3학년이니? (he)

= _____ _____ in third grade?

3 A: 저녁은 맛있었니?

B: 아니, 그렇지 않았어. 스테이크가 좋지 않았어. (the steak)

= A: _____ the dinner delicious?

B: No, it _____. _____ _____ _____ good.

star 몡 별
bright 혱 밝은
grade 몡 학년, 성적
steak 몡 스테이크
dinner 몡 저녁 (식사)
delicious 혱 맛있는

Writing Exercise

A 다음 문장을 괄호 안의 지시대로 바꿔 쓰시오. (단, 부정문에서는 줄임말을 쓰시오.)

1 He is in the swimming pool. (부정문으로)

→ _____ .

2 Sam and Julia were best friends. (의문문으로)

→ _____ ?

3 His glasses are cheap. (부정문으로)

→ _____ .

4 Coffee was popular in the 1980s. (의문문으로)

→ _____ ?

5 I am an elementary school student. (부정문으로)

→ _____ .

6 Your sisters are in the kitchen. (의문문으로)

→ _____ ?

B 우리말과 같도록 괄호 안의 말을 알맞게 배열하시오.

1 이 다큐멘터리는 지루하다. (boring, is, this documentary)

= _____ .

2 너는 한 시간 전에 깨어있었니? (awake, you, were)

= _____ an hour ago?

3 그녀는 지난 월요일에 뉴욕에 없었다. (she, in New York, not, was)

= _____ last Monday.

4 Carrie와 나는 같은 반이 아니다. (are, in the same class, Carrie and I, not)

= _____ .

5 도넛 가게에 경찰관 세 명이 있었다. (three police officers, were, there)

= _____ in the doughnut shop.

6 저 남자는 영화 감독이니? (a movie director, that man, is)

= _____ ?

C 우리말과 같도록 괄호 안의 말과 be동사를 활용하여 문장을 완성하시오. (단, 부정문에서는 줄임말을 쓰시오.)

1 책상 위에 달력이 있었다. (there, a calendar)

= _____ on the desk.

2 그것은 새 스마트폰이 아니다. (it, a new smartphone)

= _____ .

3 그들은 지금 지하철역에 있니? (they, at the subway station)

= _____ now?

4 나의 삼촌은 3년 전에 컴퓨터 프로그래머이셨다. (my uncle, a computer programmer)

= _____ three years ago.

5 Cole씨와 Smith씨는 작년에 미국 시민이 아니었다. (Mr. Cole and Ms. Smith, American citizens)

= _____ last year.

D 다음 그림을 보고 <보기>의 말을 활용하여 대화를 완성하시오.

Three hours ago  Now

| <보기> | empty | in the living room | rainy | on the sofa |

1 *A*: Is the basket full now?

B: _____ , _____ _____ . It _____ _____ now.

2 *A*: Was the weather sunny three hours ago?

B: _____ , _____ _____ . It _____ _____ three hours ago.

3 *A*: Was the puppy on the floor three hours ago?

B: _____ , _____ _____ . But it _____ _____ _____ _____ now.

4 *A*: _____ Alice and Louis _____ _____ _____ _____ now?

B: _____ , _____ _____ .

Chapter Test

[1-4] 다음 빈칸에 들어갈 알맞은 것을 고르시오.

1

We _____ 14 years old.

① be   ② am   ③ is
④ are   ⑤ was

2

Nelly _____ a champion last year.

① am   ② is   ③ was
④ are   ⑤ were

3

_____ they at the gym yesterday?

① Am   ② Is   ③ Was
④ Are   ⑤ Were

4

The room _____ warm now.

① am not   ② isn't   ③ aren't
④ wasn't   ⑤ weren't

5 다음 빈칸에 들어갈 말이 나머지 넷과 <u>다른</u> 것은?

① Mark and I _____ in England last month.
② It _____ Sunday yesterday.
③ Julie _____ 156 centimeters tall in 2020.
④ He _____ a dentist ten years ago.
⑤ The bookstore _____ not open last week.

서술형
6 be동사를 활용하여 문장을 완성하시오.

Kate _____ at the library an hour ago. She was at the restaurant an hour ago.

서술형
[7-8] 다음 문장을 괄호 안의 지시대로 바꿔 쓰시오.

7

Sam and Ann are my neighbors. (부정문으로)
→ _____ .

8

The weather is nice today. (의문문으로)
→ _____ ?

9 다음 대화의 밑줄 친 부분을 바르게 고친 것은?

A: Were you free yesterday?
B: Yes, I <u>are</u>.

① am   ② was   ③ wasn't
④ were   ⑤ weren't

[10-11] 다음 글의 빈칸에 들어갈 말이 순서대로 짝지어진 것을 고르시오.

10

> Mr. Wilson _____ a writer in 2010. He _____ a teacher now.

① is – is   ② is – was
③ was – is   ④ was – was
⑤ was – were

11

> There _____ a soccer match at school last week. It _____ so exciting.

① is – is   ② is – was
③ was – is   ④ was – was
⑤ was – were

12 다음 중 밑줄 친 부분이 어법상 어색한 대화를 모두 고르시오.

① A: Is Russia a large country?
    B: Yes, <u>it is</u>.
② A: Am I late for class?
    B: No, <u>you isn't</u>.
③ A: Are you happy now?
    B: Yes, <u>I am</u>.
④ A: Were they in the garden?
    B: No, <u>they aren't</u>.
⑤ A: Was the mobile game fun?
    B: Yes, <u>it was</u>.

13 다음 우리말을 알맞게 영작한 것은?

> 바구니 안에 신선한 당근들이 있었다.

① There be fresh carrots in the basket.
② There is fresh carrots in the basket.
③ There are fresh carrots in the basket.
④ There was fresh carrots in the basket.
⑤ There were fresh carrots in the basket.

[14-15] 다음 중 밑줄 친 부분이 어법상 <u>어색한</u> 것을 고르시오.

14 ① Pizza <u>is</u> my favorite food.
② Mom and Dad <u>were</u> not at the market.
③ <u>Was</u> the movie sad?
④ Your brother <u>are</u> very smart.
⑤ These gloves <u>are</u> old and small.

15 ① There <u>is</u> a frog on the leaf.
② There <u>are</u> some potatoes in the box.
③ There <u>is</u> a basketball on the chair.
④ There <u>are</u> five players at the stadium.
⑤ There <u>is</u> many cities in China.

서술형
16 다음 문장에서 <u>틀린</u> 부분을 바르게 고쳐 완전한 문장을 쓰시오.

> The field trip were not interesting.
> → _____.

[17-18] 다음 빈칸에 알맞은 말을 넣어 대화를 완성하시오.

17

> A: _____ breakfast ready now?
> B: Yes, it _____. Come and eat.

18

> A: _____ they at home last night?
> B: No, they _____. They went to their grandmother's house.

19 다음 중 밑줄 친 부분이 어법상 바른 것은?

① There <u>was</u> two children in the playground.
② The sky <u>were</u> clear yesterday.
③ The strawberry cupcakes <u>was</u> delicious.
④ There <u>were</u> a birthday party on Friday.
⑤ There <u>were</u> some students on the bus.

서술형 고난도

20 다음 글에서 어법상 어색한 부분을 찾아 밑줄을 치고 바르게 고쳐 쓰시오.

> There is three dogs at the park now. Their owner is Mr. Wood. They are so cute.

→ _____

서술형 고난도

[21-22] 우리말과 같도록 주어진 <조건>에 맞게 영작하시오.

21

> 식탁 위에 신문이 있었다.

> <조건>
> 1. a newspaper, on the table을 활용하시오.
> 2. 7단어로 쓰시오.

= _____.

22

> 그녀는 소방관이 아니다.

> <조건>
> 1. a firefighter를 활용하시오.
> 2. 5단어로 쓰시오.

= _____.

고난도

23 다음 중 밑줄 친 부분이 어법상 바른 것끼리 묶인 것은?

> ⓐ The books <u>is</u> on the shelf.
> ⓑ The reporter <u>was</u> very nervous.
> ⓒ The apples <u>weren't</u> delicious.
> ⓓ <u>Is</u> Ben your brother?
> ⓔ There <u>are</u> orange juice in the bottle.

① ⓐ, ⓑ, ⓒ   ② ⓐ, ⓒ, ⓔ   ③ ⓐ, ⓓ, ⓔ
④ ⓑ, ⓒ, ⓓ   ⑤ ⓑ, ⓓ, ⓔ

Chapter

02

일반동사

일반동사는 주어의 동작이나 상태를 나타내는 동사로,
나타내는 시점과 주어에 따라 형태가 달라진다.

1 일반동사

be동사와 조동사를 제외한 모든 동사로, 주어의 동작이나 상태를 나타낸다.

I **walk** to school every day.
Leaves **turn** yellow in fall.

2 일반동사 현재형의 형태

❶ 주어가 1·2인칭이나 3인칭 복수인 경우 동사원형을 쓰고, 3인칭 단수인 경우 동사원형에 -(e)s를 붙인다.

We **play** together on weekends.
Ken and Carol **run** very fast.
She **needs** a new computer.
Luke **wakes** up at 7 o'clock.

❷ 일반동사의 3인칭 단수 현재형 만드는 법

대부분의 동사	동사원형 + -s	work – work**s** know – know**s**	live – live**s** stay – stay**s**
-o, -s, -x, -ch, -sh로 끝나는 동사	동사원형 + -es	do – do**es** fix – fix**es**	pass – pass**es** catch – catch**es**
「자음 + y」로 끝나는 동사	y를 i로 바꾸고 + -es	cry – cr**ies** study – stud**ies**	fly – fl**ies** carry – carr**ies**
불규칙하게 변하는 동사	have – **has**		

Jane **lives** in Vancouver.
He **does** yoga in the evening.
My friend **has** three dogs.

Smart Check 다음 빈칸에 들어갈 알맞은 것을 고르시오.

1 They _____ horror movies on Mondays.
　① watch　　　　　　② watches　　　　　　③ watchs

2 My dad always _____ home late.
　① come　　　　　　② comes　　　　　　③ comees

3 Thomas _____ history hard.
　① study　　　　　　② studys　　　　　　③ studies

Practice

A 괄호 안에서 알맞은 것을 고르시오.

1 He (work / works) at the post office.

2 I (solve / solves) puzzles well.

3 Emma (brush / brushes) her hair before bed.

4 We (do / does) the laundry once a week.

5 Marco and Antonio (speak / speaks) Italian.

post office 우체국
solve a puzzle 수수께끼를 풀다
brush 통 빗다, 솔질하다
do the laundry 빨래를 하다
once 부 한 번

B 괄호 안의 동사를 현재형으로 바꿔 빈칸에 쓰시오.

1 He _____ colorful pants. (wear)

2 She _____ about my health. (worry)

3 Cathy _____ a blue dress. (have)

4 You and I _____ the same bus every day. (take)

5 Mr. Olson _____ history at school. (teach)

colorful 형 화려한
pants 명 바지
health 명 건강
worry 통 걱정하다
same 형 같은
take 통 타다, 가지고 가다
history 명 역사
teach 통 가르치다

C <보기>에서 알맞은 동사를 한 번씩만 골라 현재형으로 바꿔 빈칸에 쓰시오.

<보기>	know	walk	fly	miss	listen

1 An airplane _____ very high.

2 She _____ your address.

3 My neighbors _____ their dogs in the afternoon.

4 Julie sometimes _____ to the radio at 9 P.M.

5 Mom _____ her sisters very much.

miss 통 그리워하다
listen 통 듣다
airplane 명 비행기
high 부 높게, 높이
neighbor 명 이웃

D 우리말과 같도록 괄호 안의 말을 활용하여 빈칸에 쓰시오.

1 나는 교실 뒤쪽에 앉는다. (I, sit)

= _____ _____ in the back of the classroom.

2 그는 아침에 얼굴을 씻는다. (he, wash)

= _____ _____ his face in the morning.

3 나의 사촌은 토요일마다 나의 집에 머무른다. (my cousin, stay)

= _____ _____ _____ at my house on Saturdays.

4 그들은 5월마다 정원에 꽃을 심는다. (they, plant)

= _____ _____ flowers in the garden every May.

back 명 뒤쪽
classroom 명 교실
cousin 명 사촌
stay 통 머무르다
plant 통 심다

UNIT 02 | 일반동사의 과거형

1 일반동사 과거형의 형태

❶ 일반동사의 과거형은 대부분 동사원형에 -(e)d를 붙여 만든다.

대부분의 동사	동사원형 + -ed	open – open**ed** look – look**ed**	wash – wash**ed** play – play**ed**
-e로 끝나는 동사	동사원형 + -d	move – move**d** invite – invite**d**	smile – smile**d** agree – agree**d**
「자음 + y」로 끝나는 동사	y를 i로 바꾸고 + -ed	try – tr**ied** worry – worr**ied**	copy – cop**ied** hurry – hurr**ied**
「단모음 + 단자음」으로 끝나는 동사	마지막 자음을 한 번 더 쓰고 + -ed	stop – stop**ped** hug – hug**ged** ※ 예외: visit – visit**ed**	drop – drop**ped** grab – grab**bed** enter – enter**ed**

I **washed** the dishes an hour ago.
The man **hugged** his baby.

❷ 일부 일반동사의 과거형은 불규칙하게 변한다.

현재형과 과거형이 같은 동사	cut – **cut** hurt – **hurt**	hit – **hit** read – **read**	put – **put** cost – **cost**	set – **set** spread – **spread**
현재형과 과거형이 다른 동사	get – **got** sing – **sang** fall – **fell** fly – **flew** find – **found** say – **said** do – **did** break – **broke**	win – **won** swim – **swam** wake – **woke** see – **saw** stand – **stood** send – **sent** go – **went** buy – **bought**	run – **ran** drink – **drank** meet – **met** become – **became** have – **had** tell – **told** keep – **kept** catch – **caught**	sit – **sat** begin – **began** know – **knew** write – **wrote** make – **made** eat – **ate** leave – **left** bring – **brought**

Scott **put** the bag on the desk.
The girl **stood** at the door.

 Smart Check 다음 빈칸에 들어갈 알맞은 것을 고르시오.

1 The players _____ their best last year.

① try ② tryed ③ tried

2 We _____ an apple pie yesterday.

① make ② made ③ maked

Practice

Answers p.3

A 괄호 안에서 알맞은 것을 고르시오.

1 Mike (calls / called) the police last night.

2 I (wrote / writed) a letter to my grandparents.

3 She (has / had) a fight with us yesterday.

4 James (caught / catched) a cold.

5 The students (finish / finished) their homework an hour ago.

police 몡 경찰
have a fight with ~와 싸우다
catch a cold 감기에 걸리다
finish 동 끝내다

B 괄호 안의 동사를 과거형으로 바꿔 빈칸에 쓰시오.

1 I _____ my leg last week. (break)

2 Jim _____ 50 books in 2015. (read)

3 A blue bird _____ in the sky. (fly)

4 We _____ Josie at the museum. (see)

5 Her family _____ on a trip to India a month ago. (go)

leg 몡 다리
museum 몡 박물관
go on a trip 여행을 가다

C <보기>에서 알맞은 동사를 한 번씩만 골라 과거형으로 바꿔 빈칸에 쓰시오.

<보기>	find	swim	cook	study	visit

1 They _____ gold coins under the sea in 1997.

2 We _____ for the midterm exam.

3 I _____ in this lake last summer.

4 My brother _____ bacon this morning.

5 Joan _____ the village last year.

gold coin 금화
midterm exam 중간고사
lake 몡 호수
bacon 몡 베이컨
village 몡 마을

D 우리말과 같도록 괄호 안의 말을 활용하여 빈칸에 쓰시오.

1 그녀는 올림픽에서 메달을 땄다. (win, the medal)
= She _____ _____ _____ in the Olympics.

2 Alice는 어제 늦게 일어났다. (wake)
= Alice _____ up late yesterday.

3 그는 체육관에 그의 친구들을 데려왔다. (bring, his friends)
= He _____ _____ _____ to the gym.

4 그들은 3년 전에 그들의 고향을 떠났다. (leave, their hometown)
= They _____ _____ _____ three years ago.

win 동 따다, 이기다
late 부 늦게; 형 늦은
gym 몡 체육관
hometown 몡 고향

UNIT 03 | 일반동사의 부정문과 의문문

1 일반동사의 부정문

❶ 일반동사 현재형의 부정문은 「주어 + do/does not + 동사원형」의 형태이다.

주어	do/does not + 동사원형
1·2인칭이나 3인칭 복수	do not[don't] + 동사원형
3인칭 단수	does not[doesn't] + 동사원형

We do not[don't] like this movie.
This skirt does not[doesn't] fit me.

❷ 일반동사 과거형의 부정문은 「주어 + did not[didn't] + 동사원형」의 형태이다.
The kids did not[didn't] break the window.

2 일반동사의 의문문

❶ 일반동사 현재형의 의문문은 「Do/Does + 주어 + 동사원형 ~?」의 형태이며, 긍정의 대답은 「Yes, 주어 + do/does.」, 부정의 대답은 「No, 주어 + don't/doesn't.」의 형태이다.

주어	일반동사 현재형의 의문문	긍정의 대답	부정의 대답
1·2인칭이나 3인칭 복수	Do + 주어 + 동사원형 ~?	Yes, 주어 + do.	No, 주어 + don't.
3인칭 단수	Does + 주어 + 동사원형 ~?	Yes, 주어 + does.	No, 주어 + doesn't.

A: **Do they go** home by bus?
B: **Yes, they do. / No, they don't.**

A: **Does she need** a pencil?
B: **Yes, she does. / No, she doesn't.**

❷ 일반동사 과거형의 의문문은 「Did + 주어 + 동사원형 ~?」의 형태이며, 긍정의 대답은 「Yes, 주어 + did.」, 부정의 대답은 「No, 주어 + didn't.」의 형태이다.

A: **Did you write** this poem?
B: **Yes, I did. / No, I didn't.**

Smart Check 다음 빈칸에 들어갈 알맞은 것을 고르시오.

1 Ben _____ ride a bicycle.

① do not   ② does not   ③ not does

2 Does he _____ the piano well?

① play   ② plays   ③ played

Practice

A 괄호 안에서 알맞은 것을 고르시오.

1 I (don't / doesn't) want more food.

2 (Do / Does) she like chocolate cookies?

3 My father (doesn't / didn't) watch the game last night.

4 Ronnie and Steve (don't / doesn't) go to noisy places.

5 (Do / Did) you borrow some books yesterday?

food 뗑 음식
noisy 혱 시끄러운
place 뗑 장소, 곳
borrow 동 빌리다

B 괄호 안의 동사를 활용하여 부정문을 완성하시오. (단, 줄임말로 쓰시오.)

1 We _____ in an apartment now. (live)

2 She bought orange juice. She _____ milk. (buy)

3 Jason and I _____ you an hour ago. (see)

4 He _____ Italian. He speaks German. (speak)

5 Jack _____ to Busan last month. (travel)

apartment 뗑 아파트
Italian 뗑 이탈리아어
German 뗑 독일어

C 괄호 안의 동사를 활용하여 대화를 완성하시오.

1 A: _____ the sun _____ in the west? (rise)
B: No, it doesn't. It rises in the east.

2 A: _____ you _____ our graduation day? (remember)
B: Yes, I do. It snowed that day.

3 A: _____ he _____ down the stairs last night? (fall)
B: Yes, he did. He is in the hospital now.

4 A: _____ the children _____ a party on Wednesday? (have)
B: No, they didn't. They had a party on Monday.

west 뗑 서쪽
rise 동 뜨다, 오르다
east 뗑 동쪽
graduation 뗑 졸업식, 졸업
remember 동 기억하다
stair 뗑 계단
fall 동 떨어지다

D 우리말과 같도록 괄호 안의 동사를 활용하여 빈칸에 쓰시오.

1 그는 아침에 그의 방을 청소하지 않는다. (clean)
= He _____ _____ his room in the morning.

2 Susan은 한국으로 돌아갔니? (return)
= _____ Susan _____ to Korea?

3 A: 너는 George를 믿니? (trust)
B: 아니, 그렇지 않아. 그는 어제 또 거짓말했어. (tell)
= A: _____ you _____ George?
B: No, I _____. He _____ a lie again yesterday.

return 동 돌아가다
trust 동 믿다
lie 뗑 거짓말
again 뿐 또, 다시

Chapter 02

일반동사

Hackers Grammar Smart Level 1

Writing Exercise

A 밑줄 친 부분이 어법상 맞으면 O를 쓰고, 틀리면 바르게 고쳐 쓰시오.

1 Anna <u>wanted</u> some water now. → _____

2 She <u>goed</u> to the aquarium two weeks ago. → _____

3 Evan <u>catches</u> fish with his father every summer. → _____

4 The cup <u>falls</u> on the floor a minute ago. → _____

5 We <u>sang</u> a song together yesterday. → _____

6 My brother <u>bakes</u> a cake for me last month. → _____

7 Jacob lives in Canada alone. He <u>miss</u> his family. → _____

B 다음 문장을 괄호 안의 지시대로 바꿔 쓰시오.

1 The students shared their ideas.
→ (부정문으로) _____.
→ (의문문으로) _____?

2 Janet remembers his name.
→ (부정문으로) _____.
→ (의문문으로) _____?

3 She made a big mistake.
→ (부정문으로) _____.
→ (의문문으로) _____?

4 They play badminton after school.
→ (부정문으로) _____.
→ (의문문으로) _____?

5 The soccer team won the tournament yesterday.
→ (부정문으로) _____.
→ (의문문으로) _____?

6 Mr. Bean enjoys coffee in the morning.
→ (부정문으로) _____.
→ (의문문으로) _____?

C 우리말과 같도록 괄호 안의 말을 활용하여 문장을 완성하시오.

1 나의 부모님은 줄을 서서 기다리지 않으셨다. (my parents, wait)

= _____ in line.

2 너는 새로 오신 선생님을 아니? (you, know, the new teacher)

= _____ ?

3 나는 신문에서 그 이야기를 읽었다. (I, read, the story)

= _____ in the newspaper.

4 곰은 겨울마다 동굴 안에 머무른다. (a bear, stay)

= _____ in the cave every winter.

5 우리는 주말에 학교에 가지 않는다. (we, go)

= _____ to school on weekends.

6 Andrew는 우산을 가져왔니? (Andrew, bring, an umbrella)

= _____ ?

7 이 슈퍼마켓은 비싼 물건들을 팔지 않는다. (this supermarket, sell, expensive items)

= _____ .

D 다음은 Steve의 어제 일정표이다. 표에 나온 표현을 활용하여 질문에 대한 대답을 완성하시오.

8 A.M.	10 A.M.	2 P.M.	6 P.M.
wake up	study math	practice the guitar	eat dinner with family
X	X	O	X

1 *A*: Did Steve wake up at 8 A.M.?

B: _____ , _____ _____ . He _____ up at 9 A.M.

2 *A*: Did Steve study math at 10 A.M.?

B: _____ , _____ _____ . He _____ English at 10 A.M.

3 *A*: Did Steve practice the guitar at 2 P.M.?

B: _____ , _____ _____ . He _____ the guitar at 2 P.M.

4 *A*: Did Steve eat dinner with his family at 6 P.M.?

B: _____ , _____ _____ . He _____ dinner with his friends at 6 P.M.

Chapter Test

1 다음 중 동사의 3인칭 단수 현재형이 <u>잘못된</u> 것은?

① take – takes
② have – has
③ hurry – hurries
④ need – needes
⑤ touch – touches

2 다음 중 동사의 과거형이 <u>잘못된</u> 것은?

① tell – told
② hurt – hurt
③ move – moved
④ open – opened
⑤ stop – stoped

[3-5] 다음 빈칸에 들어갈 알맞은 것을 고르시오.

3

| _____ gets up at 7:30 A.M. |

① Jeremy
② You
③ I
④ My sisters
⑤ We

4

| She _____ her classmates yesterday. |

① meet
② meets
③ don't meet
④ didn't meet
⑤ doesn't meet

5

| _____ he talk loudly? |

① Is
② Was
③ Were
④ Do
⑤ Does

[6-7] 다음 빈칸에 알맞은 말을 넣어 질문에 대한 대답을 완성하시오.

6

| A: Do they drink hot water? |
| B: No, _____ _____ . |

7

| A: Does Nina swim well? |
| B: Yes, _____ _____ . |

[8-9] 다음 중 밑줄 친 부분이 어법상 <u>어색한</u> 것을 고르시오.

8
① My mom <u>goes</u> to work by subway.
② <u>Did</u> you <u>wash</u> your face?
③ Jenna <u>sent</u> a gift to me.
④ I <u>watches</u> funny movies on Thursdays.
⑤ <u>Does</u> Kelly <u>like</u> pepperoni pizza?

9
① Mr. Wood <u>doesn't eat</u> after 6 o'clock.
② Do we <u>need</u> a blanket now?
③ Did the bakery <u>close</u> three days ago?
④ Kevin <u>didn't call</u> her last night.
⑤ <u>Does</u> the cat <u>sleep</u> on the roof yesterday?

[10-11] 다음 빈칸에 들어갈 말이 순서대로 짝지어진 것을 고르시오.

10

> • Ms. Grant _____ a shower every night.
> • We _____ to the library after school.

① take – go
② take – goes
③ take – gos
④ takes – go
⑤ takes – goes

11

> • They _____ sandwiches an hour ago.
> • Bonnie _____ in Russia. She lives in Italy.

① bring – don't live
② bring – doesn't live
③ brings – didn't live
④ brought – don't live
⑤ brought – doesn't live

12 다음 중 어법상 바른 것은?

① Did Rachel waited for me?
② We didn't see our teacher last week.
③ My dog run really fast.
④ They start elementary school in 2019.
⑤ Does Mr. Taylor drives a truck?

서술형

13 우리말과 같도록 주어진 <조건>에 맞게 영작하시오.

> Eugene은 게를 좋아하지 않는다.

> <조건> 1. Eugene, like, crabs를 활용하시오.
>   2. 5단어로 쓰시오.

= _____ .

[14-15] 다음 우리말을 알맞게 영작한 것을 고르시오.

14

> 너는 너의 약을 먹었니?

① Do you take your medicine?
② Does you take your medicine?
③ Do you takes your medicine?
④ Did you take your medicine?
⑤ Did you takes your medicine?

15

> Amy는 어제 그녀의 숙제를 끝내지 않았다.

① Amy finished not her homework yesterday.
② Amy doesn't finish her homework yesterday.
③ Amy doesn't finished her homework yesterday.
④ Amy didn't finish her homework yesterday.
⑤ Amy didn't finished her homework yesterday.

Chapter 02

일반동사   Hackers Grammar Smart **Level 1**

16 다음 질문에 대한 대답으로 알맞은 것은?

> *A*: Do you want some grapes?
> *B*: _____

① Yes, I do.　　　　② Yes, I don't.
③ Yes, I did.　　　　④ No, I do.
⑤ No, I didn't.

17 다음 중 어법상 <u>어색한</u> 것은?

① They did an interview yesterday.
② I bought some cucumbers last week.
③ Sam drinks coffee an hour ago.
④ She invited me to her house.
⑤ Van Gogh painted this picture in 1885.

서술형

[18-20] 다음 문장에서 <u>틀린</u> 부분을 바르게 고쳐 완전한 문장을 쓰시오.

18
> My brother and I has short hair.
> → _____ .

19
> Martin don't remember Eric.
> → _____ .

20
> They carried the boxes together.
> → _____ .

고난도

21 다음 중 어법상 바른 것끼리 묶인 것은?

> ⓐ The Sun doesn't go around the Earth.
> ⓑ The baby grabbed the bottle.
> ⓒ Does the tourists speak Chinese?
> ⓓ Did she copy your essay?
> ⓔ Mr. Lee not met us last night.

① ⓐ, ⓑ, ⓒ　　② ⓐ, ⓑ, ⓓ　　③ ⓐ, ⓒ, ⓔ
④ ⓑ, ⓓ, ⓔ　　⑤ ⓒ, ⓓ, ⓔ

서술형 고난도

22 다음 글에서 어법상 <u>어색한</u> 부분을 찾아 쓰고 바르게 고쳐 쓰시오.

> Ryan and I went to an ice cream shop yesterday. Ryan picked mango ice cream. I haved cherry ice cream. It was delicious.

_____ → _____

서술형

[23-24] 우리말과 같도록 괄호 안의 말을 활용하여 문장을 완성하시오.

23
> 우리는 그 책을 읽지 않았다. (read the book)

= We _____ .

24
> James는 일요일마다 한국어를 공부한다. (study Korean)

= James _____ every Sunday.

Chapter

03

시제

시제는 동사의 형태를 바꿔 행동이나 사건이 발생한 시점을 표현하는 것이다.

UNIT 01 | 현재시제와 과거시제

1 현재시제

현재의 사실이나 상태, 현재의 습관이나 반복되는 일, 일반적·과학적 사실을 나타낸다.

현재의 사실이나 상태	They **are** my friends. Tom **likes** cheese pizza.
현재의 습관이나 반복되는 일	Susie **plays** tennis every day. My parents always **wake** up early.
일반적·과학적 사실	Rome **is** the capital of Italy. Water **boils** at 100℃.

2 과거시제

❶ 과거의 동작이나 상태, 역사적 사실을 나타낸다.

과거의 동작이나 상태	He **went** to the park yesterday. My hair **was** long last year.
역사적 사실	The Second World War **ended** in 1945.

❷ yesterday, last night, two weeks ago, in 1997 등의 과거를 나타내는 표현과 주로 함께 쓰인다.

They **watched** a movie *last night*.
Timothy **read** the book *four months ago*.
She **moved** to Seoul *in 2003*.

Smart Check 다음 빈칸에 들어갈 알맞은 것을 고르시오.

1 Jim _____ a soccer player now.
　① is　　　　　　　　　② was　　　　　　　　　③ are

2 I _____ to Africa five years ago.
　① travel　　　　　　　② traveled　　　　　　　③ travels

3 The sun _____ in the east every day.
　① rises　　　　　　　　② rose　　　　　　　　　③ rise

4 My brother _____ from middle school in 2012.
　① graduate　　　　　　② graduates　　　　　　③ graduated

Practice

Answers p.4

A 괄호 안에서 알맞은 것을 고르시오.

1 She (eats / ate) an apple yesterday.

2 Arnold and I (live / lived) in New York now.

3 John F. Kennedy (dies / died) in 1963.

4 They (buy / bought) the flight ticket last night.

5 The Moon (goes / went) around the Earth.

die 통 죽다
flight ticket 항공권
go around 돌다

B 괄호 안의 동사를 활용하여 빈칸에 쓰시오.

1 He _____ a credit card now. (have)

2 Marie Curie _____ her first Nobel prize in 1903. (win)

3 Eight minus five _____ three. (be)

4 She _____ the magic show last weekend. (enjoy)

credit card 신용 카드
win a prize 상을 타다
magic show 마술 쇼
enjoy 통 즐기다

C <보기>의 동사를 한 번씩만 활용하여 빈칸에 쓰시오.

<보기>	find	look	tell	dance

1 He _____ very hungry now.

2 Christopher Columbus _____ a new land in 1492.

3 My roommate _____ a secret to me yesterday.

4 They are famous dancers. They _____ very well.

find 통 발견하다, 찾다
look 통 ~하게 보이다
land 명 땅, 육지
secret 명 비밀
famous 형 유명한
dancer 명 댄서, 무용수

D 우리말과 같도록 괄호 안의 동사를 활용하여 빈칸에 쓰시오.

1 Brian은 매달 약간의 돈을 저축한다. (save)

= Brian _____ some money every month.

2 그녀는 오늘 아침에 우산을 가져왔다. (bring)

= She _____ an umbrella this morning.

3 식물들은 햇빛을 이용해서 에너지를 만든다. (make)

= Plants _____ energy with sunlight.

4 허리케인 카트리나는 2005년에 미국을 강타했다. (hit)

= Hurricane Katrina _____ America in 2005.

save 통 저축하다, 구하다
bring 통 가져오다
plant 명 식물
energy 명 에너지, 힘
sunlight 명 햇빛
hit 통 강타하다, 때리다

UNIT 02 | 미래시제

1 미래시제

❶ 앞으로 일어날 일을 나타내며, 「will + 동사원형」 또는 「be going to + 동사원형」의 형태이다. 이때 be동사는 현재형으로 쓴다.

I **will write** a letter to Laura.
→ I **am going to write** a letter to Laura.

James and Nina **will visit** Korea soon.
→ James and Nina **are going to visit** Korea soon.

❷ tomorrow, next year, soon 등의 미래를 나타내는 표현과 주로 함께 쓰인다.

Mary **will buy** a notebook *tomorrow*.
We**'re going to be** 15 years old *next year*.

2 미래시제의 부정문

「주어 + will not[won't] + 동사원형」 또는 「주어 + be동사 + not + going to + 동사원형」의 형태이다.

We will not[won't] play video games this weekend.
He's not going to stay at the old hotel.

3 미래시제의 의문문

❶ 「Will + 주어 + 동사원형 ~?」의 형태이며, 긍정의 대답은 「Yes, 주어 + will.」, 부정의 대답은 「No, 주어 + won't.」의 형태이다.

A: **Will Irene go** to middle school next year?
B: **Yes, she will. / No, she won't.**

❷ 「be동사 + 주어 + going to + 동사원형 ~?」의 형태이며, 긍정의 대답은 「Yes, 주어 + be동사.」, 부정의 대답은 「No, 주어 + be동사 + not.」의 형태이다.

A: **Are you going to sleep** early tonight?
B: **Yes, I am. / No, I'm not.**

Smart Check 다음 빈칸에 들어갈 알맞은 것을 고르시오.

1 I _____ at home next Wednesday.
① be   ② will be   ③ be going to be

2 Tony _____ make the same mistake again.
① won't be   ② not will   ③ is not going to

3 _____ Lisa cook something for us?
① Will   ② Is   ③ Is going to

Practice

Answers p.5

A 괄호 안에서 알맞은 것을 고르시오.

1 Anna will (call / calls) her mother soon.

2 I am going (finish / to finish) this book tonight.

3 Lazy students (not will / won't) get a good score.

4 Are they (going to / will) swim in this river?

finish 图 다 읽다, 끝내다
lazy 혱 게으른
score 명 점수
river 명 강

B 다음 문장을 괄호 안의 지시대로 바꿔 쓰시오.

1 Jamie is going to draw a picture. (부정문으로)

→ _____ a picture.

2 Your uncle will come back today. (의문문으로)

→ _____ back today?

3 Andy is going to walk to school tomorrow. (의문문으로)

→ _____ to school tomorrow?

4 She will buy tomatoes at the store. (부정문으로)

→ _____ tomatoes at the store.

draw a picture 그림을 그리다
uncle 명 삼촌
come back 돌아오다
store 명 가게, 상점

C <보기>의 동사와 괄호 안의 말을 한 번씩만 활용하여 문장을 완성하시오.

<보기> go   snow   meet   read

1 The children look tired. They _____ to bed soon. (will)

2 Ann got a letter. She _____ it later. (be going to)

3 It is warm outside. It _____ tonight. (will, not)

4 I'm busy. I _____ my friends. (be going to, not)

snow 图 눈이 오다; 명 눈
tired 혱 피곤한
get 图 받다
later 튀 나중에
warm 혱 따뜻한
busy 혱 바쁜

D 우리말과 같도록 괄호 안의 말을 활용하여 문장을 완성하시오.

1 우리는 다음 달에 아프리카로 여행 갈 것이다. (will, travel)

= _____ to Africa next month.

2 너는 내일 연을 날릴 거니? (be going to, fly)

= _____ the kite tomorrow?

3 Sam은 오늘 운동하지 않을 것이다. (be going to, exercise)

= _____ today.

travel 图 여행 가다
fly a kite 연을 날리다
exercise 图 운동하다

UNIT 03 | 진행시제

1 현재진행시제

❶ 지금 진행되고 있는 동작을 나타내며, 「am/are/is + V-ing」의 형태이다.

I **am doing** my homework now.
The horses **are running** in the field.

> **TIP** 소유, 감정, 상태를 나타내는 동사(have, like, know 등)는 진행형으로 쓸 수 없다. 단, **have**가 '가지다'가 아닌 '먹다, 시간을 보내다'라는 의미일 때는 진행형으로 쓸 수 있다.
> I (~~am having~~, **have**) a large bag.
> I **am having** breakfast.

❷ 동사의 V-ing형 만드는 법

대부분의 동사	동사원형 + -ing	talk – talk**ing**	play – play**ing**
「자음 + e」로 끝나는 동사	e를 빼고 + -ing	move – mov**ing** ※ 예외: be – be**ing**	write – writ**ing**
-ie로 끝나는 동사	ie를 y로 바꾸고 + -ing	lie – l**ying**	die – d**ying**
「단모음 + 단자음」으로 끝나는 동사	마지막 자음을 한 번 더 쓰고 + -ing	cut – cut**ting** ※ 예외: visit – visit**ing**	win – win**ning** enter – enter**ing**

2 과거진행시제

과거의 특정 시점에 진행되고 있던 동작을 나타내며, 「was/were + V-ing」의 형태이다.

My dad **was reading** a newspaper.
We **were making a snowman** last night.

3 진행시제의 부정문과 의문문

❶ 진행시제의 부정문은 「주어 + be동사 + not + V-ing」의 형태이다.

I'm not eating salad.

❷ 진행시제의 의문문은 「be동사 + 주어 + V-ing ~?」의 형태이며, 긍정의 대답은 「Yes, 주어 + be동사.」, 부정의 대답은 「No, 주어 + be동사 + not.」의 형태이다.

A: **Are you preparing** dinner?
B: **Yes, I am. / No, I'm not.**

Smart Check 다음 빈칸에 들어갈 알맞은 것을 고르시오.

1 He _____ for you now.

① waiting　　　　　② waited　　　　　③ is waiting

Practice

Answers p.5

A 괄호 안에서 알맞은 것을 고르시오.

1 A child (is hiding / hiding) behind the tree.

2 (Is / Does) the ice melting?

3 We were (listening not / not listening) to the music.

4 He is (siting / sitting) on the sofa.

5 Was Sally (painted / painting) the wall?

hide 통 숨다, 숨기다
behind 전 ~ 뒤에
melt 통 녹다, 녹이다
paint 통 페인트를 칠하다
wall 명 벽, 담

B 괄호 안의 동사를 활용하여 진행시제 문장을 완성하시오.

1 She _____ the mountain yesterday. (climb)

2 There are ants on the ground. They _____ a leaf. (carry)

3 My dog looks happy. It _____ its tail. (wag)

4 Bob and I weren't at home. We _____ a piano lesson. (take)

climb 통 오르다
ant 명 개미
ground 명 땅(바닥)
leaf 명 (나뭇)잎
carry 통 운반하다
tail 명 꼬리
wag 통 흔들다

C 다음 문장을 괄호 안의 지시대로 바꿔 쓰시오.

1 Charlie is playing chess. (의문문으로)
  → _____ chess?

2 The students are cleaning the room. (부정문으로)
  → _____ the room.

3 You were knocking on the door. (의문문으로)
  → _____ on the door?

4 The actor was shaking hands with her fans. (부정문으로)
  → _____ hands with her fans.

chess 명 체스
knock on the door 문을 두드리다
actor 명 배우
shake hands 악수하다

D 우리말과 같도록 괄호 안의 동사를 활용하여 빈칸에 쓰시오.

1 John은 두 시간 전에 그의 도시락을 싸고 있었니? (pack)
  = _____ John _____ his lunch box two hours ago?

2 그 고양이들은 바닥에서 자고 있지 않았다. (sleep)
  = The cats _____ _____ on the floor.

3 그들은 지금 Brook씨에게 거짓말하고 있다. (lie)
  = They _____ _____ to Ms. Brook now.

4 그녀는 저 무거운 상자를 혼자 옮기고 있니? (move)
  = _____ she _____ that heavy box alone?

pack 통 (짐 등을) 싸다
lunch box 도시락
floor 명 바닥
lie 통 거짓말하다, 눕다
heavy 형 무거운
alone 부 혼자

Writing Exercise

A 밑줄 친 부분이 어법상 맞으면 O를 쓰고, 틀리면 바르게 고쳐 쓰시오.

1 She is <u>asks</u> a question now. → _____

2 I <u>learn</u> ballet last year. → _____

3 Our solar system <u>is having</u> eight planets. → _____

4 He <u>was talking</u> with his friend two hours ago. → _____

5 Jason <u>not will</u> order a vegetable sandwich. → _____

6 Amy <u>filled</u> the bottle with water. → _____

7 My friends are <u>going travel</u> around the world. → _____

B 우리말과 같도록 괄호 안의 말을 알맞게 배열하시오.

1 나의 언니는 곧 샤워를 할 것이다. (take, my sister, a shower, will)
= _____ soon.

2 Cindy는 어제 이상한 소리를 들었니? (a strange sound, did, hear, Cindy)
= _____ yesterday?

3 그 택시 운전사는 식당 근처에 차를 주차하고 있다. (the taxi driver, parking, is, the car)
= _____ near the restaurant.

4 그들은 그 건물에 들어가고 있지 않았다. (not, were, the building, they, entering)
= _____ .

5 그는 빨간 불에 길을 건너지 않는다. (does, cross, he, not, the street)
= _____ at the red light.

6 Mark Zuckerberg는 2004년에 페이스북을 시작했다. (Mark Zuckerberg, Facebook, started)
= _____ in 2004.

7 나는 내일 내가 가장 좋아하는 드라마를 볼 것이다. (I, my favorite drama, am, watch, going to)
= _____ tomorrow.

8 너는 그 운동화를 살 거니? (going, the sneakers, are, buy, you, to)
= _____ ?

C 우리말과 같도록 괄호 안의 말을 활용하여 문장을 완성하시오. (단, 부정문에서는 줄임말을 쓰시오.)

1 나는 이번 주말에 자전거를 타지 않을 것이다. (I, ride)

= _____ a bicycle this weekend.

2 Justin은 오늘 밤에 물고기를 잡을 것이다. (Justin, catch)

= _____ fish tonight.

3 그녀는 한 시간 전에 조깅하고 있지 않았다. (she, jog)

= _____ an hour ago.

4 Alex는 월요일마다 학교에 걸어간다. (Alex, walk)

= _____ to school on Mondays.

5 우리는 지금 역사박물관에 가고 있다. (we, go)

= _____ to the history museum now.

6 그 직원은 나의 수프에 너무 많은 소금을 추가했다. (the staff, add)

= _____ too much salt to my soup.

D 다음은 Julia와 Peter의 통화 내용이다. 괄호 안의 말을 활용하여 대화를 완성하시오.

Julia: How is your summer vacation?

Peter: Great. I ⓐ_____(be) in Busan now.

Julia: Really? When did you go there?

Peter: I ⓑ_____(arrive) here two weeks ago.

Julia: ⓒ_____ _____ _____(have) a great time?

Peter: Yes, I am. I ⓓ_____(play) badminton with my cousins yesterday. Now, I ⓔ_____ _____(enjoy) the sunshine on the beach.

Julia: That sounds fun. ⓕ_____ _____ _____(come) back soon?

Peter: Yes. I ⓖ_____ _____ _____(return) next week.

Chapter Test

1 다음 중 동사의 V-ing형이 <u>잘못된</u> 것은?

① cry – crying   ② learn – learning

③ lie – lying   ④ sit – sitting

⑤ hike – hikeing

[2-4] 다음 빈칸에 들어갈 알맞은 것을 고르시오.

2

> They _____ pizza last night.

① have   ② had

③ are having   ④ was having

⑤ will have

3

> Mr. Harris _____ to the dentist tomorrow.

① go   ② went

③ will go   ④ will going

⑤ are going to go

4

> Ashley _____ in the library now.

① study   ② studied

③ is studying   ④ was studying

⑤ will studying

[5-6] 다음 빈칸에 공통으로 들어갈 알맞은 것을 고르시오.

5

> • She _____ finish her homework soon.
> • _____ Mr. Taylor water the plants in the afternoon?

① do   ② did   ③ is

④ are   ⑤ will

6

> • Sam _____ wearing jeans yesterday.
> • The weather _____ great last weekend.

① be   ② is   ③ are

④ was   ⑤ will

7 다음 중 자연스럽지 <u>않은</u> 대화를 <u>모두</u> 고르시오.

① A: Will David borrow the magazine?

   B: No, he will.

② A: Were you doing yoga?

   B: Yes, I was.

③ A: Is it going to rain next week?

   B: Yes, it is.

④ A: Are the lions chasing the zebra?

   B: No, they won't.

⑤ A: Is he going to the mall?

   B: No, he isn't.

[8-9] 다음 빈칸에 들어갈 말로 <u>어색한</u> 것을 고르시오.

8

Paul is going to take a trip _____.

① tomorrow   ② next Monday

③ next year   ④ soon

⑤ three months ago

9

I watched the video _____.

① yesterday   ② last night

③ an hour ago   ④ next weekend

⑤ in 2006

서술형

[10-11] 우리말과 같도록 주어진 <조건>에 맞게 문장을 완성하시오.

10

그들은 일요일에 그들의 조부모님을 방문할 거니?

<조건>
1. visit, their grandparents를 활용하시오.
2. 5단어로 쓰시오.

= _____ on Sunday?

11

그 선생님은 올해 1학년을 가르치지 않으실 것이다.

<조건>
1. the teacher, teach, first grade를 활용하시오.
2. 7단어로 쓰시오.

= _____ this year.

[12-14] 다음 중 밑줄 친 부분이 어법상 <u>어색한</u> 것을 고르시오.

12 ① My neighbor <u>walks</u> her dog every day.

② Penguins <u>live</u> in Antarctica.

③ Brian <u>has</u> a twin sister.

④ Egyptians <u>make</u> pyramids thousands of years ago.

⑤ Ryan and Jenny <u>ate</u> lunch at noon.

13 ① Are you <u>going to buy</u> a necklace?

② My brother and I <u>will play</u> basketball.

③ Cathy <u>won't practice</u> the piano.

④ <u>Will</u> he <u>sells</u> his phone today?

⑤ I <u>am going to exercise</u> on weekends.

14 ① The children <u>are running</u> outside.

② Nathan <u>is knowing</u> the correct answer.

③ The teacher <u>was talking</u> to the student.

④ They <u>were preparing</u> for an event.

⑤ It <u>was snowing</u> in the morning.

15 다음 우리말을 알맞게 영작한 것은?

우리는 Maggy와 Fred를 기다리고 있지 않다.

① We will wait for Maggy and Fred.

② We won't wait for Maggy and Fred.

③ We aren't waiting for Maggy and Fred.

④ We didn't wait for Maggy and Fred.

⑤ We weren't waiting for Maggy and Fred.

서술형

16 다음 문장에서 어법상 어색한 부분을 찾아 쓰고 바르게 고쳐 쓰시오.

> The package is going not to arrive on time.

_____ → _____

서술형

17 다음은 Amanda의 주말 일정표이다. 빈칸에 알맞은 말을 넣어 질문에 대한 대답을 완성하시오.

Saturday	swim at the pool
Sunday	bake chocolate chip cookies

> A: Is Amanda going to swim at the pool on Sunday?
> B: _____, _____ _____. She _____ _____ _____ _____ chocolate chip cookies on Sunday.

고난도

18 다음 중 어법상 어색한 것끼리 묶인 것은?

> ⓐ Are you meeting Dan 30 minutes ago?
> ⓑ James will going to be a famous singer.
> ⓒ We weren't listening to the radio.
> ⓓ The sky is bright last night.
> ⓔ Are they going to have pasta for dinner?

① ⓐ, ⓑ, ⓒ   ② ⓐ, ⓑ, ⓓ   ③ ⓐ, ⓓ, ⓔ
④ ⓑ, ⓒ, ⓔ   ⑤ ⓒ, ⓓ, ⓔ

서술형

19 다음 대화에서 어법상 어색한 부분을 찾아 쓰고 바르게 고쳐 쓰시오.

> A: Is Jason skating in the ice rink now?
> B: No, he wasn't. He is taking a rest.

_____ → _____

서술형

[20-22] 우리말과 같도록 괄호 안의 말을 활용하여 문장을 완성하시오.

20
> 바나나는 따뜻한 나라에서 잘 자란다. (grow)

= Bananas _____ well in warm countries.

21
> 그들은 거실을 청소하고 있었다. (clean the living room)

= They _____.

22
> 그녀는 지금 TV를 보고 있지 않다. 그녀는 책을 읽고 있다. (watch TV, read a book)

= She _____ now.
She _____.

서술형 **고난도**

23 다음 글의 밑줄 친 ⓐ~ⓔ 중 어법상 어색한 것을 찾아 기호를 쓰고 바르게 고쳐 쓰시오.

> I ⓐam going to go on a picnic with my friends today. It ⓑis raining an hour ago, but it ⓒwill be sunny soon. I ⓓwill making some gimbab now, and my sister is helping me. My friends ⓔwill love it.

(1) _____ → _____
(2) _____ → _____

Chapter

04

조동사

조동사는 be동사나 일반동사와 함께 쓰여 여러 가지 의미를 더하는 말이다.

UNIT 01 | can, may

1 조동사

주어의 인칭이나 수에 따라 형태가 변하지 않으며, 「조동사 + 동사원형」의 형태로 쓴다.

My brother **can** *drive* a truck.

---

2 can

❶ 능력·가능(~할 수 있다)을 나타내며, 이때 be able to로 바꿔 쓸 수 있다.

I **can** play the guitar. = I **am able to** play the guitar.
Penguins **cannot[can't]** fly. = Penguins **are not[aren't] able to** fly.
Can she ride a bicycle? = **Is** she **able to** ride a bicycle?

❷ 허가(~해도 된다), 요청(~해주겠니?)

You **can** borrow my eraser.
You **cannot[can't]** enter the room.

A: **Can** I see your passport?
B: Yes, you **can**. / Of course. / No, you **can't**. / Sorry, you **can't**.

Can you close the door?

TIP could는 능력·가능을 나타내는 can의 과거형으로 쓰이거나, can보다 정중한 허가·요청을 나타낸다.
I **could not[couldn't]** remember her name. <능력·가능>
Could you lend me your phone? <요청>

---

3 may

❶ 약한 추측(~일지도 모른다)

It **may** snow tomorrow.
The news **may not** be true.

❷ 허가(~해도 된다)

You **may** sleep now.
We **may not** play here.

A: **May** I ask a question?
B: Yes, you **may**. / Of course. / No, you **may not**. / Sorry, you **may not**.

Smart Check 다음 빈칸에 들어갈 알맞은 것을 고르시오.

1 Brian _____ read Russian.

① can   ② is   ③ able to

Practice

Answers p.6

A 괄호 안에서 알맞은 것을 고르시오.

1 You may (go / going) home now.

2 We (are able to / are able) wash the car.

3 The boy could (lifted / lift) the books.

4 His sister (may / mays) need help with her homework.

5 (Is / Does) he able to swim in the ocean?

6 My mother (not may / may not) be in her room.

wash a car 세차하다
lift 통 들어 올리다
help 형 도움; 통 돕다
ocean 명 바다

B can 또는 can't와 괄호 안의 동사를 활용하여 빈칸에 쓰시오.

1 You look tired. You _____ _____ a break. (have)

2 This dog has short legs. It _____ _____ high. (jump) .

3 Benny lived in Korea for a long time. She _____ _____ Korean. (speak)

4 He doesn't have much money. He _____ _____ a new camera. (buy)

tired 형 피곤한
have a break 잠시 휴식을 취하다
short 형 짧은
high 부 높게
for a long time 오랫동안
much 형 많은; 부 많이

C may 또는 may not과 괄호 안의 동사를 활용하여 문장을 완성하시오.

1 It's dark. You _____ on the light. (turn)

2 Daniel _____ the rumor. But it is real. (believe)

3 Ann had lunch six hours ago. She _____ hungry now. (be)

4 It's too windy outside. You _____ the window. (open)

dark 형 어두운
turn on a light 불을 켜다
rumor 명 소문
real 형 진짜의
believe 통 믿다
windy 형 바람이 많이 부는
outside 부 밖에(서)

D 우리말과 같도록 괄호 안의 동사를 활용하여 빈칸에 쓰시오.

1 내가 지금 TV를 봐도 되니? (watch)

= _____ I _____ TV now?

2 다음 주말에 비가 올지도 모른다. (rain)

= It _____ _____ next weekend.

3 나를 위해 노래를 불러주겠니? (sing)

= _____ you _____ a song for me?

4 Baker씨는 김치를 만들 수 있니? (make)

= _____ Mr. Baker _____ _____ _____ kimchi?

watch 통 보다
rain 통 비가 오다; 명 비
sing a song 노래를 부르다

UNIT 02 | must, have to, should

1 must

❶ 의무(~해야 한다)

You **must** wear a seat belt.

We **must not** lie to our parents.
> → must not은 강한 금지(~하면 안 된다)를 나타낸다.

❷ 강한 추측(~임이 틀림없다)

That boy **must** be Oliver.

She **must** be very happy.

> **TIP** 강한 추측을 나타내는 **must**의 부정은 **cannot[can't]**(~일 리가 없다)를 쓴다.
> That boy **cannot[can't]** be Oliver.

2 have to

의무(~해야 한다)를 나타내며, must와 바꿔 쓸 수 있다. 주어가 3인칭 단수일 때는 has to를 쓴다.

I **have to** meet my friend.

Cindy **has to** repair her laptop.

Does he **have to** go now?

You **don't have to** worry about me.
> → don't/doesn't have to는 불필요(~할 필요가 없다)를 나타낸다.

3 should

충고·의무(~해야 한다)를 나타낸다.

We **should** wake up early tomorrow.

You **should not[shouldn't]** forget this.

Smart Check 다음 빈칸에 들어갈 가장 알맞은 것을 고르시오.

1 Her grandfather is sick. She _____ be sad.
 ① must ② have to ③ must not

2 Liam has many cups. He _____ buy more.
 ① has to ② don't have to ③ doesn't have to

3 My brother _____ clean his desk. It's dirty.
 ① must not ② should ③ doesn't have to

Practice

A 밑줄 친 부분의 의미를 <보기>에서 골라 그 기호를 쓰시오.

<보기> ⓐ ~해야 한다 ⓑ ~하면 안 된다 ⓒ ~임이 틀림없다 ⓓ ~할 필요가 없다

1 Eric <u>should</u> wear warm clothes.　　　　　[　　　]

2 You <u>don't have to</u> do the dishes now.　　　[　　　]

3 The students <u>must not</u> break the rules.　　　[　　　]

4 That woman has blond hair. She <u>must</u> be Alice.　[　　　]

5 Children <u>shouldn't</u> drink coffee.　　　　[　　　]

warm 휑 따뜻한
clothes 명 옷
do the dishes 설거지를 하다
break a rule 규칙을 어기다
blond hair 금발 머리

B 다음 두 문장의 의미가 같도록 have to를 활용하여 문장을 완성하시오.

1 I must find my credit card.　　→ I ＿＿＿＿＿＿＿ my credit card.

2 Jason must study hard.　　→ Jason ＿＿＿＿＿＿＿ hard.

3 They must be quiet here.　　→ They ＿＿＿＿＿＿＿ quiet here.

4 She must tell the truth.　　→ She ＿＿＿＿＿＿＿ the truth.

find 동 찾다
quiet 휑 조용한
truth 명 사실

C must not 또는 don't/doesn't have to와 괄호 안의 동사를 활용하여 문장을 완성하시오.

1 The milk smells strange. You ＿＿＿＿＿＿＿ it. (drink)

2 The weather is nice. I ＿＿＿＿＿＿＿ an umbrella. (bring)

3 She ＿＿＿＿＿＿＿. The store is very close. (drive)

4 Mr. Smith ＿＿＿＿＿＿＿ much. His bones are weak. (exercise)

smell 동 ~한 냄새가 나다
strange 휑 이상한
close 휑 가까운
bone 명 뼈
weak 휑 약한
exercise 동 운동하다

D 우리말과 같도록 괄호 안의 말을 활용하여 빈칸에 쓰시오.

1 너는 나를 따라올 필요가 없다. (have to, follow)

= You ＿＿＿＿ ＿＿＿＿ ＿＿＿＿ ＿＿＿＿ me.

2 Hall씨는 부엌에 있는 것이 틀림없다. (must, be)

= Ms. Hall ＿＿＿＿ ＿＿＿＿ in the kitchen.

3 우리는 나쁜 말을 하면 안 된다. (must, say)

= We ＿＿＿＿ ＿＿＿＿ ＿＿＿＿ bad words.

4 나의 할머니는 혼자 걸으시면 안 된다. (should, walk)

= My grandmother ＿＿＿＿ ＿＿＿＿ alone.

follow 동 따라오다, 따라가다
kitchen 명 부엌
say 동 말하다
word 명 말, 단어
alone 뷔 혼자

Writing Exercise

A 다음 문장을 괄호 안의 지시대로 바꿔 쓰시오.

1 Anna should use the oven. (부정문으로)

→ _____ the oven.

2 The workers must paint this wall today. (부정문으로)

→ _____ this wall today.

3 He is able to post articles on the website. (의문문으로)

→ _____ articles on the website?

4 Jackson can explain the story. (부정문으로)

→ _____ the story.

5 You may park the car on the corner. (부정문으로)

→ _____ the car on the corner.

6 Ms. Harris can take care of the baby. (의문문으로)

→ _____ care of the baby?

B 우리말과 같도록 괄호 안의 말을 알맞게 배열하시오.

1 Charles는 그 기차를 놓치면 안 된다. (not, Charles, miss, should)

= _____ the train.

2 그들은 이메일을 보낼 필요가 없다. (don't, send, to, have, they)

= _____ an e-mail.

3 너는 마당에 사과 나무를 심어도 된다. (can, you, plant)

= _____ an apple tree in the yard.

4 학생들은 그들의 점수를 알고 있을지도 모른다. (know, students, may)

= _____ their scores.

5 방문객들은 건물 안에서 음식을 먹으면 안 된다. (not, must, visitors, eat)

= _____ food in the building.

6 그녀는 케이크를 구울 수 있다. (she, to, able, bake, is)

= _____ a cake.

C 우리말과 같도록 괄호 안의 말을 활용하여 문장을 완성하시오.

1 나의 사촌은 바둑을 둘 수 있다. (my cousin, play)

= _____ baduk.

2 Mary는 줄을 서서 기다릴 필요가 없다. (Mary, wait)

= _____ in line.

3 아빠는 나에게 화가 나신 것이 틀림없다. (dad, be)

= _____ angry with me.

4 너는 너의 일을 나중에 해도 된다. (you, do)

= _____ your work later.

5 오전 7시에 Nicole를 깨워주겠니? (you, wake)

= _____ up Nicole at 7 A.M.?

6 운전자들은 어린이 보호 구역에서 속도를 줄여야 한다. (drivers, slow)

= _____ down in school zones.

7 Jacob은 농구를 잘할지도 모른다. (Jacob, be)

= _____ good at basketball.

D 다음 그림을 보고 <보기>와 괄호 안의 말을 한 번씩만 활용하여 문장을 완성하시오.

1  **2**  **3**  **4**

<보기>	can	may	must	have to

1 _____ fast. (ostriches, run)

2 _____ our dog to this playground. (we, bring)

3 _____ your order? (I, take)

4 _____ a ticket for her child. (Ms. Hill, buy)

Chapter 04

조동사

Hackers Grammar Smart Level 1

Chapter Test

서술형

[1-3] 다음 빈칸에 가장 알맞은 말을 <보기>에서 한 번씩만 골라 쓰시오.

<보기>	can	may not	should

1

We _____ go to bed. It's already 11 P.M.

2

_____ you help me?

3

You _____ play outside. Today is hot.

[4-5] 다음 밑줄 친 부분과 바꿔 쓸 수 있는 것을 고르시오.

4

I <u>must</u> brush my teeth after dinner.

① can   ② may   ③ have to
④ shouldn't   ⑤ am able to

5

You <u>may</u> leave the classroom now.

① do   ② can   ③ must
④ should   ⑤ don't have to

6 다음 중 어법상 <u>어색한</u> 것은?

① He doesn't have to writes a report.
② May I sit next to you?
③ This restaurant must be very famous.
④ Should I take the subway?
⑤ Laura isn't able to meet us today.

[7-8] 다음 빈칸에 들어갈 가장 알맞은 것을 고르시오.

7

The train will leave at 6:20 A.M. I _____ wake up early tomorrow.

① cannot   ② may   ③ must not
④ should   ⑤ don't have to

8

We _____ cross the street. The traffic light is red.

① could   ② may   ③ should
④ must not   ⑤ don't have to

서술형

9 다음 문장에서 어법상 <u>어색한</u> 부분을 찾아 쓰고 바르게 고쳐 쓰시오.

You must are kind to the children.

_____ → _____

서술형

[10-12] 우리말과 같도록 문장을 완성하시오.

10

> 저 여자는 모델일지도 모른다.

= That woman _____ be a model.

11

> TV를 꺼주겠니?

= _____ you turn off the TV?

12

> 너는 그 책값을 지불할 필요가 없다.

= You _____ pay for the book.

13 다음 중 자연스럽지 않은 대화는?

① A: May I speak to Amanda?
 B: Sorry, you may not. She's not here.

② A: Should I wear a helmet?
 B: Yes, you should.

③ A: Do we have to return the book?
 B: Yes. Let's go to the library today.

④ A: Must I finish my homework today?
 B: No, you don't have to.

⑤ A: Can I go to Sam's house?
 B: No, you can. You should clean your room first.

14 다음 중 어법상 바른 것을 모두 고르시오.

① Jack can be able to smell the roses.

② May I borrow your cell phone?

③ You not must use the stairs.

④ My sister has to buy new sneakers.

⑤ Hannah should listens to my advice.

서술형

15 다음 대화에서 어법상 어색한 부분을 찾아 쓰고 바르게 고쳐 쓰시오.

> A: It's so cold! Could you making some hot chocolate?
> B: Sure. Should I put marshmallows in it?
> A: Yes, please.

_____ → _____

[16-17] 다음 중 밑줄 친 부분의 의미가 나머지 넷과 다른 것을 고르시오.

16 ① Students <u>must</u> wear uniforms.

② You <u>must</u> keep your promise.

③ Alice <u>must</u> be lazy. She is always late.

④ You <u>must</u> eat broccoli.

⑤ We <u>must</u> hurry. The movie will start soon.

17 ① James <u>can</u> build a snowman.

② The teacher <u>can</u> speak Russian.

③ I <u>can</u> solve the puzzle easily.

④ <u>Can</u> polar bears swim fast?

⑤ <u>Can</u> I have some soup?

18 다음 빈칸에 공통으로 들어갈 가장 알맞은 것은?

> • You _____ drink enough water every day.
> • Benji isn't answering the phone. He _____ be very busy now.

① can   ② may   ③ must
④ have to   ⑤ should

서술형 고난도

19 다음 글에서 어법상 어색한 부분을 찾아 쓰고 바르게 고쳐 쓰시오.

> We should use not plastic cups because they are polluting the earth. We have to use glasses instead.

_____ → _____

고난도

20 다음 중 어법상 바른 것끼리 묶인 것은?

> ⓐ Amy must is very nervous.
> ⓑ We has to print our homework.
> ⓒ Could I drink a cup of green tea?
> ⓓ Bill doesn't have to pack a bag.
> ⓔ You may not take off your shoes.

① ⓐ, ⓑ, ⓒ   ② ⓐ, ⓑ, ⓓ   ③ ⓐ, ⓓ, ⓔ
④ ⓑ, ⓒ, ⓔ   ⑤ ⓒ, ⓓ, ⓔ

서술형

21 다음 표지판을 보고 must와 괄호 안의 말을 활용하여 문장을 완성하시오.

(1)   (2)

(1) You _____ here. (stop)
(2) You _____ here. (take pictures)

서술형

22 우리말과 같도록 괄호 안의 말을 활용하여 문장을 완성하시오.

> 그는 농구 선수일 리가 없다. (be a basketball player)

= He _____.

서술형 고난도

23 우리말과 같도록 주어진 <조건>에 맞게 영작하시오.

> 방문객들은 그들의 이름을 써야 한다.

> <조건>
> 1. visitors, write, their names를 활용하시오.
> 2. 6단어로 쓰시오.

= _____.

Chapter

05

동사의 종류

동사의 종류에 따라 필수 문장 요소가 달라진다.

UNIT 01 | 주격 보어가 필요한 동사

1 ### 주격 보어가 필요한 동사

주어를 보충 설명하는 주격 보어가 필요한 동사로, 「주어 + 동사 + 주격 보어」 형태의 문장을 이룬다. 주격 보어 자리에는 명사나 형용사가 온다.

주어	+	be, become, turn, keep, get, stay 등	+	주격 보어 (명사, 형용사)

Ms. Johnson **is** a doctor.
The singer **became** popular.

2 ### 감각동사

감각을 나타내는 동사인 look, sound, smell, taste, feel의 주격 보어 자리에는 형용사만 온다.

주어	+	look(~하게 보이다) sound(~하게 들리다) smell(~한 냄새가 나다) taste(~한 맛이 나다) feel(~하게 느끼다)	+	주격 보어 (형용사)

The children **look** friendly.
Your voice **sounded** scary.
This strawberry cake **smells** delicious.
Lemons **taste** sour.
The scarf **feels** soft.

> **TIP** 감각동사 뒤에 명사가 올 때는 전치사 like와 함께 「감각동사 + like + 명사」의 형태로 쓴다.
> The baby **looks like** an angel.
> Her hands **smelled like** roses.

Smart Check 다음 빈칸에 들어갈 알맞은 것을 고르시오.

1 Her skirt looked _____.
　① beautifully　　　　② nicely　　　　③ pretty

2 It sounded like _____.
　① thunder　　　　② noisy　　　　③ boring

Practice

Answers p.7

A 괄호 안에서 알맞은 것을 고르시오.

1 These potato chips taste (salt / salty).

2 The weather is (warm / warmly).

3 Your tea smells (good / well).

4 Those kittens look (love / lovely).

5 The concert hall became (quiet / quietly).

salt 몡 소금
salty 혱 짠
tea 몡 차
kitten 몡 새끼 고양이
concert hall 콘서트홀, 연주회장

B 다음 빈칸에 like가 필요하면 like를 쓰고, 필요하지 않으면 X를 쓰시오.

1 His idea sounds _____ nice.

2 Her hair feels _____ a broom.

3 These grapes taste _____ sweet.

4 The dogs looked _____ lions.

5 It smells _____ coffee.

idea 몡 생각, 아이디어
broom 몡 빗자루
sweet 혱 단, 달콤한

C 밑줄 친 부분이 어법상 맞으면 O를 쓰고, 틀리면 바르게 고쳐 쓰시오.

1 This soap smells <u>greatly</u>.　　　→ _____

2 He sounds <u>angry</u>.　　　→ _____

3 The food turned <u>badly</u>.　　　→ _____

4 This juice tastes <u>peaches</u>.　　　→ _____

5 Her wedding dress looks <u>perfectly</u>.　→ _____

soap 몡 비누
peach 몡 복숭아
perfectly 뮈 완벽하게

D 우리말과 같도록 괄호 안의 말을 활용하여 빈칸에 쓰시오.

1 나의 토마토 수프는 이상한 맛이 났다. (strange)
= My tomato soup _____ _____.

2 이 야채 샌드위치는 신선하게 보인다. (fresh)
= This vegetable sandwich _____ _____.

3 그 향수는 나무 같은 냄새가 난다. (wood)
= The perfume _____ _____ _____.

4 Tommy는 어젯밤에 외롭게 느꼈다. (lonely)
= Tommy _____ _____ last night.

strange 혱 이상한
fresh 혱 신선한
vegetable 몡 야채
wood 몡 나무, 목재
perfume 몡 향수
lonely 혱 외로운

UNIT 02 | 두 개의 목적어가 필요한 동사

1 주어 + 수여동사 + 간접 목적어 + 직접 목적어

수여동사는 '-에게 ~을 (해)주다'라는 의미를 나타내며, 간접 목적어(-에게)와 직접 목적어(~을)가 모두 필요한 동사이다.

주어	+	give, send, bring, pass, show, teach, tell, write, read, lend, buy, cook, find, make, get, build, ask 등	+	간접 목적어 (-에게)	+	직접 목적어 (~을)

He **sent** *her a gift*.
I can **make** *you a paper plane*.
Andy **asked** *the teacher some questions*.

2 주어 + 수여동사 + 직접 목적어 + to/for/of + 간접 목적어

「주어 + 수여동사 + 간접 목적어 + 직접 목적어」는 「주어 + 수여동사 + 직접 목적어 + to/for/of + 간접 목적어」로 바꿔 쓸 수 있다. 이때 쓰는 전치사 to/for/of는 동사에 따라 다르다.

❶ to를 쓰는 동사: give, send, bring, pass, show, teach, tell, write, read, lend 등

She **showed** *me a picture*.
→ She **showed** *a picture* **to** *me*.

❷ for를 쓰는 동사: buy, cook, find, make, get, build 등

I will **buy** *my brother a toy robot*.
→ I will **buy** *a toy robot* **for** *my brother*.

❸ of를 쓰는 동사: ask 등

Can I **ask** *you a favor*?
→ Can I **ask** *a favor* **of** *you*?

Smart Check 다음 빈칸에 들어갈 알맞은 것을 고르시오.

1 Please lend _____.
　① a pencil me　　　　　　② me a pencil　　　　　　③ to me a pencil

2 Mr. Allen teaches English _____ us.
　① to　　　　　　② for　　　　　　③ of

Practice

Answers p.7

A 괄호 안에서 알맞은 것을 고르시오.

1 Mr. Brown gave advice (to / of) his students.

2 Her mom bought a new laptop (to / for) her.

3 My brother asked a question (to / of) me.

4 Jake showed his ID card (to / for) the security guard.

advice 몡 조언
laptop 몡 노트북, 휴대용 컴퓨터
ID card 신분증
security guard 경비원

B <보기>의 동사를 한 번씩만 활용하여 대화를 완성하시오.

<보기>	pass	write	lend	make

1 A: Can you _____ me the water?

   B: Sure.

2 A: Rachel _____ some cookies for us last night.

   B: Were they tasty?

3 A: Larry _____ a letter to his girlfriend yesterday.

   B: Wow, he is so romantic.

4 A: I didn't bring my wallet today.

   B: It's okay. I can _____ you some money.

tasty 혱 맛있는
letter 몡 편지
romantic 혱 낭만적인
wallet 몡 지갑

C 다음 두 문장의 의미가 같도록 빈칸에 알맞은 말을 쓰시오.

1 The server got us napkins.

   → The server _____ _____ _____ _____ .

2 Mr. Flores taught his nephew science.

   → Mr. Flores _____ _____ _____ _____ _____ .

3 Franco told the rumor to me.

   → Franco _____ _____ _____ _____ .

server 몡 종업원
napkin 몡 냅킨
nephew 몡 조카
science 몡 과학
rumor 몡 소문

D 우리말과 같도록 괄호 안의 말을 알맞게 배열하시오.

1 그들은 Wilson씨에게 그 개를 찾아줬다. (for, found, Ms. Wilson, the dog)

   = They _____ .

2 그는 그의 아버지께 그 기사를 읽어드렸다. (to, the article, read, his father)

   = He _____ .

3 나는 지난주에 그녀에게 선물을 보내줬다. (her, sent, a present)

   = I _____ last week.

article 몡 기사
present 몡 선물

목적격 보어가 필요한 동사

1 목적격 보어가 필요한 동사

목적어를 보충 설명하는 목적격 보어가 필요한 동사로, 「주어 + 동사 + 목적어 + 목적격 보어」 형태의 문장을 이룬다. 목적격 보어 자리에는 명사, 형용사, to부정사가 온다.

주어	+	call, make, keep, find, want, ask, tell, expect, allow, advise, order 등	+	목적어	+	목적격 보어 (명사, 형용사, to부정사)

❶ 목적격 보어로 명사를 쓰는 동사: call, make 등

We **call** her *a genius*.
The program **made** the book *a bestseller*.

❷ 목적격 보어로 형용사를 쓰는 동사: make, keep, find 등

Elizabeth always **makes** me *angry*.
The air conditioner will **keep** us *cool*.

❸ 목적격 보어로 to부정사를 쓰는 동사: want, ask, tell, expect, allow, advise, order 등

My sister **wants** me *to cook* lunch.
The man **asked** Reina *to give* directions.
I **expected** you *to arrive* on time.

Smart Check 다음 빈칸에 들어갈 알맞은 것을 고르시오.

1 They _____ the kid Thomas.
① keep ② ask ③ call

2 This documentary will make you _____.
① to be sad ② sad ③ sadly

3 My mother doesn't allow me _____ games.
① play ② to play ③ played

4 The doctor _____ them to eat healthy food.
① advised ② kept ③ made

Practice

Answers p.8

A 괄호 안에서 알맞은 것을 고르시오.

1 Honey makes food (sweet / sweetly).

2 He told the children (be / to be) silent.

3 Ms. Young (found / advised) her house dirty.

4 I asked her (turn / to turn) off the heater.

5 The coach allowed us (to sit / sitting) down.

honey 명 꿀
silent 형 조용한
dirty 형 더러운
turn off (전기, 기계 등을) 끄다
heater 명 난방기, 히터
coach 명 코치
sit down 앉다

B 다음 빈칸에 알맞은 말을 <보기>에서 한 번씩만 골라 쓰시오.

<보기>	wrong	to study	to be

1 I expected this box _____ light.

2 Charles found the answer _____ .

3 Our grandmother wanted us _____ hard.

wrong 형 틀린, 잘못된
light 형 가벼운
answer 명 답, 대답

C 밑줄 친 부분이 어법상 맞으면 O를 쓰고, 틀리면 바르게 고쳐 쓰시오.

1 My neighbors called <u>a liar him</u>.   → _____

2 He advised his daughter <u>sleeping</u> early.   → _____

3 She asked me <u>to move</u> my seat.   → _____

4 The firefighter ordered them <u>ran</u>.   → _____

neighbor 명 이웃
liar 명 거짓말쟁이
daughter 명 딸
seat 명 자리, 좌석
firefighter 명 소방관

D 우리말과 같도록 괄호 안의 말을 활용하여 빈칸에 쓰시오.

1 Brenda는 그녀의 성적이 높기를 기대했다. (expect, her grade, be)
= Brenda _____ _____ _____ _____ high.

2 헬멧은 너의 머리를 안전하게 유지한다. (keep, your head, safe)
= A helmet _____ _____ _____ _____ .

3 우리는 새끼 개를 강아지라고 부른다. (call, a baby dog, a puppy)
= We _____ _____ _____ _____ .

4 나의 부모님은 내가 변호사가 되기를 원하신다. (want, me, become)
= My parents _____ _____ _____ _____ a lawyer.

grade 명 성적, 등급
high 형 높은
safe 형 안전한
helmet 명 헬멧
puppy 명 강아지
lawyer 명 변호사

Writing Exercise

A 다음 빈칸에 알맞은 말을 <보기>에서 한 번씩만 골라 쓰시오.

<보기>	sounds very good	felt hungry	found the summer
	allowed the visitors	gave snacks	build the children

1 Matilda _____ to her friends.

2 The man _____ to enter the room.

3 His vacation plan _____.

4 They will _____ a school.

5 I skipped breakfast, so I _____.

6 Ryan is from a cold country, so he _____ hot in Korea.

B 우리말과 같도록 괄호 안의 말을 알맞게 배열하시오.

1 그 사과 파이는 맛있는 냄새가 난다. (delicious, smells)

= The apple pie _____.

2 저에게 저 숟가락을 건네주시겠어요? (me, pass, that spoon)

= Could you _____?

3 이 도넛은 그 빵집을 유명하게 만들었다. (famous, the bakery, made)

= This doughnut _____.

4 이 스웨터는 비단처럼 느껴진다. (like, feels, silk)

= This sweater _____.

5 Maki 선생님은 학생들에게 일본어를 가르치실 것이다. (to, Japanese, students, teach)

= Ms. Maki will _____.

6 사람들은 숫자 7을 행운의 숫자라고 부른다. (the number seven, call, a lucky number)

= People _____.

7 나는 Brian에게 규칙적으로 운동하라고 조언했다. (to, Brian, advised, exercise)

= I _____ regularly.

8 나의 어머니는 나의 여동생에게 배낭을 사주실 것이다. (my sister, will buy, for, a backpack)

= My mother _____.

C 우리말과 같도록 <보기>의 동사와 괄호 안의 말을 활용하여 빈칸에 쓰시오.

<보기>	be	taste	lend	get	order

1 그녀의 체온은 정상이었다. (normal)

= Her body temperature _____ _____.

2 나에게 너의 교과서를 빌려주겠니? (your textbook)

= Can you _____ _____ _____ _____?

3 한국 음식은 외국인들에게 매운 맛이 날지도 모른다. (spicy)

= Korean food may _____ _____ to foreigners.

4 아빠는 우리에게 집 안에 머무르라고 명령하셨다. (stay)

= Dad _____ _____ _____ _____ in the house.

5 그의 고모는 어제 그에게 표를 가져다줬다. (the ticket)

= His aunt _____ _____ _____ _____ _____ yesterday.

D 다음은 Sophie와 Brandon이 주고받은 문자 메시지이다. <보기>의 동사와 괄호 안의 말을 활용하여 빈칸에 쓰시오.

<보기>	look	bring	ask	make

Sophie: What did you do last weekend?

Brandon: I went to Jejudo. The scenery ⓐ_____ _____. (beautiful)

Sophie: Did you take a picture with a dolhareubang?

Brandon: Yes, I did. I ⓑ_____ _____ _____ _____ a picture of me with it. (my mother, take)

Brandon: And I will ⓒ_____ _____ _____ _____ tomorrow. (you, a souvenir) I bought it for you.

Sophie: Thanks a lot! You always ⓓ_____ _____ _____. (me, happy)

Chapter Test

[1-3] 다음 빈칸에 알맞은 말을 <보기>에서 한 번씩만 골라 쓰시오.

<보기>	became	sounded	brought

1

Sally _____ the class president.

2

Harry _____ her the guitar.

3

My voice _____ strange in the morning.

4 다음 빈칸에 들어갈 알맞은 것은?

Mason _____ the paper to me.

① made ② bought ③ gave
④ found ⑤ asked

5 다음 중 밑줄 친 부분이 어법상 어색한 것은?

① Ms. Bryant is busy now.
② Seawater smells salty.
③ Their music sounds terribly.
④ This blanket feels heavy.
⑤ The lemonade tasted sour.

6 다음 중 자연스럽지 않은 대화는?

① A: Please show me your passport.
　B: Here it is.
② A: Did you lend him your jacket?
　B: No. I lent my sweater to him.
③ A: It's snowing outside.
　B: I didn't expect snow to fall.
④ A: Did Max call you?
　B: No. He sent a text message for me.
⑤ A: How was the new mobile game?
　B: I found it boring.

7 다음 (A)~(C)에 들어갈 말이 바르게 짝지어진 것은?

- David looks __(A)__ today.
- The cat __(B)__ a mouse to us.
- Did the book __(C)__ her a famous writer?

	(A)	(B)	(C)
①	happy	brought	make
②	happily	got	find
③	happy	got	find
④	happily	brought	make
⑤	happy	brought	find

8 다음 빈칸에 들어갈 말로 어색한 것은?

Ms. Cooper _____ us the letter.

① read ② wrote ③ gave
④ wanted ⑤ got

9 다음 빈칸에 들어갈 말이 나머지 넷과 <u>다른</u> 것은?

① Edward gave some pencils _____ me.
② She passed the ball _____ her friend.
③ My grandfather read the book _____ us.
④ They showed a map _____ the tourists.
⑤ We made a cake _____ our teacher.

10 다음 빈칸에 공통으로 들어갈 알맞은 것은?

- Nancy told a secret _____ Nate.
- He allowed them _____ buy a new washing machine.

① for ② on ③ to
④ at ⑤ of

[11-12] 다음 우리말을 알맞게 영작한 것을 고르시오.

11
Smith 선생님은 학생들에게 과학을 가르치신다.

① Mr. Smith teaches students to science.
② Mr. Smith teaches science students.
③ Mr. Smith teaches students science.
④ Mr. Smith teaches students for science.
⑤ Mr. Smith teaches science of students.

12
그들은 내가 돕기를 원했다.

① They wanted me help.
② They wanted to me help.
③ They wanted to help me.
④ They wanted me to help.
⑤ They wanted me helping.

13 다음 중 밑줄 친 부분의 쓰임이 나머지 넷과 <u>다른</u> 것은?

① Jordan's shoes <u>made</u> him tall.
② This movie <u>made</u> her a star.
③ The sun <u>made</u> me hot.
④ That new toy <u>made</u> my dog excited.
⑤ The cook <u>made</u> us delicious soup.

서술형

[14-15] 다음 두 문장의 의미가 같도록 알맞은 전치사를 이용하여 문장을 완성하시오.

14
Amy passed James the salt and pepper.
→ Amy passed _____.

15
The man built his children a sandcastle.
→ The man built _____.

16 다음 중 어법상 바른 것을 <u>모두</u> 고르시오.

① Those strawberries tasted sweetly.
② That cloud looks like a bird.
③ The story sounds like interesting.
④ Your pajamas feel soft.
⑤ The popcorn smells wonderfully.

17 다음 문장에서 **틀린** 부분을 바르게 고쳐 완전한 문장을 쓰시오.

> Did you write an e-mail Mr. Anderson?
> → _____ ?

고난도

18 다음 중 어법상 바른 것끼리 묶인 것은?

> ⓐ The gloves will keep your hands warm.
> ⓑ Emily showed her picture us.
> ⓒ Mr. Brown asked a question of me.
> ⓓ I told my sister to wash the dishes.
> ⓔ We bought some flowers to Thomas.

① ⓐ, ⓑ, ⓒ   ② ⓐ, ⓒ, ⓓ   ③ ⓐ, ⓓ, ⓔ
④ ⓑ, ⓒ, ⓔ   ⑤ ⓑ, ⓓ, ⓔ

서술형

[19-20] 우리말과 같도록 괄호 안의 말을 활용하여 문장을 완성하시오.

19
> 그의 계획들은 흥미진진하게 들린다. (exciting)

= His plans _____ .

20
> 새 이웃은 친절해 보인다. (friendly)

= The new neighbor _____ .

서술형

21 다음 대화에서 어법상 **어색한** 부분을 찾아 쓰고 바르게 고쳐 쓰시오.

> A: Who was on the phone?
> B: It was Julia. I asked a favor to her.

_____ → _____

서술형 고난도

[22-23] 우리말과 같도록 주어진 <조건>에 맞게 영작하시오.

22
> 나는 나의 할머니께 안경을 찾아드렸다.

> <조건>
> 1. find, my grandmother, the glasses를 활용하시오.
> 2. 7단어로 쓰시오.

= _____ .

23
> 그녀는 우리에게 많은 책을 읽으라고 조언했다.

> <조건>
> 1. advise, read, many books를 활용하시오.
> 2. 7단어로 쓰시오.

= _____ .

서술형 고난도

24 다음 글의 밑줄 친 ⓐ~ⓔ 중 어법상 **어색한** 것을 찾아 기호를 쓰고 바르게 고쳐 쓰시오.

> My family has a puppy, and it looks ⓐlovely. Its name ⓑis Marie, but my brother calls ⓒit Marley. I asked him ⓓcall it Marie, but he didn't listen. He makes me ⓔangry.

_____ → _____

Chapter

06

문장의 종류

특정한 의도를 나타내기 위해 명령문, 감탄문, 의문문 등
다양한 종류의 문장을 사용할 수 있다.

UNIT 01 | 명령문, 청유문, 감탄문

1 명령문

상대방에게 지시하거나 요구하는 문장이며, 주어 You가 생략되어 있다.

긍정 명령문(~해라)	동사원형
부정 명령문(~하지 마라)	Don't[Do not] + 동사원형

Do your homework.

Please **don't[do not] run** here. (= **Don't[Do not] run** here, *please*.)
↳ 명령문 맨 앞이나 맨 뒤에 please를 붙이면 더 정중한 표현이 된다.

TIP · 「명령문 + and ~」: ···해라, 그러면 ~
Exercise regularly, and you will become healthy.

· 「명령문 + or ~」: ···해라, 그렇지 않으면 ~
Study hard, or you will fail the test.

2 청유문

상대방에게 권유하거나 제안하는 문장이다.

긍정 청유문((우리) ~하자)	Let's + 동사원형
부정 청유문((우리) ~하지 말자)	Let's not + 동사원형

Let's drink milk.
Let's not be nervous.

3 감탄문

기쁨이나 놀라움 등의 감정을 나타내는 문장으로, '정말 ~이구나/하구나!'의 의미이다. 문장 맨 뒤의 「주어 + 동사」는 생략할 수도 있다.

What 감탄문(명사 강조)	What + (a/an) + 형용사 + 명사 + (주어 + 동사)!
How 감탄문(형용사나 부사 강조)	How + 형용사/부사 + (주어 + 동사)!

What a funny book *(this is)*!
How easy *(the quiz was)*!
How slowly *turtles go*!
↳ How 감탄문이 부사를 강조할 때는 문장 맨 뒤의 「주어 + 동사」를 생략할 수 없다.

TIP **What** 감탄문이 복수명사나 셀 수 없는 명사를 강조할 때는 **a/an**을 쓰지 않는다.
What cute babies (they are)!

  다음 빈칸에 들어갈 알맞은 것을 고르시오.

1 _____ the window.
① Close   ② Closing   ③ Closed

Practice

Answers p.9

A 괄호 안에서 알맞은 것을 고르시오.

1 (Wash / Washing) the dishes, please.

2 (Not / Don't) enter the building.

3 What a (big forest / forest big) it is!

4 Let's (save / saves) energy.

5 (What / How) delicious this pie is!

6 Drink this hot chocolate, (or / and) you will get warm.

> wash the dishes 설거지를 하다
> enter 图 들어가다
> forest 图 숲
> save 图 절약하다, 구하다
> energy 图 에너지, 동력 자원
> delicious 图 맛있는
> warm 图 따뜻한

B 다음 문장을 명령문으로 바꿔 쓰시오.

1 You should turn left. → _____ left.

2 You shouldn't lock the door. → _____ the door.

3 You should be fair. → _____ fair.

4 You shouldn't eat too fast. → _____ too fast.

> turn left 좌측으로 돌다
> lock 图 잠그다
> fair 图 공정한, 공평한

C 다음 문장을 감탄문으로 바꿔 쓰시오.

1 That smartphone is very small.
→ How _____ _____ _____ _____ !

2 These are very sweet bananas.
→ What _____ _____ _____ _____ !

3 My brother dances really well.
→ How _____ _____ _____ _____ !

4 You are a very careful driver.
→ What _____ _____ _____ _____ _____ !

> small 图 작은
> dance 图 춤을 추다; 图 춤
> careful 图 조심스러운
> driver 图 운전자

D 우리말과 같도록 괄호 안의 말을 활용하여 빈칸에 쓰시오.

1 우리의 시간을 낭비하지 말자. (waste, our time)
= _____ _____ _____ _____ _____ .

2 James는 정말 용감한 소년이구나! (a brave boy)
= _____ _____ _____ _____ _____ James is!

3 서둘러라, 그렇지 않으면 너는 비행기를 놓칠 것이다. (hurry up)
= _____ _____ , _____ you will miss the plane.

> waste 图 낭비하다
> brave 图 용감한
> hurry up 서두르다
> miss 图 놓치다
> plane 图 비행기

UNIT 02 | 의문사 의문문 I

1 who(누구)

❶ 사람에 대해 물을 때 쓰며, 목적격인 경우 whom으로도 쓸 수 있다.

Who is her homeroom teacher?
Who *calls* you every morning?
└→ 의문사가 주어인 경우 3인칭 단수 동사가 온다.
Who(m) do you know in this room?

❷ whose는 '누구의'라는 의미의 형용사로 쓰여 명사 앞에서 명사를 꾸밀 수 있다.

Whose *gloves* are these?

2 what(무엇)

❶ 동물이나 사물, 또는 사람의 직업이나 성격에 대해 물을 때 쓴다.

What are you eating?
What does Mr. Cooper do?

❷ '무슨, 어떤'이라는 의미의 형용사로 쓰여 명사 앞에서 명사를 꾸밀 수 있다.

What *vegetable* is that?

3 which(어느 것)

❶ 정해진 범위 안에서의 선택을 물을 때 쓴다.

Which do you want, strawberries or melons?
Which do you like better, spring or fall?

❷ '어느, 어떤'이라는 의미의 형용사로 쓰여 명사 앞에서 명사를 꾸밀 수 있다.

Which *character* do you like in the movie?

TIP what은 정해지지 않은 범위에서 질문할 때 쓰고, which는 정해진 범위 안에서의 선택을 물을 때 쓴다.
What is your favorite subject?
Which do you prefer, history or science?

Smart Check 다음 빈칸에 들어갈 알맞은 것을 고르시오.

1 _____ was he doing at noon?
① Who   ② What   ③ Which

2 _____ is faster, an airplane or a ship?
① Who   ② What   ③ Which

Practice

Answers p.9

A 다음 빈칸에 Who, Who(m), Whose 중 알맞은 것을 넣어 대화를 완성하시오.

1 A: _____ son is Austin?   B: He is Mr. Miller's son.

2 A: _____ is your best friend?   B: My best friend is Amy.

3 A: _____ did Bella meet?   B: She met Liam.

4 A: _____ used my scissors?   B: I used them.

son 몡 아들
meet 통 만나다
use 통 사용하다
scissors 몡 가위

B 괄호 안에서 알맞은 것을 고르시오.

1 A: (Who / What) will be the class president?
   B: Jason will be the class president.

2 A: (What / Which) is your favorite Mexican food?
   B: My favorite Mexican food is taco.

3 A: Who (make / makes) breakfast on Sundays?
   B: My dad makes breakfast on Sundays.

4 A: (What / Which) do you like more, the steak or the lobster?
   B: I like the steak more.

class president 반장
breakfast 몡 아침 (식사)
steak 몡 스테이크
lobster 몡 바닷가재

C 자연스러운 대화가 되도록 질문과 대답을 연결하시오.

1 Whom did you play with?   •   • ⓐ Some milk.

2 Who ate my sandwiches?   •   • ⓑ My cousins.

3 Which is larger, Russia or China? •   • ⓒ Russia.

4 What did Gina buy yesterday?   •   • ⓓ Your sister ate them.

cousin 몡 사촌

D 우리말과 같도록 괄호 안의 말을 활용하여 빈칸에 쓰시오.

1 이것은 누구의 지갑이니? (wallet)
   = _____ _____ is this?

2 너는 오늘 학교에서 무엇을 배웠니? (learn)
   = _____ _____ _____ _____ at school today?

3 너는 치킨과 피자 중 어느 것을 선호하니? (prefer)
   = _____ _____ _____ _____, chicken or pizza?

4 누가 그 질문에 대한 답을 아니? (know)
   = _____ _____ the answer to the question?

wallet 몡 지갑
learn 통 배우다
prefer 통 선호하다

UNIT 03 | 의문사 의문문 II

1 **where**(어디에(서))

장소를 물을 때 쓴다.

Where is the library?   **Where** did you buy the shoes?

---

2 **when**(언제)

시간이나 날짜를 물을 때 쓰며, 시간을 물을 때는 what time으로 바꿔 쓸 수 있다.

When(= **What time**) does the train leave?   **When** is Sophie's birthday?

---

3 **why**(왜)

이유를 물을 때 쓰며, because(왜냐하면)를 사용하여 대답할 수 있다.

A: **Why** was your father angry?

B: *Because* I broke his computer.

TIP ·「Why don't you + 동사원형 ~?」: (너는) ~하는 게 어때?
> **Why don't you try** on the suit?

·「Why don't we + 동사원형 ~?」: (우리) ~하지 않겠니? (= How[What] about + V-ing ~?, Let's + 동사원형.)
> **Why don't we go** to an amusement park?
> = **How[What] about going** to an amusement park?
> = **Let's go** to an amusement park.

---

4 **how**(어떻게)

방법이나 상태를 물을 때 쓴다.

How do you go home?   **How** is she today?

---

5 **how + 형용사/부사**(얼마나 ~한/하게)

높이, 기간, 거리, 무게 등의 구체적인 정보를 물을 때 쓴다.

How tall is the tower? <높이, 키>   **How long** will you stay in Korea? <기간, 길이>

How far is it from here to the park? <거리>   **How heavy** are those bags? <무게>

How old are they? <나이>   **How often** does he go to the gym? <빈도>

How many eggs do I need? <개수>   **How much** money did you spend? <양, 가격>

Smart Check 다음 빈칸에 들어갈 알맞은 것을 고르시오.

1 *A*: _____ were you late for school today?   *B*: Because I missed the bus.

    ① When   ② Why   ③ Where

Practice

A 괄호 안에서 알맞은 것을 고르시오.

1 *A*: (When / Where) did you call me?
    B: An hour ago.

2 *A*: (How / Where) can I find a printer?
    B: On the desk over there.

3 *A*: (When / How) do birds fly?
    B: They use their wings.

printer 몡 프린터
over there 저쪽에
wing 몡 날개

B 자연스러운 대화가 되도록 질문과 대답을 연결하시오.

1 How was the cartoon? •   • ⓐ The bookstore.

2 What time does the gallery close? •   • ⓑ It is May 5.

3 When is Children's Day? •   • ⓒ Because he was busy.

4 Where will you go tomorrow? •   • ⓓ It was fun.

5 Why did he quit the club? •   • ⓔ At 9 P.M.

cartoon 몡 만화
gallery 몡 미술관
close 동 문을 닫다
May 몡 5월
Children's Day 어린이날
quit 동 그만두다
club 몡 동아리

C 다음 대화의 빈칸에 알맞은 말을 <보기>에서 골라 쓰시오.

<보기> tall   heavy   often   much

1 *A*: How _____ is your backpack?   *B*: It is 5 kilograms.

2 *A*: How _____ does the bus come?   *B*: It comes every 10 minutes.

3 *A*: How _____ is that yellow hat?   *B*: It is 15 dollars.

4 *A*: How _____ are you?   *B*: I'm 163 centimeters tall.

backpack 몡 배낭
hat 몡 모자

D 우리말과 같도록 괄호 안의 말을 활용하여 빈칸에 쓰시오.

1 그는 어떻게 좋은 성적을 받았니? (get)
    = _____ _____ _____ _____ good grades?

2 너는 밖에서 노는 게 어때? (play)
    = _____ _____ _____ _____ outside?

3 Ella는 지난 주말에 어디를 여행했니? (travel)
    = _____ _____ _____ _____ last weekend?

4 그는 얼마나 많은 펜을 가지고 있니? (pens, have)
    = _____ _____ _____ _____ _____ _____ ?

grade 몡 성적, 학년
outside 뷔 밖에서
travel 동 여행하다

UNIT 04 | 부정의문문, 선택의문문, 부가의문문

1 부정의문문

부정어 not을 포함한 의문문으로, '~하지 않니?'의 의미이다. 질문의 형태와 상관없이 대답의 내용이 긍정이면 Yes, 부정이면 No로 답한다.

A: Aren't you hungry?
B: **Yes**, *I am.* (= Yes, I am hungry.) / **No**, *I'm not.* (= No, I'm not hungry.)

2 선택의문문

or를 사용하여 상대방의 선택을 묻는 의문문이며, 제시된 것 중 하나를 선택하여 대답한다.

A: Is this *your coat* **or** *Cameron's coat*?　　*B*: **It's my coat.**
A: Which do you like better, *day* **or** *night*?　　*B*: **Night.**

3 부가의문문

❶ 상대방에게 확인이나 동의를 구하기 위해 문장 뒤에 덧붙이는 의문문이다. 질문의 형태와 상관없이 대답의 내용이 긍정이면 Yes, 부정이면 No로 답한다.

　　A: Anna doesn't live in Seattle, **does she**?
　　B: **Yes**, *she does.* (= Yes, she lives in Seattle.) / **No**, *she doesn't.* (= No, she doesn't live in Seattle.)

❷ 부가의문문 만드는 법

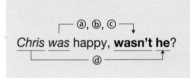

ⓐ 긍정문 뒤에는 부정의 부가의문문을, 부정문 뒤에는 긍정의 부가의문문을 덧붙인다. (단, 부정형은 줄임말로 쓴다.)
ⓑ 부가의문문의 동사는 앞 문장의 동사에 따라 다르게 쓴다. (be동사 → be동사, 일반동사 → do/does/did, 조동사 → 조동사)
ⓒ 부가의문문의 시제는 앞 문장의 시제와 같은 시제를 쓴다.
ⓓ 부가의문문의 주어는 앞 문장의 주어와 맞는 인칭대명사를 사용한다.

Ms. Davis works for a bank, **doesn't she**?
Your brother can't make pancakes, **can he**?

> **TIP** 명령문과 청유문의 부가의문문은 긍정문인지 부정문인지와 상관없이 각각 'will you?'와 'shall we?'를 쓴다.
> *Take a break,* **will you**?
> *Let's not climb a mountain today,* **shall we**?

Smart Check 다음 빈칸에 들어갈 알맞은 것을 고르시오.

1 *A*: Didn't she skip lunch?　　*B*: _____.
　① Yes, she didn't　　② No, she didn't　　③ No, she did

2 Brad and Joan studied together, _____?
　① did they　　② didn't they　　③ didn't he

Practice

A 괄호 안에서 알맞은 것을 고르시오.

1 (Doesn't / Isn't) the weather nice?

2 Tom doesn't eat cucumbers, (does / is) he?

3 Was it Jenny's umbrella (or / and) Sam's umbrella?

4 A: Which color do you prefer, pink or purple?
B: (Yes, I do. / Purple.)

5 A: Don't you remember his name?
B: (Yes / No), I don't.

weather 명 날씨
cucumber 명 오이
purple 명 자주색
remember 동 기억하다

B 질문에 대한 대답이 괄호 안의 내용과 일치하도록 빈칸에 쓰시오.

1 A: Didn't you take the bus yesterday?
B: _____, _____ _____. (아니, 나는 어제 그 버스를 탔어.)

2 A: Doesn't he like desserts?
B: _____, _____ _____. (응, 그는 디저트를 좋아하지 않아.)

3 A: Isn't Ms. Wilson good at cooking?
B: _____, _____ _____. (응, 그녀는 요리를 잘하지 않아.)

4 A: Weren't the books interesting?
B: _____, _____ _____. (아니, 그것들은 흥미로웠어.)

take a bus 버스를 타다
dessert 명 디저트, 후식
good at ~을 잘하는
interesting 형 흥미로운

C 다음 빈칸에 알맞은 부가의문문을 쓰시오.

1 They usually walk to school, _____ _____?

2 Your father can win the race, _____ _____?

3 My dog wasn't in the living room, _____ _____?

4 Be kind to your sister, _____ _____?

5 Emily looked sad yesterday, _____ _____?

usually 부 보통, 대개
race 명 경주
living room 거실

D 우리말과 같도록 괄호 안의 말을 활용하여 빈칸에 쓰시오.

1 그녀는 지난 월요일에 한가하지 않았니? (free)
= _____ _____ _____ last Monday?

2 너는 소금과 설탕 중 어느 것이 필요하니? (salt, sugar)
= _____ do you need, _____ _____ _____?

3 Tommy와 Jim은 제시간에 도착하지 않았어, 그렇지? (arrive)
= Tommy and Jim _____ _____ on time, _____ _____?

free 형 한가한, 자유로운
need 동 필요하다
arrive 동 도착하다
on time 제시간에

Hackers Grammar Smart Level 1 · Chapter 06 · 문장의 종류

Writing Exercise

A 밑줄 친 부분이 어법상 맞으면 O를 쓰고, 틀리면 바르게 고쳐 쓰시오.

1 <u>Wearing</u> a helmet, or you will get hurt. → _____

2 <u>How</u> sharp knives these are! → _____

3 <u>Let's not</u> take the elevator. → _____

4 You and Kelly watched TV last night, <u>did you</u>? → _____

5 <u>What</u> early Peter wakes up! → _____

6 Which do you prefer, an e-mail <u>or</u> a letter? → _____

7 <u>Isn't</u> she have brothers and sisters? → _____

8 <u>Doesn't</u> turn on the heater. → _____

B 우리말과 같도록 괄호 안의 말을 활용하여 빈칸에 쓰시오.

1 누가 그 창문을 깼니? (break, the window)

= _____ _____ _____ _____?

2 이 음악 축제는 정말 신나는구나! (exciting)

= _____ _____ this music festival is!

3 그는 어제 피곤하지 않았니? (tired)

= _____ _____ _____ yesterday?

4 저 아이는 몇 살이니? (that child)

= _____ _____ _____ _____ _____?

5 파티에 당신의 친구들을 초대하세요. (invite, your friends)

= _____ _____ _____ _____ to the party.

6 우리 지금 우리의 가방을 싸지 않겠니? (pack, our bags)

= Why _____ _____ _____ _____ _____ now?

7 그는 언제 그의 전화번호를 바꿨니? (change, his phone number)

= _____ _____ _____ _____ _____ _____ _____?

C 우리말과 같도록 괄호 안의 말을 알맞게 배열하시오.

1 저것은 정말 비싼 목걸이구나! (what, is, an, necklace, expensive, that)

= _____ !

2 함께 사진을 찍자. (take, let's, a picture)

= _____ together.

3 너는 여름과 겨울 중 어느 계절을 더 좋아하니? (season, like more, you, summer, which, winter, do, or)

= _____ , _____ ?

4 Gerald는 어디에 그의 차를 주차했니? (his car, Gerald, did, park, where)

= _____ ?

5 Stephanie는 그 시험을 통과할 수 있어, 그렇지 않니? (pass, can, Stephanie, the test, she, can't)

= _____ , _____ ?

6 너는 얼마나 자주 이를 닦니? (often, you, how, do, your teeth, brush)

= _____ ?

D 다음은 **Michael**에 대한 정보이다. 빈칸에 알맞은 말을 넣어 대화를 완성하시오.

Name: Michael Jones
Age: 17
Birthday: March 20
Height: 176 cm
Blood Type: AB
Hometown: Chicago
Role Model: Yuna Kim

1 *A*: Michael is 16 years old, _____ _____ ?   *B*: _____ , _____ _____ .

2 *A*: _____ is Michael's birthday?   *B*: His birthday is March 20.

3 *A*: _____ _____ is Michael?   *B*: He is 176 centimeters tall.

4 *A*: _____ is Michael's blood type?   *B*: His blood type is AB.

5 *A*: _____ is Michael's hometown?   *B*: His hometown is Chicago.

6 *A*: _____ is Michael's role model?   *B*: His role model is Yuna Kim.

Chapter 06

문장의 종류

Hackers Grammar Smart Level 1

Chapter Test

[1-2] 다음 대화의 빈칸에 들어갈 알맞은 것을 고르시오.

1

> A: _____ is Mr. Adams?
> B: He is my English teacher.

① Who ② Whose ③ Whom
④ Where ⑤ Why

2

> A: _____ color is your cell phone?
> B: It is silver.

① Whose ② What ③ Whom
④ When ⑤ How

[3-4] 다음 빈칸에 들어갈 알맞은 것을 고르시오.

3

> _____ funny stories they are!

① How ② What ③ Why
④ Which ⑤ Who

4

> _____ have dinner at the new restaurant.

① Let ② Let's ③ What
④ Why don't ⑤ How about

서술형 고난도
5 다음 빈칸에 공통으로 들어갈 알맞은 말을 쓰시오.

> • _____ speak loudly in the library.
> • _____ you like scary movies?

6 다음 중 자연스럽지 <u>않은</u> 대화는?

① A: What is her job?
  B: She is an engineer.
② A: Which flavor do you want, grape or watermelon?
  B: I want the watermelon flavor.
③ A: Whose computer is this?
  B: This is Karen's computer.
④ A: When does the plane arrive?
  B: At the airport.
⑤ A: Why don't we go for a walk?
  B: Sure.

7 다음 빈칸에 들어갈 말이 나머지 넷과 <u>다른</u> 것은?

① _____ boring movies they are!
② _____ a cloudy day it is!
③ _____ soft the ice cream was!
④ _____ fun games they are!
⑤ _____ a lucky man he is!

서술형
[8-9] 다음 문장을 감탄문으로 바꿔 쓰시오.

8

> They are really big pumpkins.
> → _____ _____ _____ they are!

9

> The orange was very sour.
> → _____ _____ the orange was!

서술형

10 다음 빈칸에 알맞은 말을 넣어 질문에 대한 대답을 완성하시오.

> A: Didn't you visit Busan in May?
> B: _____, _____ _____.
>   I visited Busan in April.

11 다음 중 어법상 바른 것을 <u>모두</u> 고르시오.

① Aren't they middle school students?
② How did you solve the problem?
③ Don't feeds the birds in the park.
④ Clean your room, and Mom will get angry.
⑤ What is your skirt, this or that?

12 다음 우리말을 알맞게 영작한 것은?

> Jane은 고등학생이 아니야, 그렇지?

① Jane is a high school student, is she?
② Jane is a high school student, isn't she?
③ Jane isn't a high school student, she isn't?
④ Jane isn't a high school student, is she?
⑤ Jane isn't a high school student, isn't she?

13 다음 빈칸에 들어갈 말이 순서대로 짝지어진 것은?

> _____ animal do you like better, cats
> _____ dogs?

① What – or   ② What – and
③ Which – but   ④ Which – or
⑤ Which – and

서술형

[14-15] 다음 문장에서 <u>틀린</u> 부분을 바르게 고쳐 완전한 문장을 쓰시오.

14
> Let go to the gym at 6:30 together.
> → _____ .

15
> Don't is rude to other people.
> → _____ .

[16-17] 다음 질문에 대한 대답으로 알맞은 것을 고르시오.

16
> A: How do you go to school?
> B: _____

① Because I take a subway to school.
② It is two kilometers to school.
③ I ride a bike to school.
④ At 8 o'clock.
⑤ That is my school.

17
> A: Why did you buy those apples?
> B: _____

① My dad and I bought them.
② On December 15.
③ I bought them at the supermarket.
④ I will buy some apples.
⑤ Because I will make an apple pie.

서술형

18 다음 대화에서 어법상 <u>어색한</u> 부분을 찾아 쓰고 바르게 고쳐 쓰시오.

> A: Isn't that café open on Sunday?
> B: No, it is. It's open from Monday to Saturday.

_____ → _____

서술형 **고난도**

19 우리말과 같도록 주어진 <조건>에 맞게 영작하시오.

> 그녀는 정말 아름다운 목소리를 가지고 있구나!

> <조건>   1. 감탄문으로 쓰시오.
>   2. have, a beautiful voice를 활용하시오.
>   3. 6단어로 쓰시오.

= _____ !

서술형 **고난도**

20 다음 대화의 밑줄 친 ⓐ~ⓔ 중 어법상 <u>어색한</u> 것을 찾아 기호를 쓰고 바르게 고쳐 쓰시오.

> A: I invited Jim for dinner. ⓐ How about ordering pizza?
> B: Good. ⓑ Which do you prefer, pepperoni or Hawaiian?
> A: I prefer Hawaiian pizza. But Jim doesn't eat pineapple, ⓒ is he?
> B: No, he ⓓ doesn't.
> A: Then ⓔ let's order pepperoni pizza.
> B: OK.

_____ → _____

고난도

21 다음 중 어법상 바른 것끼리 묶인 것은?

> ⓐ Please don't take pictures in the museum.
> ⓑ How a great you look!
> ⓒ Eric sent you the letter, did he?
> ⓓ Hold the door, will you?
> ⓔ Where did you lose your wallet?

① ⓐ, ⓑ, ⓒ   ② ⓐ, ⓑ, ⓓ   ③ ⓐ, ⓓ, ⓔ
④ ⓑ, ⓒ, ⓔ   ⑤ ⓒ, ⓓ, ⓔ

서술형

[22-24] 우리말과 같도록 괄호 안의 말을 활용하여 문장을 완성하시오.

22
> 돈을 낭비하지 말자. (waste, money)

= _____ .

23
> Chris는 바이올린을 연주할 수 있어, 그렇지 않니? (play, the violin)

= Chris _____ , _____ ?

24
> 너는 얼마나 많은 지우개를 가지고 있니? (have, erasers)

= How _____ ?

Chapter
07

명사와 관사

명사는 사람, 사물, 장소, 개념 등의 이름을 나타내는 말이며,
관사는 명사 앞에 쓰여 명사의 수나 성격을 나타내는 말이다.

UNIT 01 | 셀 수 있는 명사와 셀 수 없는 명사

1 셀 수 있는 명사

❶ 하나, 둘 등으로 셀 수 있는 명사이며, 단수일 때는 명사 앞에 a(n)을 붙이고 복수일 때는 복수형으로 쓴다.

I have **a notebook**. Joseph has three **notebooks**.

❷ 셀 수 있는 명사의 복수형은 대부분 명사에 -(e)s를 붙여 만들며, 일부는 불규칙하게 변한다.

대부분의 명사	명사 + -s	cat - cat**s**	desk - desk**s**
-s, -x, -ch, -sh로 끝나는 명사	명사 + -es	bus - bus**es** watch - watch**es**	fox - fox**es** dish - dish**es**
「자음 + o」로 끝나는 명사	명사 + -es	potato - potato**es** ※ 예외: piano - pianos	tomato - tomato**es** photo - photos
「자음 + y」로 끝나는 명사	y를 i로 바꾸고 + -es	baby - bab**ies**	country - countr**ies**
-f, -fe로 끝나는 명사	f, fe를 v로 바꾸고 + -es	wolf - wol**ves** ※ 예외: roof - roofs	knife - kni**ves** cliff - cliffs
불규칙하게 변하는 명사	man - **men** ox - **oxen**	woman - **women** goose - **geese**	child - **children** mouse - **mice** tooth - **teeth** foot - **feet**
단수형과 복수형이 같은 명사	sheep - **sheep**	deer - **deer**	fish - **fish**

TIP 한 쌍이 짝을 이루는 명사(glasses, gloves, shoes, socks, pants, scissors 등)는 항상 복수형으로 쓰며, 단위를 나타내는 명사 pair를 활용하여 수량을 나타낸다.

Mom bought me *two pairs of* **gloves**.

- -

2 셀 수 없는 명사

❶ 하나, 둘 등으로 셀 수 없는 명사로 항상 단수 취급하며, 명사 앞에 a(n)을 붙일 수 없고 복수형으로도 쓸 수 없다.

Tom is drinking **milk**.

❷ 셀 수 없는 명사의 종류
ⓐ 사람이나 장소 등의 고유한 이름을 나타내는 명사: Jenny, Mr. Han, Korea, New York 등
ⓑ 추상적인 개념을 나타내는 명사: love, friendship, kindness, help, advice, information 등
ⓒ 일정한 형태가 없는 물질을 나타내는 명사: water, juice, rice, bread, paper, sand 등

❸ 셀 수 없는 명사는 그것을 담는 그릇이나 단위를 나타내는 말인 단위명사를 활용하여 수량을 나타내고, 복수형은 단위명사에 -(e)s를 붙여 만든다.

<잔> **a glass of** water/milk/juice	<컵/잔> **a cup of** tea/coffee	<병> **a bottle of** water/juice
<캔> **a can of** coke/soda/paint	<그릇> **a bowl of** soup/rice/cereal	<덩어리> **a loaf of** bread
<장/점> **a piece of** paper/furniture	<조각> **a slice[piece] of** pizza/cheese/bread/cake	

We ordered **a glass of** *juice* and **two bowls of** *cereal*.

Smart Check 다음 빈칸에 들어갈 말로 <u>어색한</u> 것을 고르시오.

1 They will buy _____ .

① a car   ② waters   ③ two pieces of cake

Practice

Answers p.10

A 다음 명사의 복수형을 쓰시오.

1 church – _____

2 city – _____

3 leaf – _____

4 dog – _____

5 man – _____

6 roof – _____

7 foot – _____

8 tomato – _____

9 sheep – _____

10 box – _____

church 몡 교회
city 몡 도시
leaf 몡 (나뭇)잎

B 괄호 안에서 알맞은 것을 고르시오.

1 She will grow (tree / a tree) in the yard.

2 There were two (pianoes / pianos) in the room.

3 They traveled to (Spain / a Spain) last month.

4 Gerald needs (advice / advices) about his homework.

5 Jack bought three loaves of (bread / breads) at the bakery.

6 There are (magazine / magazines) on the shelf.

grow 통 기르다
yard 몡 마당
magazine 몡 잡지
shelf 몡 선반, 책꽂이

C 괄호 안의 말을 활용하여 문장을 완성하시오.

1 Bring seven _____, please. (can, soda)

2 He ate two _____ yesterday. (slice, pizza)

3 Can you pass me a _____? (bottle, water)

4 The waiter is carrying five _____. (cup, coffee)

5 Ms. Clark has three _____. (pair, glasses)

6 The teacher will give ten _____ to us. (piece, paper)

bring 통 가져오다
pass 통 건네주다
waiter 몡 종업원
carry 통 나르다

D 우리말과 같도록 괄호 안의 명사를 활용하여 문장을 완성하시오.

1 Ava는 연못에서 거위 다섯 마리를 봤다. (goose)

= Ava saw _____ at the pond.

2 나는 식탁 위에 밥 네 그릇을 놓았다. (rice)

= I put _____ on the table.

3 접시 위에 체리 세 개가 있다. (cherry)

= There are _____ on the plate.

4 우정은 우리의 삶에서 중요하다. (friendship)

= _____ is important in our lives.

pond 몡 연못
plate 몡 접시
important 몡 중요한
life 몡 삶

UNIT 02 | 관사

1 부정관사 a(n)

셀 수 있는 명사의 단수형 앞에 쓴다.

정해지지 않은 막연한 하나를 가리킬 때	Ms. Bell is **a** *designer*.
'하나의(one)'를 나타낼 때	He ate **a** *sandwich* yesterday.
'~마다(per)'를 나타낼 때	I clean my room once **a** *day*.

TIP a와 an은 뒤따라오는 단어의 첫소리에 따라 구별해서 쓴다.
- 「a + 첫소리가 자음으로 발음되는 단어」: **a** dog, **a** chair, **a** university, **a** week, **a** year, **a** delicious apple
- 「an + 첫소리가 모음으로 발음되는 단어」: **an** umbrella, **an** orange, **an** hour, **an** empty room

2 정관사 the

셀 수 있는 명사와 셀 수 없는 명사 앞에 모두 쓸 수 있다.

앞에서 언급된 명사가 반복될 때	I bought *a flower*. **The** *flower* smelled nice.
정황상 서로 알고 있는 것을 말할 때	Could you pass me **the** *pen*?
구나 절의 수식을 받는 명사 앞에	**The** *clock on the desk* is new.
유일한 것을 말할 때	Stars are shining in **the** *sky*. **TIP** 「the + 유일한 것」: **the** sun, **the** earth, **the** moon, **the** world 등
악기 이름 앞에	Dan will play **the** *cello* at the concert.

3 관사를 쓰지 않는 경우

운동, 식사, 과목 이름 앞에	Let's play *tennis* tomorrow. I always have *lunch* at noon. Her favorite subject is *math*.
「by + 교통·통신수단」	They can go to the bookstore *by bus*. You should send it *by e-mail*. **TIP** 「by + 교통·통신수단」: **by** car, **by** subway, **by** train, **by** phone, **by** fax 등
장소나 건물이 본래의 목적으로 쓰일 때	James went to *bed* two hours ago. We go to *school* on weekdays.

Smart Check 다음 빈칸에 들어갈 알맞은 것을 고르시오.

1 I usually eat soup for _____ dinner.

① a   ② the   ③ 필요 없음

Practice

Answers p.11

A 괄호 안에서 알맞은 것을 고르시오.

1 (A / The) moon rises in the evening.

2 My aunt became (a / an) artist.

3 Mike has (a / an) great idea.

4 It is cold outside. Please close (a / the) door.

5 Camilla is (a / an) honest girl.

rise 图 뜨다, 오르다
aunt 图 고모, 이모
artist 图 화가, 예술가
idea 图 생각, 아이디어
honest 图 정직한

B 다음 빈칸에 a(n)과 the 중 알맞은 것을 쓰고, 필요하지 않으면 **X**를 쓰시오.

1 My brother's hobby is _____ soccer.

2 _____ sofa in the living room is comfortable.

3 Ms. Wilson teaches _____ music at a high school.

4 I have to buy _____ eraser today.

5 Peter went to Singapore by _____ ship.

hobby 图 취미
living room 거실
comfortable 图 편안한
high school 고등학교
eraser 图 지우개

C 다음 문장의 밑줄 친 부분을 바르게 고쳐 쓰시오.

1 We should go back to a store on the first floor. → _____

2 Cindy sleeps seven hours the day. → _____

3 Did you have the breakfast this morning? → _____

4 There was a party yesterday. A party wasn't fun. → _____

5 I don't have to go to a school on a national holiday. → _____

go back 돌아가다
floor 图 층, 바닥
fun 图 재미있는
national holiday 국경일

D 우리말과 같도록 괄호 안의 명사를 활용하여 문장을 완성하시오.

1 그녀는 작가가 될 거니? (writer)

= Is she going to be _____ ?

2 Perry씨는 우편으로 너에게 편지를 보낼 것이다. (mail)

= Ms. Perry will send you a letter _____ .

3 나는 리코더를 연습해야 한다. (recorder)

= I should practice _____ .

4 역사는 나에게 너무 어렵다. (history)

= _____ is too difficult for me.

writer 图 작가
mail 图 우편
recorder 图 리코더, 녹음기
practice 图 연습하다
history 图 역사
difficult 图 어려운

Chapter 07

Writing Exercise

A 밑줄 친 부분이 어법상 맞으면 O를 쓰고, 틀리면 바르게 고쳐 쓰시오.

1 I visited Busan by <u>plane</u> in July.   → _____

2 This book has five short <u>storys</u>.   → _____

3 He's not <u>an university</u> student.   → _____

4 Emily prepared two <u>glass</u> of grape juice.   → _____

5 I find <u>an information</u> on the Internet.   → _____

6 There is <u>a big elephant</u> in the field.   → _____

7 You should take a break once <u>hour</u>.   → _____

8 The man has three ducks and five <u>sheep</u>.   → _____

B 우리말과 같도록 괄호 안의 말을 활용하여 문장을 완성하시오.

1 그는 클라리넷을 잘 연주할 수 있다. (play, clarinet)
= He can _____ well.

2 나는 공원에서 사슴 일곱 마리를 봤다. (see, deer)
= I _____ at the park.

3 그 집에는 가구 다섯 점이 있다. (be, furniture)
= There _____ in the house.

4 여자 세 명이 해변을 따라 걷고 있었다. (woman, walk)
= _____ along the beach.

5 우리는 보통 우리의 친구들과 함께 저녁을 먹는다. (eat, dinner)
= We usually _____ with our friends.

6 Steve는 필통을 샀다. 그 필통은 검은색이었다. (pencil case, be)
= Steve bought a pencil case. _____ black.

7 나는 버스에서 빈 자리 하나를 발견했다. (find, empty seat)
= I _____ on the bus.

8 Doris는 그녀의 여행 가방에 바지 두 벌을 챙겼다. (pack, pants)
= Doris _____ in her suitcase.

C 다음 그림을 보고 알맞은 단위명사와 괄호 안의 명사를 활용하여 대화를 완성하시오.

Luna: Did you go shopping in the morning?	
Mia: Yes, I did. I bought four ⓐ_____ (bread), some vegetables, and three	
ⓑ_____ (socks).	
Luna: Why did you buy vegetables?	
Mia: Because I am going to make two ⓒ_____ (vegetable soup).	
Luna: That sounds delicious!	
Mia: By the way, will you come to my house and have a ⓓ_____ (tea)?	
Luna: Sure. I'll bring two ⓔ_____ (cake).	

D <보기>의 명사를 한 번씩만 활용하여 대화를 완성하시오.

<보기>	year	air conditioner	science	basketball	book

Mary: It's very hot. We should turn on ⓐ_____.
Steven: Good idea. And let's not play ⓑ_____ today.
Mary: Okay.
Steven: Oh, can I ask you a question? I read a book about ⓒ_____ last night, but I
couldn't understand ⓓ_____.
Mary: Sure. What is it?
Steven: Why do the seasons change?
Mary: Because the Earth moves around the Sun once ⓔ_____. Let's read that part
together one more time.

Chapter Test

[1-2] 다음 중 명사의 복수형이 <u>잘못된</u> 것을 고르시오.

1　① bus – buses　② cookie – cookies
③ wolf – wolfes　④ child – children
⑤ lady – ladies

2　① fox – foxes　② potato – potatoes
③ egg – eggs　④ fish – fish
⑤ butterfly – butterflys

[3-4] 다음 빈칸에 들어갈 알맞은 것을 고르시오.

3
> Josh borrowed a _____ from Dan.

① paint　② cup　③ maps
④ salt　⑤ boxes

4
> There is a loaf of _____ on the table.

① juice　② rice　③ pizza
④ paper　⑤ bread

5　다음 빈칸에 들어갈 말로 <u>어색한</u> 것은?

> There are _____ in this picture.

① woman　② dishes　③ oxen
④ soldiers　⑤ toys

6　다음 빈칸에 들어갈 말이 나머지 넷과 <u>다른</u> 것은?

① They are looking for _____ bench.
② There is _____ monkey on the road.
③ He met his grandfather _____ week ago.
④ Samantha has _____ black umbrella.
⑤ I ate _____ orange after lunch.

7　다음 중 밑줄 친 부분이 어법상 바른 것은?

① I gave a <u>glasses of water</u> to the old man.
② The chef used three <u>slice of cheese</u>.
③ Four <u>cans of paints</u> are on the floor.
④ My sister ordered two <u>pieces of cake</u>.
⑤ Jake had a <u>bowls of cereals</u> for breakfast.

8　다음 중 밑줄 친 부분이 어법상 <u>어색한</u> 것은?

① We played <u>the basketball</u> after school.
② Mariah went to Chicago by <u>train</u>.
③ <u>The cat</u> on the roof is white.
④ A bird is flying in <u>the sky</u>.
⑤ Mr. Wilson picked <u>an apple</u> from the tree.

9　주어진 문장의 밑줄 친 <u>a</u>와 쓰임이 같은 것은?

> I brush my teeth three times <u>a</u> day.

① Ms. Walker is <u>a</u> pilot.
② Amy visits the library once <u>a</u> day.
③ I sent him <u>a</u> photo.
④ He made <u>a</u> sandwich for his brother.
⑤ There is <u>a</u> dog behind the fence.

[10-11] 다음 글의 빈칸에 들어갈 말이 순서대로 짝지어진 것을 고르시오. (단, X는 필요 없음을 의미함)

10
Carol has _____ necklace. She bought _____ necklace in Italy.

① a – a   ② an – the   ③ a – the
④ the – a   ⑤ an – an

11
Mr. Ross arrived in _____ London last night. He ate _____ dinner there.

① a – a   ② a – the   ③ X – a
④ X – X   ⑤ a – X

서술형
12 다음 빈칸에 공통으로 들어갈 알맞은 관사를 쓰시오.

• Close _____ window. It's raining.
• _____ sun rises in the east.

서술형
[13-14] 괄호 안의 명사를 알맞은 형태로 바꿔 빈칸에 쓰시오.

13
Taylor wanted _____ about his bad habit. (advice)

14
_____ were swimming in the lake. (goose)

서술형
[15-18] 우리말과 같도록 괄호 안의 말을 활용하여 문장을 완성하시오.

15
Charlie는 플루트를 아름답게 연주했다. (flute)

= Charlie played _____ beautifully.

16
Ellis씨는 오늘 수박 한 통을 살 것이다. (watermelon)

= Ms. Ellis will buy _____ today.

17
나는 서랍 안에 양말 한 켤레를 넣었다. (socks)

= I put _____ in the drawer.

18
그들은 매일 버스를 타고 학교에 간다. (school, bus)

= They go to _____ by _____ every day.

19 다음 중 어법상 어색한 것은?

① Ms. Johns gave love to the cat.
② There are two children in the classroom.
③ Baseball is my favorite sport.
④ The ladybug on the leaf looks pretty.
⑤ You have a hour for the exam.

20 다음 우리말을 알맞게 영작한 것은?

> 병원 옆에 있는 건물은 은행이다.

① Building next to the hospital is a bank.
② Buildings next to the hospital is a bank.
③ A buildings next to the hospital is a bank.
④ An building next to the hospital is a bank.
⑤ The building next to the hospital is a bank.

고난도

21 다음 중 어법상 바른 것끼리 묶인 것은?

> ⓐ Moon was shining brightly.
> ⓑ I want a slice of pizza for dinner.
> ⓒ Snakes eat mouses and rats.
> ⓓ You should take the medicine once a day.
> ⓔ Math is a difficult subject for everyone.

① ⓐ, ⓑ, ⓒ　　② ⓐ, ⓒ, ⓓ　　③ ⓐ, ⓓ, ⓔ
④ ⓑ, ⓒ, ⓔ　　⑤ ⓑ, ⓓ, ⓔ

서술형

[22-23] 다음 문장에서 어법상 어색한 부분을 찾아 쓰고 바르게 고쳐 쓰시오.

22

> Mr. Anderson told me the news by a phone.

_____ → _____

23

> I will go to the bed at 11 P.M.

_____ → _____

서술형　고난도

24 다음 대화에서 어법상 어색한 부분을 찾아 쓰고 바르게 고쳐 쓰시오.

> A: Can I have two bowls of soups please?
> B: Sure. Do you want anything else?
> A: Do you have bananas too?
> B: Sorry. We only have strawberrys.

(1) _____ → _____
(2) _____ → _____

고난도

25 다음 중 밑줄 친 부분이 어법상 어색한 것은?

> ①A girl was looking at ②the peach on the tree. It looked delicious. She asked for ③help from her father. Her father picked ④the peach for her. She ate it after ⑤the breakfast.

서술형　고난도

26 다음 글의 밑줄 친 ⓐ~ⓔ중 어법상 어색한 것을 찾아 기호를 쓰고 바르게 고쳐 쓰시오.

> There is a large park in my town. My family goes to ⓐthe park once ⓑan week by ⓒcar. My father and I usually play ⓓbadminton in the park. Sometimes, some musicians play ⓔviolin there.

(1) _____ → _____
(2) _____ → _____

Chapter

08

대명사

대명사는 앞에서 언급된 특정한 명사를 반복하지 않기 위해
대신해서 쓰는 말이다.

UNIT 01 | 인칭대명사

1 인칭대명사

인칭대명사는 사람이나 사물의 이름을 대신하는 말로, 인칭·수·격에 따라 형태가 다르다.

인칭·수	격	주격	소유격	목적격	소유대명사	재귀대명사
1인칭	단수	I	my	me	mine	myself
	복수	we	our	us	ours	ourselves
2인칭	단수	you	your	you	yours	yourself
	복수					yourselves
3인칭	단수	he	his	him	his	himself
		she	her	her	hers	herself
		it	its	it	-	itself
	복수	they	their	them	theirs	themselves

I have a sister. **I** love **her**.

Thomas sold **his** clothes. **He** didn't like **them**.

This book is **mine**(= **my** book). Where is **yours**(= **your** book)?

TIP 사람을 나타내는 명사의 소유격과 소유대명사는 명사에 **-'s**를 붙여 만들며, **-s**로 끝나는 복수명사에는 **-'**만 붙여 만든다.

Tell me **Sam's** plan.

Your shoes are here. **Tina's**(= **Tina's** shoes) are there.

I will go to my **grandparents'** house.

2 재귀대명사의 쓰임

재귀대명사는 '~ 자신, 직접'의 의미로, 인칭대명사의 소유격이나 목적격에 -self(단수)/-selves(복수)를 붙인 형태이다.

❶ 동사나 전치사의 목적어가 주어와 같은 대상일 때 목적어로 재귀대명사를 쓴다. 이때 재귀대명사는 생략할 수 없다.

They introduced **themselves**.

Mr. Smith was talking to **himself**.

❷ 문장의 주어나 목적어를 강조하기 위해 강조하는 말 바로 뒤나 문장 맨 뒤에 재귀대명사를 쓴다. 이때 재귀대명사는 생략할 수 있다.

I (**myself**) solved the problem.

We saw *the singer* (**herself**).

Smart Check 다음 빈칸에 들어갈 알맞은 것을 고르시오.

1 My brother broke _____ leg.

① he   ② his   ③ him

Practice

Answers p.12

A 다음 문장의 밑줄 친 부분을 알맞은 인칭대명사로 바꿔 쓰시오.

1 The boy is running on the track.   → _____

2 You may know Jenny.   → _____

3 I like this bag's color.   → _____

4 She will meet her friends.   → _____

5 He surprised Bella and me yesterday.   → _____

6 Diane and Chris joined the book club.   → _____

track 명 경주로, 길
surprise 통 놀라게 하다
join 통 가입하다

B 괄호 안에서 알맞은 것을 고르시오.

1 Brian bought an umbrella. He used (it / its) today.

2 We respect Mr. Brown. (He / Himself) is always kind to neighbors.

3 Kangaroos carry (their / its) babies in the pouch.

4 I found Kitty's necklace, but I couldn't find (my / mine).

5 She likes (myself / herself) in the painting.

6 Our car isn't fast, but (theirs / them) is fast.

respect 통 존경하다
neighbor 명 이웃
carry 통 데리고 있다, 가지고 다니다
pouch 명 주머니
necklace 명 목걸이
painting 명 그림

C 밑줄 친 부분을 생략할 수 있으면 O를 쓰고, 생략할 수 없으면 X를 쓰시오.

1 I am proud of myself.   → _____

2 We made this video ourselves.   → _____

3 Ms. Hill doesn't trust herself.   → _____

4 The students themselves study hard.   → _____

5 My uncle talked about himself for an hour.   → _____

proud of ~을 자랑스러워하는
video 명 비디오, 영상
trust 통 신뢰하다, 믿다

D 우리말과 같도록 괄호 안의 말을 활용하여 빈칸에 쓰시오.

1 우리는 너의 옛날 사진을 봤다. (old picture)
= We saw _____ _____ _____.

2 나에게 연필을 빌려주겠니? (a pencil)
= Can you lend _____ _____ _____?

3 Rachel은 그녀의 숙제를 직접 할 것이다. (homework)
= Rachel will do _____ _____ _____.

old 형 옛날의, 나이 든
picture 명 사진, 그림
lend 통 빌려주다

UNIT 02 | this, that, it

1 this, that

❶ this(이 사람, 이것)

가까이 있는 사람이나 사물을 가리킬 때 쓰는 지시대명사로, 복수형은 these이다.

This is my cousin.
Are **these** fresh tomatoes?

❷ that(저 사람, 저것)

멀리 있는 사람이나 사물을 가리킬 때 쓰는 지시대명사로, 복수형은 those이다.

That is our basketball coach.
Those are Ethan's gloves.

❸ this/these/that/those는 '이 ~, 저 ~'라는 의미의 지시형용사로 쓰여 명사 앞에서 명사를 꾸밀 수 있다.

This *family* is from Brazil.
Those *restaurants* close at 10 P.M.

2 비인칭 주어 it

날씨, 온도, 계절, 시간, 요일, 날짜, 명암, 거리를 나타낼 때 쓰며, 해석하지 않는다.

It is sunny today. <날씨>
It is 19℃ now. <온도>
It will be summer soon. <계절>
A: What time is **it** now?　　　　B: **It** is 7 o'clock. <시간>
A: What day is **it** today?　　　　B: **It's** Thursday. <요일>
A: What date was **it** yesterday?　　B: **It** was June 23. <날짜>
It's bright in here. <명암>
It is 200 meters to the café. <거리>

> **TIP** 인칭대명사 it은 특정한 대상을 가리킬 때 쓰며, '그것'이라고 해석한다.
> I watched *a TV show* last week. **It** was interesting.

Smart Check 다음 빈칸에 들어갈 알맞은 것을 고르시오.

1 I read _____ magazines last night.
　① this　　　　　　　　② these　　　　　　　③ that

2 _____ was Friday yesterday.
　① This　　　　　　　　② Its　　　　　　　　③ It

3 What is _____ in the sky?
　① this　　　　　　　　② that　　　　　　　③ those

Practice

Answers p.12

A 괄호 안에서 알맞은 것을 고르시오.

1 (This / These) is my roommate Kevin.

2 I will eat (this / these) oranges for breakfast.

3 (That / It) is 9 P.M. now.

4 (That / Those) are my favorite characters.

roommate 몧 룸메이트
character 몧 등장인물, 성격

B 비인칭 주어와 <보기>의 말을 활용하여 질문에 대한 대답을 완성하시오.

<보기>	snowy	January 5	7 kilometers

1 *A*: What is the date today?

　B: _____.

2 *A*: How was the weather this morning?

　B: _____.

3 *A*: How far is it from your house to school?

　B: _____.

snowy 몧 눈이 많이 내리는
January 몧 1월

C 다음 대화의 빈칸에 알맞은 말을 <보기>에서 한 번씩만 골라 쓰시오.

<보기>	this	these	that	those	it

1 *A*: What day was _____ yesterday?　　*B*: Wednesday.

2 *A*: _____ is my friend Mark.　　*B*: Hello, Mark. I'm Lisa.

3 *A*: Look at _____ dogs over there.　　*B*: Wow, they're so cute!

4 *A*: What is _____ on the tree?　　*B*: It's a kite.

5 *A*: What do you have in your hand?　　*B*: _____ are golf balls.

look at ~을 보다
over there 저쪽에
cute 몧 귀여운
kite 몧 연
golf ball 골프공

D 우리말과 같도록 괄호 안의 말을 알맞게 배열하시오.

1 지난겨울에는 추웠다. (cold, was, it)

= _____ last winter.

2 그녀는 저 그림들을 7년 전에 샀다. (paintings, bought, she, those)

= _____ seven years ago.

3 이 사고는 많은 사람들을 다치게 했다. (accident, many people, this, hurt)

= _____.

accident 몧 사고
people 몧 사람들
hurt 동 다치게 하다

UNIT 03 | one, some, any

1 one

앞에서 언급된 명사와 같은 종류의 불특정한 대상을 가리킬 때 쓰며, 복수형은 ones이다.

Eric lost his *wallet*. He'll buy a new **one**.
I like these *spoons*. Do you have silver **ones**?

> **TIP** 앞에서 언급된 특정한 대상을 가리킬 때는 **it**이나 **they/them**을 쓴다.
> Bill bought *a watch*. **It** was expensive.
> Susan wrote *poems*. She showed **them** to me.

2 some, any

'약간(의), 조금(의), 몇몇(의)'라는 의미이며, 대명사나 형용사로 쓰인다. 형용사로 쓰일 때는 셀 수 있는 명사, 셀 수 없는 명사 모두와 함께 쓸 수 있다.

❶ some은 주로 긍정문과 권유·요청을 나타내는 의문문에 쓴다.

I made **some** *sandwiches*. Do you want **some**?
Could you lend me **some** *money*?

❷ any는 주로 부정문과 의문문에 쓴다.

He didn't get **any** *letters*. I didn't get **any**, either.
Did Rachel give you **any** *information*?

Smart Check　다음 빈칸에 들어갈 알맞은 것을 고르시오.

1 My tennis racket is broken. I should borrow _____.

　① one　　　　　　　　② it　　　　　　　　③ them

2 I don't have _____ coins.

　① some　　　　　　　② any　　　　　　　③ ones

3 There is _____ sand in my shoes.

　① one　　　　　　　② some　　　　　　　③ any

4 I have a ring. Monica gave _____ to me.

　① any　　　　　　　② them　　　　　　　③ it

Practice

A 괄호 안에서 알맞은 것을 고르시오.

1 Do you want (some / any) juice?

2 He found the book. (It / One) was under the desk.

3 I didn't bring an eraser. Can I borrow (it / one)?

4 Does Jack have (some / any) cousins?

5 Jane will buy gray jeans. She won't buy black (one / ones).

eraser 몡 지우개
borrow 통 빌리다
cousin 몡 사촌
gray 혱 회색의
jeans 몡 (청)바지

B 다음 빈칸에 알맞은 말을 <보기>에서 골라 쓰시오.

> <보기>   one   ones   it   them

1 This computer is too slow. Can I use a faster _____?

2 What is her name? I can't remember _____.

3 Lucas wore sunglasses yesterday. He didn't wear _____ today.

4 The students need some balls. They want light _____.

slow 혱 느린
remember 통 기억하다
wear 통 쓰고 있다, 입고 있다
sunglasses 몡 선글라스
need 통 필요하다
light 혱 가벼운; 몡 빛

C 다음 빈칸에 some과 any 중 알맞은 것을 쓰시오.

1 Will you have _____ rice?

2 I couldn't get _____ help from my brother.

3 Charlie took _____ pictures at the photo studio.

4 Do you have _____ good ideas?

5 Could you make me _____ tea?

get 통 받다
help 몡 도움; 통 돕다
take a picture 사진을 찍다
photo studio 사진관

D 우리말과 같도록 괄호 안의 말을 활용하여 빈칸에 쓰시오.

1 Laura는 어제 몇몇 박물관을 방문했다. (museums)

= Laura visited _____ _____ yesterday.

2 이 영화는 지루하다. 나는 무서운 것을 원한다. (scary)

= This movie is boring. I want a _____ _____.

3 그는 오후 8시 이후에 음식을 전혀 먹지 않는다. (food)

= He doesn't eat _____ _____ after 8 P.M.

4 엄마는 컵케이크를 구우셨다. 나는 작은 것들을 좀 먹었다. (small)

= Mom baked cupcakes. I had some _____ _____.

museum 몡 박물관
scary 혱 무서운
boring 혱 지루한
bake 통 굽다

Writing Exercise

A 다음 대화의 빈칸에 알맞은 말을 <보기>에서 한 번씩만 골라 쓰시오.

<보기>	these	that	those	it

1 A: My phone is very old.　　　　　　　B: When did you buy _____?

2 A: Can you see _____ birds over there?　B: Yes, I can see them.

3 A: _____ are my friends from Canada.　B: Hello. Nice to meet you.

4 A: Look at _____ airplane in the sky.　B: It looks very small.

<보기>	one	ones	some	any

5 A: Can you bring me _____ milk?　　B: Of course.

6 A: Is there a library near here?　　　　　B: There is _____ in the next block.

7 A: I called you last night.　　　　　　　B: Really? I didn't get _____ calls.

8 A: Where are your glasses?　　　　　　　B: I lost them. I have to buy new _____.

B 우리말과 같도록 괄호 안의 말을 활용하여 문장을 완성하시오.

1 알래스카는 매우 춥다. (be, very cold)

= _____ in Alaska.

2 이것은 Logan의 텀블러가 아니다. (Logan, tumbler)

= This is not _____.

3 이 복숭아들은 얼마니? (peaches)

= How much are _____?

4 Olivia는 다른 학생들에게 자기 소개를 했다. (introduce)

= Olivia _____ to the other students.

5 Ella는 그 수업에 대한 약간의 정보가 필요하다. (information)

= Ella needs _____ about the class.

6 Brian은 너의 쿠키를 먹었지만, 나는 너의 것을 먹지 않았다. (eat)

= Brian ate your cookies, but I _____.

7 그녀는 이 코트가 마음에 들지 않는다. 그녀는 검은 것을 원한다. (black)

= She doesn't like this coat. She wants a _____.

C 우리말과 같도록 괄호 안의 말을 알맞게 배열하시오.

1 저 토끼들은 사랑스러워 보인다. (lovely, rabbits, those, look)

= _____ .

2 우리의 삼촌은 우리에게 책을 읽어주실 것이다. (a book, read, uncle, us, will, our)

= _____ .

3 Mason은 조언을 전혀 듣지 않는다. (advice, listen to, doesn't, any, Mason)

= _____ .

4 Moore 선생님은 그들에게 약간의 기회를 주셨다. (them, chances, some, gave, Ms. Moore)

= _____ .

5 그녀의 교복은 저 노란 것이다. (yellow, is, school uniform, her, that, one)

= _____ .

6 Matthew는 그의 것을 끝내지 않았다. (his, Matthew, finish, didn't)

= _____ .

7 나의 이웃은 나에게 이것을 빌려줬다. (me, lent, my neighbor, to, this)

= _____ .

8 Joanna는 그녀 자신을 매우 잘 알고 있다. (herself, knows, very well, Joanna)

= _____ .

D 다음은 Susan의 일기이다. 괄호 안의 인칭대명사를 알맞은 형태로 바꿔 빈칸에 쓰시오.

September 3

Dear Diary,

Yesterday, I took care of my little brother Owen because ⓐ_____(we) parents went to ⓑ_____(they) friend's house. At lunchtime, Owen said, "I'm hungry." So, I ⓒ_____(I) made ⓓ_____(he) some pasta. Suddenly, I heard a big sound from the living room. Owen fell down and hurt ⓔ_____(he), so he was crying. I put a Band-Aid on ⓕ_____(he) knee and called my parents. ⓖ_____(they) came back soon and hugged ⓗ_____(we).

Chapter 08 · 대명사 · Hackers Grammar Smart Level 1

Chapter Test

[1-3] 다음 빈칸에 들어갈 알맞은 것을 고르시오.

1

_____ vegetables are fresh.

① This   ② These   ③ That
④ They   ⑤ It

2

There were _____ books on the desk.

① it   ② one   ③ ones
④ some   ⑤ any

3

Beth bought a red jacket. I bought a blue _____.

① it   ② one   ③ ones
④ some   ⑤ any

서술형

[4-5] 우리말과 같도록 빈칸에 알맞은 말을 쓰시오.

4

언덕 위에 있는 집은 그들의 것이다.

= The house on the hill is _____.

5

Charles는 그 울타리를 직접 칠했다.

= Charles _____ painted the fence.

[6-7] 다음 중 어법상 어색한 것을 고르시오.

6
① Nicole was angry at herself.
② The socks on the floor are his.
③ That is two kilometers from here to the park.
④ This robot can fold its arms.
⑤ Mr. Williams will meet us tomorrow.

7
① These watermelon is so sweet.
② Paul forgot her phone number.
③ I put your salad in the refrigerator.
④ Sally told me that rumor.
⑤ Their cousin will visit them next month.

[8-9] 다음 대화의 빈칸에 들어갈 알맞은 것을 고르시오.

8
A: Is _____ your brother over there?
B: Yes. He is my older brother.

① they   ② these   ③ that
④ those   ⑤ them

9
A: Did you buy the laptop for your sister?
B: No. I bought it for _____.

① I   ② my   ③ myself
④ me   ⑤ mine

서술형

10 다음 대화의 빈칸에 공통으로 들어갈 알맞은 말을 쓰시오.

> A: May I turn on the light? _____ is too dark in here.
> B: Sure. Press the white button. _____ is next to you.

11 다음 중 밑줄 친 부분이 어법상 바른 것은?

① <u>This</u> is 6:48 now.
② There are <u>any</u> shirts in the drawer.
③ The backpack on the chair isn't <u>my</u>.
④ My brother brought <u>those</u> pants to me.
⑤ <u>This</u> letters are from Ms. Anderson.

12 다음 대화의 빈칸에 들어갈 말이 순서대로 짝지어진 것은?

> A: Whose pen is this? Is it _____?
> B: No, it isn't. I will ask Brian. He lost _____ pen yesterday.

① your – his
② your – him
③ yours – him
④ yours – his
⑤ you – his

13 주어진 문장의 밑줄 친 <u>it</u>과 쓰임이 <u>다른</u> 것은?

> <u>It</u> is windy outside.

① <u>It</u> is Thursday today.
② <u>It</u> will be spring soon.
③ <u>It</u> is bright inside the bedroom.
④ <u>It</u> was 10 o'clock in the morning.
⑤ <u>It</u> is a beautiful bracelet.

[14-15] 다음 중 자연스럽지 <u>않은</u> 대화를 고르시오.

14 ① A: You can use this ladder.
  B: This is too short. I need a longer one.
② A: Do you have any plans this weekend?
  B: Yes. I will read some books.
③ A: Who were you talking to?
  B: I was talking to myself.
④ A: Can you lend me some money?
  B: Sorry. I don't have some now.
⑤ A: I like Greg's new T-shirt.
  B: Why don't you buy one?

15 ① A: How's the weather in Africa?
  B: It's very hot.
② A: When is your birthday?
  B: It is October 15.
③ A: Who are that boys at the door?
  B: They are my cousins.
④ A: Are these Ms. Lake's cups?
  B: Yes, they are hers.
⑤ A: Is it far from here to the bank?
  B: Yes. You cannot walk there.

16 다음 빈칸에 들어갈 말이 나머지 넷과 <u>다른</u> 것은?

① That hat looks good. Do you have a brown _____?
② These shoes are so dirty. Wear clean _____.
③ I already watched that movie. I'll watch a different _____.
④ Can you show me a cheaper car? That _____ is too expensive.
⑤ Our house is old. Let's move to a new _____.

17 다음 빈칸에 공통으로 들어갈 알맞은 재귀대명사를 쓰시오.

> • Ms. Smith saw _____ in the mirror.
> • My grandmother _____ made this.

18 다음 중 어법상 바른 것끼리 묶인 것은?

> ⓐ It is July 7 today.
> ⓑ Mr. Evans washed him clothes.
> ⓒ This is Jenna e-mail address.
> ⓓ Are there any onions in the box?
> ⓔ She lost my umbrella. It was new.

① ⓐ, ⓑ, ⓒ   ② ⓐ, ⓒ, ⓓ   ③ ⓐ, ⓓ, ⓔ
④ ⓑ, ⓒ, ⓔ   ⑤ ⓑ, ⓓ, ⓔ

[19-20] 우리말과 같도록 괄호 안의 말을 활용하여 문장을 완성하시오.

19
> 몇몇 아이들이 거리에서 노래하고 있다. (children)

= _____ are singing on the street.

20
> 어제는 12월 31일이었다. (December 31)

= _____ yesterday.

21 다음 대화의 밑줄 친 ⓐ~ⓔ 중 어법상 어색한 것을 찾아 기호를 쓰고 바르게 고쳐 쓰시오.

> A: ⓐThis bookshelf is too small in my room. I need a larger ⓑit.
> B: ⓒIt is rainy today. Let's go to the mall tomorrow.
> A: Okay. By the way, I baked ⓓany cookies. Do you want ⓔsome?
> B: Sure. They smell good!

(1) _____ → _____
(2) _____ → _____

[22-23] 다음 대화에서 어법상 어색한 부분을 찾아 쓰고 바르게 고쳐 쓰시오.

22
> A: These knife is so sharp.
> B: Yes. Be careful with it.

_____ → _____

23
> A: There aren't some oranges on the plate.
> B: There are some in the fridge.

_____ → _____

24 다음 글에서 어법상 어색한 부분을 찾아 쓰고 바르게 고쳐 쓰시오.

> I myself planted some sunflowers yesterday. Ones were beautiful.

_____ → _____

Chapter

09

형용사/부사와 비교구문

형용사는 명사나 대명사를 꾸미거나, 주어나 목적어를 보충 설명한다.
부사는 동사, 형용사, 다른 부사, 문장 전체를 꾸민다.
형용사나 부사를 사용하여 원급, 비교급, 최상급 비교를 표현할 수 있다.

UNIT 01 | 형용사

1 형용사의 쓰임

❶ 주로 명사 앞에서 명사를 꾸민다.

I need a **new** *watch*.
He found **popular** *magazines*.

> **TIP** -thing, -body, -one으로 끝나는 대명사를 꾸밀 때는 형용사가 대명사 뒤에 온다.
> They want *something* **spicy**.

❷ 보어로 쓰여 주어나 목적어를 보충 설명한다.

Charlie is **sleepy** now. <주격 보어>
The slippers keep *my feet* **warm**. <목적격 보어>

2 수량을 나타내는 형용사

❶ many, much, a lot of, lots of

many((수가) 많은)	셀 수 있는 명사의 복수형
much((양이) 많은) +	셀 수 없는 명사
a lot of / lots of((수·양이) 많은)	셀 수 있는 명사의 복수형, 셀 수 없는 명사

Many *kids* are playing in the playground.
She couldn't get **much** *help*.
My brother received **a lot of**[**lots of**] *presents*.

❷ a few, few, a little, little

a few(약간의, 조금 있는)	셀 수 있는 명사의 복수형
few(거의 없는) +	
a little(약간의, 조금 있는)	셀 수 없는 명사
little(거의 없는) +	

I dropped **a few** *cookies*.
There were **few** *people* on the street.

Please give me **a little** *advice*.
Mom added **little** *sugar* to the sauce.

Smart Check 다음 빈칸에 들어갈 말로 <u>어색한</u> 것을 고르시오.

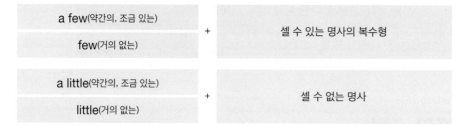

1 He had a _____ day today.

① busy   ② happily   ③ wonderful

Practice

Answers p.13

A 다음 문장의 밑줄 친 형용사가 수식하는 부분에 동그라미를 치시오.

1 A giraffe has <u>brown</u> spots on its body.

2 She saw someone <u>rude</u> at the café.

3 Joe borrowed <u>old</u> books from the library.

4 They don't need anybody <u>lazy</u>.

giraffe 몡 기린
spot 몡 점, 얼룩
body 몡 몸
rude 톙 무례한, 예의 없는
lazy 톙 게으른

Chapter 09

B 괄호 안에서 알맞은 것을 고르시오.

1 There is a (love / lovely) hamster in the cage.

2 There is (few / little) jam in the jar.

3 Elisa made her parents (angry / angrily).

4 The readers want (something new / new something).

cage 몡 우리, 새장
jar 몡 병
reader 몡 독자

C 다음 빈칸에 알맞은 말을 괄호 안에서 골라 쓰시오.

1 (many / much)

① George spent _____ time on his homework.

② I caught _____ fish last weekend.

2 (a few / a little)

① This plant needs _____ water.

② Kristina made _____ friends at her new school.

3 (few / little)

① _____ students got a perfect score.

② We have _____ experience in foreign countries.

spend 퇭 (시간·돈을) 쓰다, 들이다
catch 퇭 잡다
plant 몡 식물
perfect score 만점, 백점
experience 몡 경험
foreign country 외국

D 우리말과 같도록 괄호 안의 말을 활용하여 빈칸에 쓰시오.

1 나에게 시원한 무언가를 주겠니? (cool, something)

= Can you give me _____ _____ ?

2 그들은 많은 야채를 샀다. (vegetables)

= They bought _____ _____ _____ _____ .

3 Carol은 인터뷰에서 긴장했다. (be, nervous)

= Carol _____ _____ at the interview.

nervous 톙 긴장한, 불안해하는
interview 몡 인터뷰, 면접

UNIT 02 | 부사

부사의 쓰임

동사, 형용사, 다른 부사, 문장 전체를 꾸민다.

I *eat* **slowly**.

His speech was **really** *great*.

Mindy speaks Chinese **very** *well*.

Suddenly, *the woman fell down*.

2 부사의 형태

부사는 대부분 형용사에 -ly를 붙여 만든다.

대부분의 형용사	형용사 + -ly	kind – kind**ly**	wise – wise**ly**
「자음 + y」로 끝나는 형용사	y를 i로 바꾸고 + -ly	easy – eas**ily**	happy – happ**ily**
-le로 끝나는 형용사	e를 없애고 + -y	simple – simp**ly**	gentle – gent**ly**
불규칙하게 변하는 부사	good – **well**		
형용사와 형태가 같은 부사	late(늦은) – late(늦게) hard(어려운, 단단한) – hard(열심히) fast(빠른) – fast(빠르게) **TIP** -ly가 붙으면 의미가 달라지는 부사 　late(늦게) – late**ly**(최근에) 　hard(열심히) – hard**ly**(거의 ~않다)	early(이른) – early(일찍) high(높은) – high(높게, 높이) close(가까이) – close**ly**(면밀히) high(높게) – high**ly**(매우, 대단히)	

I finished the test **easily**.　　　　　　　The eagles are flying **high**.

He became a **highly** successful pianist.

TIP **friendly**(친절한), **lovely**(사랑스러운), **lonely**(외로운), **weekly**(주간의), **likely**(그럴듯한)는 -ly로 끝나지만 부사가 아닌 형용사이다.

Sam is a very **friendly** *person*.

3 빈도부사

어떤 일이 얼마나 자주 발생하는지를 나타내는 부사이며, be동사나 조동사 뒤 또는 일반동사 앞에 온다.

100%					0%
always (항상)	usually (보통, 대개)	often (종종, 자주)	sometimes (때때로, 가끔)	seldom (거의 ~않다)	never (결코 ~않다)

Kevin *is* **always** kind.

We *can* **sometimes** see the aurora.

My sister **never** *eats* walnuts.

Smart Check　　다음 빈칸에 들어갈 알맞은 것을 고르시오.

1 We walked very _____.

① calm　　　　　　　　　② quiet　　　　　　　　　③ carefully

Practice

Answers p.14

A 다음 문장의 밑줄 친 부사가 수식하는 부분에 동그라미를 치시오.

1 The moon shines <u>brightly</u> in the sky.

2 Mr. Davis is holding the baby <u>so</u> gently.

3 <u>Sadly</u>, my brother entered the army.

4 I had <u>very</u> delicious pasta yesterday.

shine ⑧ 빛나다
brightly ⑨ 밝게
hold ⑧ 안고 있다, 잡다
gently ⑨ 부드럽게
enter the army 군대에 입대하다

B 괄호 안에서 알맞은 것을 고르시오.

1 Bats (are usually / usually are) active at night.

2 (Lucky / Luckily), I took the bus on time.

3 Tony gave me (high / highly) useful information.

bat ⑨ 박쥐
active ⑱ 활동적인
on time 제시간에
useful ⑱ 유용한
information ⑨ 정보

C 다음 표를 보고 <보기>의 빈도부사와 괄호 안의 말을 활용하여 문장을 완성하시오.
(단, 현재형으로 쓰시오.)

	Mon	Tue	Wed	Thu	Fri
Ken	🏊	🏊	📖	🏊	🏊
Lily	🚶	🚶	🚶	🚶	🚶
Daniel	🥛	🥛	🥛	🥛	🥛

<보기>	always	usually	seldom	never

1 Ken _____. (go swimming)

2 Ken _____. (read a book)

3 Lily _____. (walk to school)

4 Daniel _____. (drink coffee)

D 우리말과 같도록 괄호 안의 말을 활용하여 빈칸에 쓰시오.

1 그들은 지난 주말에 아주 열심히 일했다. (work, real)

= They _____ _____ hard last weekend.

2 Jones씨는 차를 빠르게 운전한다. (drive, fast)

= Ms. Jones _____ the car _____.

3 나는 결코 이 순간을 잊지 않을 것이다. (never, forget)

= I _____ _____ _____ this moment.

work ⑧ 일하다
drive ⑧ 운전하다
forget ⑧ 잊다
moment ⑨ 순간

UNIT 03 | 원급/비교급/최상급 비교

1 원급 비교:「as + 형용사/부사의 원급 + as」

비교하는 두 대상의 정도가 비슷하거나 같음을 나타내며, '…만큼 ~한/하게'라는 의미이다.

Rachel is **as tall as** Nelson.
I wake up **as early as** my dad.

2 비교급 비교:「형용사/부사의 비교급 + than」

비교하는 두 대상 간 정도의 차이를 나타내며, '…보다 더 ~한/하게'라는 의미이다.

Your hair is **longer than** Lisa's hair.
I play soccer **better than** you.

> **TIP** 비교급 앞에 **much, even, far, a lot** 등을 써서 '훨씬'이라는 의미로 비교급을 강조할 수 있다.
> This cake is **much** *bigger* than that.

3 최상급 비교:「the + 형용사/부사의 최상급」

셋 이상의 비교 대상 중 하나의 정도가 가장 높음을 나타내며, '가장 ~한/하게'라는 의미이다. 보통 in이나 of를 사용하여 비교 범위를 나타낸다.

Mercury is **the smallest** planet *in our solar system*.
Ian is **the smartest** *of his friends*.

4 비교급과 최상급 만드는 법

비교급/최상급 만드는 법		원급 – 비교급 – 최상급
대부분의 형용사/부사	+ -er/-est	warm – warm**er** – warm**est**
-e로 끝나는 형용사/부사	+ -r/-st	wide – wide**r** – wide**st**
「자음 + y」로 끝나는 형용사/부사	y를 i로 바꾸고 + -er/-est	heavy – heav**ier** – heav**iest**
「단모음 + 단자음」으로 끝나는 형용사/부사	마지막 자음을 한 번 더 쓰고 + -er/-est	big – big**ger** – big**gest**
대부분의 2음절 이상인 형용사/부사	more/most + 원급	popular – **more** popular – **most** popular
「형용사 + ly」 형태의 부사		slowly – **more** slowly – **most** slowly
불규칙하게 변하는 형용사/부사	good/well – **better** – best many/much – **more** – most	bad/ill – **worse** – **worst** little – **less** – **least**

Smart Check 다음 빈칸에 들어갈 알맞은 것을 고르시오.

1 That bed was more comfortable _____ this bed.

① as   ② in   ③ than

Practice

Answers p.14

A 다음 형용사나 부사의 비교급과 최상급을 쓰시오.

1 strong - _____ - _____

2 nice - _____ - _____

3 pretty - _____ - _____

4 quickly - _____ - _____

5 little - _____ - _____

6 difficult - _____ - _____

7 thin - _____ - _____

strong [형] 강한, 힘센
pretty [형] 예쁜, 귀여운
quickly [부] 빨리
difficult [형] 어려운
thin [형] 얇은, 가는

B 괄호 안에서 알맞은 것을 고르시오.

1 Samantha studies as (hard / harder) as her sister.

2 January is the (most cold / coldest) month in winter.

3 His room is much (clean / cleaner) than Karen's room.

4 This band is (more famous / famouser) than my favorite band.

5 Jejudo is the (bigger / biggest) island in Korea.

January [명] 1월
winter [명] 겨울
clean [형] 깨끗한
famous [형] 유명한
island [명] 섬

C 다음 표를 보고 괄호 안의 말을 활용하여 문장을 완성하시오.

Model	A	B	C
Price	$5	$3	$2
Weight	1 kg	2 kg	1 kg

1 Model A is _____ Model C. (heavy)

2 Model A is _____ Model B. (light)

3 Model C is _____ of the three. (cheap)

4 Model B is _____ Model C. (expensive)

model [명] 모델, 디자인
price [명] 가격
weight [명] 무게
heavy [형] 무거운
light [형] 가벼운
cheap [형] 싼
expensive [형] 비싼

D 우리말과 같도록 괄호 안의 말을 활용하여 문장을 완성하시오.

1 이것은 마을에서 가장 오래된 집이다. (old)

= This is _____ house in the town.

2 나의 나무는 너의 나무만큼 자랐다. (tall)

= My tree grew _____ your tree.

3 오렌지는 포도보다 더 맛있다. (delicious)

= Oranges are _____ grapes.

town [명] 마을
grow [동] 자라다
delicious [형] 맛있는
grape [명] 포도

Writing Exercise

A 밑줄 친 부분이 어법상 맞으면 O를 쓰고, 틀리면 바르게 고쳐 쓰시오.

1 You should exercise <u>regularly</u>. → _____

2 Don't make <u>noisily</u> sounds, please. → _____

3 Homemade food is <u>healthiest</u> than fast food. → _____

4 There isn't <u>much</u> snow on the roof. → _____

5 He <u>eats sometimes</u> snacks after meals. → _____

6 Yesterday was the <u>baddest</u> day of my life. → _____

7 The chef will make <u>something special</u> for us. → _____

8 <u>A little</u> people were singing together. → _____

B 우리말과 같도록 괄호 안의 말을 활용하여 문장을 완성하시오.

1 그 병 안에는 주스가 거의 없었다. (juice)
= There was _____ in the bottle.

2 나의 통학 버스는 보통 제시간에 떠난다. (leave)
= My school bus _____ on time.

3 그녀는 트램펄린 위에서 높게 뛸 수 있다. (jump, high)
= She can _____ on a trampoline.

4 Jacob은 잘못된 무언가를 알아채지 못했다. (wrong, anything)
= Jacob didn't notice _____.

5 나는 원어민만큼 스페인어를 잘 말한다. (well)
= I speak Spanish _____ a native speaker.

6 Cooper씨는 결코 온라인으로 옷을 사지 않을 것이다. (buy)
= Mr. Cooper _____ clothes online.

7 나는 나의 돼지 저금통에 동전을 거의 가지고 있지 않다. (coins)
= I have _____ in my piggy bank.

8 그것은 그 대회에서 가장 흥미진진한 공연이었다. (exciting, performance)
= It was _____ in the contest.

C 우리말과 같도록 괄호 안의 말을 알맞게 배열하시오.

1 사막에는 비가 거의 오지 않는다. (rains, seldom, it)

= _____ in deserts.

2 그의 인형은 나의 것보다 훨씬 더 귀엽다. (cuter, mine, his doll, than, much, is)

= _____ .

3 그녀는 매달 약간의 돈을 저축한다. (saves, little, she, money, a)

= _____ every month.

4 Linda는 월요일마다 주간 신문을 읽는다. (newspaper, a, reads, weekly, Linda)

= _____ on Mondays.

5 수학은 나에게 모든 과목 중에서 가장 어렵다. (the, of, math, difficult, is, all subjects, most)

= _____ for me.

6 많은 관광객들이 에펠탑의 사진을 찍었다. (took, tourists, of, lots, pictures)

= _____ of the Eiffel Tower.

D 다음은 현장 학습 장소에 대한 학생들의 투표 결과이다. 괄호 안의 말을 활용하여 문장을 완성하시오.

Place	Everland	The National Museum	Gyeongbokgung
Distance	40 km	10 km	10 km
Ticket Price	$15	$8	$5
Vote			

1 The National Museum is _____ Gyeongbokgung. (close)

2 Gyeongbokgung has _____ ticket price of the three. (cheap)

3 Everland tickets are _____ the National Museum tickets. (expensive)

4 Everland is _____ place of the three. (popular)

Chapter Test

1 다음 중 형용사와 부사의 형태가 <u>잘못된</u> 것은?

① simple – simply ② safe – safely

③ good – goodly ④ lucky – luckily

⑤ interesting – interestingly

2 다음 중 원급, 비교급, 최상급 형태가 <u>잘못된</u> 것은?

① sunny – sunnier – sunniest

② many – much – most

③ long – longer – longest

④ colorful – more colorful – most colorful

⑤ loudly – more loudly – most loudly

[3-4] 다음 빈칸에 들어갈 말로 <u>어색한</u> 것을 고르시오.

3

A _____ cat was sitting on the bench.

① fat ② small ③ wildly

④ sleepy ⑤ friendly

4

The tree is _____ taller than the building.

① very ② much ③ even

④ far ⑤ a lot

5 다음 중 밑줄 친 부분이 어법상 바른 것은?

① The lion <u>quiet</u> watched the deer.

② The chef <u>quick</u> turned off the fire.

③ Amy was <u>late</u> for the class.

④ The living room is very <u>brightly</u>.

⑤ The wind blew <u>strong</u> from the west.

[6-7] 다음 중 괄호 안의 말이 들어갈 가장 알맞은 위치를 고르시오.

6

George ① goes ② to ③ the ④ beach in ⑤ summer. (often)

7

I ① will ② tell ③ the ④ truth to ⑤ you. (always)

서술형
[8-10] 우리말과 같도록 괄호 안의 말을 활용하여 문장을 완성하시오.

8

그 상자는 바위만큼 무겁다. (heavy)

= The box is _____ a rock.

9

한라산은 대한민국에서 가장 높은 산이다. (high)

= Hallasan is _____ mountain in South Korea.

10

건강은 돈보다 더 중요하다. (important)

= Health is ＿＿＿＿＿＿＿＿＿＿＿＿＿＿ money.

14

Today, New York is 31℃, London is 26℃, and Seoul is 34℃. Seoul is ＿＿＿＿＿＿＿＿ of the three. (hot, city)

[11-12] 다음 우리말을 알맞게 영작한 것을 고르시오.

11

그 아이들은 달팽이만큼 느리게 걸었다.

① The children walked slowly a snail.
② The children walked more slowly than a snail.
③ The children walked as slowly a snail.
④ The children walked as slowly as a snail.
⑤ The children walked the most slowly a snail.

15 다음 중 어법상 바른 것은?

① There are much books in the library.
② Charles seldom brushes his hair.
③ Mom was much angry than Dad.
④ Is there exciting anything tonight?
⑤ Mr. Brown put few salt in his soup.

[16-17] 다음 빈칸에 들어갈 말이 순서대로 짝지어진 것을 고르시오.

12

John은 나의 친구들 중에서 가장 키가 작다.

① John is shortest of my friends.
② John is shorter than my friends.
③ John is the most shortest of my friends.
④ John is as short as my friends.
⑤ John is the shortest of my friends.

16

• Jenny moved the vase to the terrace ＿＿＿＿＿.
• The new curtain looked ＿＿＿＿＿ on the window.

① careful – nice　　② careful – nicely
③ careful – nicer　　④ carefully – nice
⑤ carefully – nicely

서술형

[13-14] 다음 글을 읽고 괄호 안의 말을 활용하여 문장을 완성하시오.

13

Hanna is 167 centimeters tall. Julia is 167 centimeters tall, too. Julia is ＿＿＿＿＿＿＿ Hanna. (tall)

17

• Mr. Burns ＿＿＿＿＿ recommended this song.
• The birds are flying ＿＿＿＿＿ in the sky.

① high – high　　② high – highly
③ highly – high　　④ highly – highly
⑤ high – higher

18 우리말과 같도록 괄호 안의 말을 알맞게 배열하시오.

> 러시아는 인도보다 훨씬 더 크다. (much, Russia, than, is, bigger, India)

= _____ .

19 우리말과 같도록 주어진 <조건>에 맞게 문장을 완성하시오.

> 너는 이 실험실에서 위험한 어떤 것도 만지면 안 된다.

> <조건>
> 1. should, touch, dangerous, anything을 활용하시오.
> 2. 6단어로 쓰시오.

= _____

in this laboratory.

[20-21] 다음 문장에서 어법상 <u>어색한</u> 부분을 찾아 쓰고 바르게 고쳐 쓰시오.

20
> There is a few milk in the glass.

_____ → _____

21
> This movie is most boring of the four.

_____ → _____

22 다음 중 어법상 바른 것끼리 묶인 것은?

> ⓐ A few old toys were in the box.
> ⓑ This book is as thickest as a dictionary.
> ⓒ Mr. Grant is looking for somebody clever.
> ⓓ Don't add many sugar to your coffee.
> ⓔ My dog is braver than other dogs.

① ⓐ, ⓑ, ⓒ   ② ⓐ, ⓑ, ⓓ   ③ ⓐ, ⓒ, ⓔ
④ ⓑ, ⓓ, ⓔ   ⑤ ⓒ, ⓓ, ⓔ

23 다음 글에서 어법상 <u>어색한</u> 부분을 찾아 쓰고 바르게 고쳐 쓰시오.

> Eric found a lot of pens in his drawer. He uses never pens, so he gave them to his sister. She studies much hard than him.

(1) _____ → _____
(2) _____ → _____

24 다음 대화의 밑줄 친 ⓐ~ⓔ 중 어법상 <u>어색한</u> 것을 찾아 기호를 쓰고 바르게 고쳐 쓰시오.

> A: I heard ⓐ<u>a few</u> scary stories about the house on the hill.
> B: Tell me one.
> A: My friend Josh ⓑ<u>usually walks</u> by the house. Last week, he heard ⓒ<u>strange something</u>, and the door opened ⓓ<u>suddenly</u>.
> B: Someone may live in that house.
> A: ⓔ<u>Actual</u>, nobody lives in that house!

(1) _____ → _____
(2) _____ → _____

Chapter

10

---

to부정사와 동명사

to부정사는 「to + 동사원형」의 형태로 문장 안에서 명사·형용사·부사 역할을 한다.
동명사는 「동사원형 + -ing」의 형태로 문장 안에서 명사 역할을 한다.

UNIT 01 │ to부정사의 명사적 용법

1 to부정사

to부정사는 「to + 동사원형」의 형태로 문장 안에서 명사·형용사·부사 역할을 한다.

She hopes **to become** a singer. <명사 역할>
Ken needs a coat **to wear**. <형용사 역할>
They went to the supermarket **to buy** milk. <부사 역할>

> **TIP** to부정사의 부정형: 「**not to** + 동사원형」
> We decided **not to watch** this movie.

2 to부정사의 명사적 용법

❶ 주어(~하는 것은)

to부정사가 주어로 쓰일 때는 주로 주어 자리에 가주어 it을 쓰고 진주어 to부정사(구)를 뒤로 보낸다.

To read many books is helpful.
→ **It** is helpful **to read** many books.

> **TIP** 주어로 쓰인 **to부정사(구)**는 항상 단수 취급한다.

❷ 목적어(~하는 것을, ~하기를)

to부정사는 동사 want, hope, decide, plan, need, promise, like, start 등의 목적어로 쓰인다.

Jenny *wants* **to travel** to Paris.
He *promised* **to marry** her.

❸ 보어(~하는 것(이다))

to부정사가 보어로 쓰일 때는 주어의 상태나 성질을 보충 설명한다.

My hobby is **to collect** stamps.

❹ 「의문사 + to부정사」는 문장 안에서 명사처럼 쓰인다.

what + to부정사 무엇을 ~할지	where + to부정사 어디에(서)/어디로 ~할지
when + to부정사 언제 ~할지	how + to부정사 어떻게 ~할지

I don't know **what to eat**.
Tell me **when to send** the letter.

Smart Check 다음 빈칸에 들어갈 알맞은 것을 고르시오.

1 It is difficult _____ this puzzle.

① to solve   ② solves   ③ solved

Practice

Answers p.15

A 밑줄 친 to부정사의 쓰임을 <보기>에서 골라 그 기호를 쓰시오.

> <보기>   ⓐ 주어   ⓑ 목적어   ⓒ 보어

1 To write a memo is useful.   [   ]
2 My dream is to go to space.   [   ]
3 Brian likes to read novels.   [   ]
4 It is interesting to watch action movies.   [   ]
5 We needed to leave at 8 o'clock.   [   ]

useful 휑 유용한
dream 휑 꿈
space 휑 우주, 공간
novel 휑 소설
action movie 액션 영화
leave 통 떠나다, 두고 오다

B <보기>의 동사를 한 번씩만 활용하여 문장을 완성하시오.

> <보기>   keep   meet   wear   exercise

1 It is not easy _____ a secret.
2 Ms. Green is choosing what _____ for the party.
3 My vacation plan is _____ every day.
4 He hopes _____ his old friends again.

keep 통 지키다, 유지하다
wear 통 입다, 매다
exercise 통 운동하다
secret 휑 비밀
choose 통 고르다
vacation plan 방학 계획

C 다음 문장을 가주어 it을 사용한 문장으로 바꿔 쓰시오.

1 To walk alone at night is scary.
  → _____.

2 To eat slowly is healthy.
  → _____.

3 To sleep in this bed is comfortable.
  → _____.

alone 휜 혼자
scary 휑 무서운
slowly 휜 천천히, 느리게
healthy 휑 건강에 좋은, 건강한
comfortable 휑 편안한

D 우리말과 같도록 괄호 안의 말을 활용하여 빈칸에 쓰시오.

1 그들의 직업은 화재에서 사람들을 구하는 것이다. (save)
  = Their job is _____ _____ people in fires.

2 Amy의 오빠는 그녀의 숙제를 돕기로 약속했다. (promise, help)
  = Amy's brother _____ _____ _____ with her homework.

3 그녀는 어디에서 머리를 자를지 결정했다. (cut)
  = She decided _____ _____ _____ her hair.

4 제시간에 공항에 도착하는 것은 불가능하다. (arrive)
  = _____ is impossible _____ _____ at the airport on time.

save 통 구하다
job 휑 직업, 일
fire 휑 화재, 불
arrive 통 도착하다
impossible 휑 불가능한
airport 휑 공항

UNIT 02 | to부정사의 형용사적/부사적 용법

1 to부정사의 형용사적 용법

to부정사는 형용사 역할을 할 때 '~할, ~하는'의 의미로 명사나 대명사를 뒤에서 꾸민다.

Liam has *homework* **to do**.

We need *more time* **to play**.

> **TIP** -thing, -body, -one으로 끝나는 대명사를 형용사와 to부정사가 동시에 꾸밀 때는 「-thing/-body/-one + 형용사 + to부정사」의 형태로 쓴다.
>
> He is looking for *someone* **strong to lift** the box.

2 to부정사의 부사적 용법

to부정사는 부사 역할을 할 때 동사, 형용사, 부사, 문장 전체를 꾸미며, 목적, 감정의 원인, 결과 등을 나타낸다.

❶ 목적(~하기 위해)

They went to the library **to study**.
= They went to the library **in order to study**.
→ 목적의 의미를 강조하기 위해 to 대신 in order to를 쓸 수 있다.

❷ 감정의 원인(~해서, ~하니)

주로 감정을 나타내는 형용사(happy, glad, sad, sorry, surprised 등) 뒤에 쓰인다.

I'm *happy* **to know** you.
Emily was *surprised* **to see** me here.

❸ 결과((…해서 결국) ~하다)

He grew up **to be** a lawyer.
My grandmother lived **to be** 98 years old.

> **TIP** • 「**too** + 형용사/부사 + **to부정사**」: …하기에 너무 ~한/하게
>
> She was **too busy to watch** TV.
>
> • 「형용사/부사 + **enough** + **to부정사**」: …할 만큼 충분히 ~한/하게
>
> Frank is **tall enough to ride** the roller coaster.

Smart Check   다음 빈칸에 들어갈 알맞은 것을 고르시오.

1 My dog needs some food _____.

① eats   ② ate   ③ to eat

2 Harry went outside _____ a walk.

① take   ② to take   ③ takes

Practice

Answers p.15

A <보기>의 동사를 활용하여 대화를 완성하시오.

<보기>	say	cut	wash

1 *A*: Do you have anything _____ _____ this rope?

  B: Yes. I have a pair of scissors.

2 *A*: How was the interview?

  B: There wasn't enough time _____ _____ everything.

3 *A*: There are a lot of dishes _____ _____ in the sink.

  B: Don't worry. I will do the dishes.

rope 명 밧줄
scissors 명 가위
interview 명 인터뷰, 면접
enough 형 충분한
sink 명 싱크대
do the dishes 설거지를 하다

B 밑줄 친 to부정사의 의미를 <보기>에서 골라 그 기호를 쓰시오.

<보기>	ⓐ ~하기 위해	ⓑ ~해서, ~하니	ⓒ (…해서 결국) ~하다

1 I was sad to hear that news.   [   ]

2 We visited the flower shop to buy carnations.   [   ]

3 Napoleon lived to be 51 years old.   [   ]

4 She came home early to get some rest.   [   ]

flower shop 꽃가게
carnation 명 카네이션
get some rest 약간의 휴식을 취하다

C to부정사를 이용하여 다음 두 문장을 한 문장으로 연결하시오.

1 Sophia raised her hand. She asked a question.

  → Sophia raised her hand _____ _____ a question.

2 Mary was surprised. She saw a mouse in the kitchen.

  → Mary was surprised _____ _____ a mouse in the kitchen.

3 He sent me a text message. He talked about our teacher.

  → He sent me a text message _____ _____ _____ _____

  about our teacher.

raise 동 들다, 올리다
text message 문자 메시지

D 우리말과 같도록 괄호 안의 말을 활용하여 빈칸에 쓰시오.

1 Anne은 스페인어를 배우기 위해 방과 후 수업을 듣는다. (learn)

  = Anne takes the after-school class _____ _____ Spanish.

2 루브르 박물관에는 볼 많은 그림이 있다. (see, many paintings)

  = The Louvre Museum has _____ _____ _____ _____ .

3 그들은 그 책을 이해할 만큼 충분히 똑똑하다. (understand, smart)

  = They are _____ _____ _____ _____ the book.

learn 동 배우다
after-school 형 방과 후의
museum 명 박물관
understand 동 이해하다
smart 형 똑똑한

UNIT 03 | 동명사의 쓰임

1 동명사

동명사는 「동사원형 + -ing」의 형태로 문장 안에서 명사처럼 주어, 목적어, 보어로 쓰인다.

Natalie enjoys **watching** videos on the Internet.

> **TIP** 동명사의 부정형은 동명사 앞에 **not**을 붙여 만든다.
> **Not wearing** a life jacket is dangerous.

2 동명사의 쓰임

❶ 주어(~하는 것은)

주어로 쓰인 동명사(구)는 항상 단수 취급한다.

Playing soccer with my friends *is* fun.

❷ 동사의 목적어(~하는 것을)

동명사는 동사 enjoy, finish, avoid, keep, mind, give up, stop, practice 등의 목적어로 쓰인다.

Jason *finished* **doing** his homework.
Stop **shaking** your legs.

> **TIP** 동사 **like, love, hate, start, begin** 등은 동명사와 **to**부정사를 모두 목적어로 쓴다.
> Thomas *likes* **drinking[to drink]** hot tea.

❸ 전치사의 목적어(~하는 것(을))

She is thinking *about* **changing** her hairstyle.

❹ 보어(~하는 것(이다))

My problem is **eating** too much instant food.

3 동명사 관용 표현

go + V-ing ~하러 가다	be busy + V-ing ~하느라 바쁘다
be worth + V-ing ~할 가치가 있다	feel like + V-ing ~하고 싶다
be good at + V-ing ~하는 것을 잘하다	thank … for + V-ing ~한 것에 대해 …에게 감사해하다

Let's **go swimming** in the afternoon.
The temple **is worth visiting**.

Smart Check 다음 빈칸에 들어갈 알맞은 것을 고르시오.

1 My uncle enjoys _____ mountains.
　　① climbed　　　　　② climb　　　　　③ climbing

Practice

Answers p.15

A 밑줄 친 동명사의 쓰임을 <보기>에서 골라 그 기호를 쓰시오.

<보기>   ⓐ 주어   ⓑ 동사의 목적어   ⓒ 전치사의 목적어   ⓓ 보어

1 My goal is <u>studying</u> abroad.   [   ]
2 He doesn't mind <u>sharing</u> his room.   [   ]
3 <u>Drinking</u> coffee is not good for children. [   ]
4 I worried about <u>performing</u> on the stage.   [   ]
5 The machine stopped <u>working</u> suddenly.   [   ]

goal 몡 목표
abroad 児 해외에서
share 동 함께 쓰다
perform 동 공연하다, 수행하다
machine 몡 기계
work 동 작동하다
suddenly 児 갑자기

B 밑줄 친 부분이 어법상 맞으면 O를 쓰고, 틀리면 바르게 고쳐 쓰시오.

1 Thank you for <u>come</u> to the event.   → _____
2 <u>Being</u> honest is important in our lives. → _____
3 I'm nervous about <u>talk</u> to him.   → _____
4 Mr. Wilson gave up <u>smoke</u> last year.   → _____

event 몡 행사, 사건
honest 혱 정직한
important 혱 중요한
smoke 동 (담배를) 피우다

C <보기>의 동사를 한 번씩만 활용하여 빈칸에 쓰시오.

<보기>   play   use   bite   brush

1 She practiced _____ chopsticks.
2 His bad habit is _____ his nails.
3 Not _____ your teeth makes them weak.
4 Sandra kept _____ computer games last night.

bite 동 물어뜯다
brush 동 닦다
chopstick 몡 젓가락
nail 몡 손톱
weak 혱 약한

D 우리말과 같도록 괄호 안의 말을 활용하여 빈칸에 쓰시오.

1 매운 음식을 주문하는 것을 피해주세요. (avoid, order)
   = Please _____ _____ spicy food.
2 나는 나의 개를 산책시키고 싶다. (feel like, walk)
   = I _____ _____ _____ my dog.
3 안전벨트를 매는 것은 필수적이다. (wear seat belts, be)
   = _____ _____ _____ necessary.
4 경찰관들은 그 여자를 쫓느라 바빴다. (be busy, chase)
   = The police officers _____ _____ _____ the woman.

order 동 주문하다
spicy 혱 매운
walk a dog 개를 산책시키다
seat belt 안전벨트
necessary 혱 필수적인
chase 동 쫓다
police officer 경찰관

Writing Exercise

A 괄호 안의 말을 활용하여 문장을 완성하시오.

1 Jacob _____ a bicycle yesterday. (practiced, ride)

2 They came to Korea _____. (meet, their cousins)

3 She is not sure _____ during the holidays. (what, do)

4 I'm _____ noise in the theater. (sorry for, make)

5 It is bad for plants _____. (not, get, enough sunlight)

6 Mr. Thompson _____. (decided, eat out)

7 My mom _____ on rainy days. (hates, drive)

B 우리말과 같도록 괄호 안의 말을 알맞게 배열하시오.

1 시간을 현명하게 쓰는 것은 중요하다. (important, is, spend, to, time, it)
= _____ wisely.

2 쿠키를 굽는 것은 나를 행복하게 만든다. (cookies, me, makes, baking, happy)
= _____.

3 그의 아버지는 줄을 서서 기다리는 것을 좋아하지 않으신다. (like, his father, waiting, doesn't)
= _____ in lines.

4 John은 자라서 유명한 감독이 되었다. (be, grew up, a famous director, John, to)
= _____.

5 나의 여동생은 벽에 포스터를 걸고 싶어 한다. (hang, wants, my sister, a poster, to)
= _____ on the wall.

6 그녀는 그 건물을 찾기 위해 지도를 가져왔다. (find, in order, brought, to, a map, the building, she)
= _____.

7 Nicole은 부산에서 볼 멋진 무언가를 알고 있다. (something, see, Nicole, to, knows, wonderful)
= _____ in Busan.

C 우리말과 같도록 괄호 안의 말을 활용하여 문장을 완성하시오.

1 그는 대회에서 연주할 새 바이올린이 필요하다. (need, a new violin, play)

= He _____ at the contest.

2 Reina는 그녀가 가장 좋아하는 배우를 봐서 기뻤다. (be glad, see, her favorite actor)

= Reina _____ .

3 Michael은 저녁 식사를 요리하기로 약속했다. (promise, cook, dinner)

= Michael _____ .

4 그들은 여행을 준비하느라 바빴다. (be busy, prepare)

= They _____ for the trip.

5 우리는 그 문제를 어떻게 푸는지 배웠다. (learn, solve, the problem)

= We _____ .

6 나의 계획은 오늘 오후에 너의 집에 도착하는 것이다. (be, arrive)

= My plan _____ at your house this afternoon.

D 다음 그림을 보고 괄호 안의 말을 활용하여 문장을 완성하시오. (단, 현재형으로 쓰시오.)

1	2	3	4

1 Sharon _____ sick people. (hope, help)

2 Ryan _____ care of animals. (like, take)

3 Ms. Bell _____ English to students. (enjoy, teach)

4 Tyler _____ a beautiful dress. (plan, make)

Chapter 10

to부정사와 동명사

Hackers Grammar Smart Level 1

Chapter Test

[1-3] 다음 빈칸에 들어갈 알맞은 것을 고르시오.

1

You need _____ up now.

① wake   ② wakes   ③ woke
④ to wake   ⑤ waking

2

Sarah stopped _____ the piano.

① play   ② plays   ③ played
④ to playing   ⑤ playing

3

_____ is good to exercise regularly.

① This   ② It   ③ They
④ That   ⑤ What

서술형
[4-5] 다음 문장에서 어법상 어색한 부분을 찾아 쓰고 바르게 고쳐 쓰시오.

4

Natalie finished to write the essay.

_____ → _____

5

They were angry to hearing the news.

_____ → _____

서술형
6 다음 빈칸에 공통으로 들어갈 알맞은 말을 쓰시오.

- James picked a movie _____ watch.
- I bought some noodles in order _____ cook pasta.

7 다음 빈칸에 들어갈 말이 순서대로 짝지어진 것은?

- Sam wants _____ the bakery in Paris.
- We enjoyed _____ in the forest.

① visit – walk   ② to visit – to walk
③ to visit – walking   ④ visiting – to walk
⑤ visiting – walking

[8-9] 다음 중 밑줄 친 부분의 쓰임이 나머지 넷과 다른 것을 고르시오.

8   ① To ride a roller coaster is exciting.
② It is her hobby to collect comic books.
③ My goal is to lose weight this year.
④ It isn't easy to learn Chinese.
⑤ To read ten books a day is impossible.

9   ① Ms. Lopez gave up smoking last year.
② His dream was becoming an artist.
③ I don't mind changing my seat.
④ They kept asking the same question.
⑤ You cannot avoid meeting him forever.

10 다음 빈칸에 들어갈 알맞은 것을 <u>모두</u> 고르시오.

> The writer began _____ a science fiction novel.

① write　　② writes　　③ to write
④ to writing　　⑤ writing

11 다음 중 어법상 <u>어색한</u> 것은?

① Do you know how make an apple pie?
② Mr. Jackson likes listening to jazz music.
③ It is fun to talk with my best friend.
④ His plan is going shopping after school.
⑤ We hope to pass the exam.

고난도

[12-13] 주어진 문장의 밑줄 친 to부정사와 용법이 같은 것을 고르시오.

12

> My brother likes <u>to swim</u> in the pool.

① They went to the gym <u>to play</u> volleyball.
② I was scared <u>to hear</u> the strange sound.
③ The boy grew up <u>to be</u> a scientist.
④ Kevin started <u>to prepare</u> for a trip.
⑤ Maria washed her hands <u>to hold</u> the baby.

13

> They ran <u>to catch</u> the train to Busan.

① I want fresh salad <u>to eat</u>.
② There wasn't anyone <u>to clean</u> the room.
③ Please lend me a knife <u>to use</u>.
④ Susan searched for places <u>to go</u>.
⑤ Benjamin called her <u>to check</u> the schedule.

서술형

[14-17] 우리말과 같도록 괄호 안의 말을 활용하여 문장을 완성하시오.

14

> 그녀는 그 새를 보기 위해 창문을 열었다. (see the bird)

= She opened the window _____.

15

> 나에게 어디에 이 상자를 놓을지 말해주겠니? (put this box)

= Can you tell me _____?

16

> Robert는 그 벽을 칠하느라 바빴다. (be busy, paint the wall)

= Robert _____.

17

> 나는 엘리베이터를 타는 것을 무서워한다. (be afraid of, take an elevator)

= I _____.

18 다음 중 밑줄 친 부분이 어법상 바른 것은?

① Mr. Foster decided <u>to sell not</u> his car.
② Do you know where <u>get</u> a ticket?
③ Matt is good at <u>solve</u> math problems.
④ I feel like <u>having</u> ice cream for dessert.
⑤ Lily wanted <u>sharing</u> the secret with me.

[19-20] 우리말과 같도록 괄호 안의 말을 알맞게 배열하시오.

19
약속을 지키는 것은 중요하다. (important, it, promises, is, keep, to)

= _____ .

20
George는 입을 따뜻한 무언가를 찾았다. (found, to, something, George, warm, wear)

= _____ .

21 다음 두 문장을 한 문장으로 바르게 연결한 것은?

- Eva went to the mall.
- She bought a wallet.

① Eva went to the mall buy a wallet.
② Eva went to the mall buying a wallet.
③ Eva went to the mall to buying a wallet.
④ Eva went to the mall to buy a wallet.
⑤ Eva went to the mall order to buy a wallet.

22 다음 대화에서 어법상 <u>어색한</u> 부분을 찾아 쓰고 바르게 고쳐 쓰시오.

A: Do you remember to visit when the dentist?
B: No. I need checking the calendar.

(1) _____ → _____
(2) _____ → _____

23 다음 중 어법상 바른 것끼리 묶인 것은?

ⓐ Paul's hobby is skiing.
ⓑ Her job is edit newspaper articles.
ⓒ The student asked what to do next.
ⓓ Carol started to running to the building.
ⓔ The water is too cold to take a shower.

① ⓐ, ⓑ, ⓒ   ② ⓐ, ⓒ, ⓔ   ③ ⓐ, ⓓ, ⓔ
④ ⓑ, ⓒ, ⓓ   ⑤ ⓑ, ⓓ, ⓔ

24 주어진 <조건>에 맞게 다음 두 문장을 한 문장으로 연결하시오.

- I was happy.
- I met my old teacher.

<조건> 1. to부정사를 이용하시오.
       2. 8단어로 쓰시오.

→ _____ .

25 다음 글의 밑줄 친 ⓐ~ⓔ 중 어법상 <u>어색한</u> 것을 찾아 기호를 쓰고 바르게 고쳐 쓰시오.

Yesterday, Kate's father promised ⓐ<u>to take</u> her to a lake. She loves going ⓑ<u>fishing</u>, so she was excited ⓒ<u>to hear</u> that. She couldn't sleep well because she kept ⓓ<u>to think</u> about ⓔ<u>going</u> to the lake.

_____ → _____

Chapter

11

전치사

전치사는 명사나 대명사 앞에 와서 장소나 시간 등을 나타내는 말이다.

UNIT 01 | 장소를 나타내는 전치사

1 at, on, in

at(~에, ~에서)	비교적 좁은 장소나 하나의 지점	**at** home **at** the airport **at** the corner	**at** school **at** the station **at** the party
on(~ 위에, ~에)	표면에 접촉한 상태	**on** the table **on** the floor	**on** the chair **on** the wall
in(~ 안에, ~에)	비교적 넓은 장소나 공간의 내부	**in** Paris **in** the cabinet	**in** Korea **in** the building

Mina waited for me **at** the train station.
Your gloves are **on** the sofa.
He put his books **in** the backpack.

2 장소를 나타내는 기타 전치사

❶ over((표면과 떨어져서) ~ 위에), under(~ 아래에)

There is a cloud **over** the mountain.
I found my cell phone **under** the desk.

❷ in front of(~ 앞에), behind(~ 뒤에)

Lisa was standing **in front of** *me*.
  └→ 전치사 뒤에 인칭대명사가 올 때는 목적격을 쓴다.

The zebra hid **behind** the trees.

❸ near(~ 근처에), next to(~ 옆에), across from(~ 맞은편에)

Is there a swimming pool **near** your house?
She is doing yoga **next to** her sister.
The bank is **across from** the flower shop.

Smart Check   다음 빈칸에 들어갈 알맞은 것을 고르시오.

1 They hung the picture _____ the wall.
  ① at   ② on   ③ in

2 I lived _____ California last year.
  ① at   ② on   ③ in

3 The kids built a snowman _____ the mailbox.
  ① at   ② over   ③ next to

Practice

A 괄호 안에서 알맞은 것을 고르시오.

1 I left my bag (at / in) the car.

2 Jessica wears a hairband (at / on) her head.

3 We met our teacher (at / on) the park.

4 The musician was playing (on / in) the bridge.

5 Mark saw Ashley (at / in) the bus stop.

6 She bought this necklace (on / in) Turkey.

leave ⑧ 두고 오다, 떠나다
wear ⑧ 쓰고 있다, 입고 있다
hairband ⑲ 머리띠
musician ⑲ 음악가
bridge ⑲ 다리
bus stop 버스 정류장

B 다음 빈칸에 알맞은 전치사를 <보기>에서 한 번씩만 골라 쓰시오.

<보기>	at	in	under	across from

1 He kept his uniform _____ the closet.

2 The tennis ball is _____ the sofa.

3 You should cross the street. I am _____ you.

4 Laura and her friends were _____ school all day.

keep ⑧ 보관하다
uniform ⑲ 교복, 유니폼
closet ⑲ 벽장
cross the street 길을 건너다

C 다음 그림을 보고 빈칸에 알맞은 전치사를 <보기>에서 골라 쓰시오.

<보기>	on	behind	next to

1 The bookshelf is _____ the desk.

2 There is a trophy _____ the desk.

3 The cat is sitting _____ the box.

bookshelf ⑲ 책장
trophy ⑲ 트로피

D 우리말과 같도록 괄호 안의 말을 활용하여 빈칸에 쓰시오.

1 나는 봉투 위에 우표를 붙였다. (the envelope)
   = I put a stamp _____ _____ _____ .

2 잠자리들이 호수 위에서 날고 있다. (the lake)
   = Dragonflies are flying _____ _____ _____ .

3 그의 자리는 너의 자리 앞에 있다. (your seat)
   = His seat is _____ _____ _____ _____ .

4 그 비행기는 곧 공항에 도착할 것이다. (the airport)
   = The airplane will arrive _____ _____ _____ soon.

envelope ⑲ 봉투
put ⑧ 붙이다, 놓다, 넣다
stamp ⑲ 우표
lake ⑲ 호수
dragonfly ⑲ 잠자리
seat ⑲ 자리
arrive ⑧ 도착하다

UNIT 02 | 시간을 나타내는 전치사

1 at, on, in(~에)

at	시각, 시점	**at** 6 o'clock **at** noon	**at** 8:30 P.M. **at** night
on	요일, 날짜, 기념일	**on** Tuesday **on** March 17 **on** my birthday	**on** Sunday **on** December 3, 2018 **on** New Year's Day
in	월, 계절, 연도, 세기, 아침·오후·저녁	**in** April **in** 2007 **in** the morning/afternoon/evening **TIP** 특정한 날의 아침·오후·저녁을 나타낼 때는 **on**을 쓴다. 　　**on** Saturday morning	**in** fall **in** the 21st century 　　**on** Halloween evening

Let's eat breakfast **at** 7:30.
Vincent van Gogh died **on** July 29, 1890.
My family goes camping **in** October.

2 시간을 나타내는 기타 전치사

❶ before(~ 전에), after(~ 후에)
Eric played soccer **before** class.
They went to bed **after** dinner.

❷ for/during(~ 동안)
for 뒤에는 숫자를 포함한 기간 표현이 오고, during 뒤에는 특정 기간을 나타내는 명사가 온다.
Ms. Collins walked her dog **for** *three hours*.
Will you wear a hanbok **during** *the holidays*?

❸ by/until(~까지)
by는 어떤 행동이나 상황이 특정 시점까지 완료되는 것을 나타내고, until은 계속되는 것을 나타낸다.
Students should finish their homework **by** Friday.
You can borrow this magazine **until** January 13.

❹ around(~쯤)
He will come back **around** 9 o'clock.

다음 빈칸에 들어갈 알맞은 것을 고르시오.

1 We learned to cook _____ one year.
　① for　　　　　　　② during　　　　　　　③ until

Practice

Answers p.17

A 괄호 안에서 알맞은 것을 고르시오.

1 The last train leaves (at / in) 11 P.M.

2 Andrew and Betty married (on / in) 2010.

3 Americans usually eat turkey (at / on) Thanksgiving Day.

marry 통 결혼하다
turkey 명 칠면조
Thanksgiving Day 추수 감사절

B 다음 빈칸에 알맞은 전치사를 <보기>에서 한 번씩만 골라 쓰시오.

<보기>	on	for	during	by

1 Judy talked with her parents _____ 40 minutes.

2 He looked so nervous _____ the test.

3 My mom does volunteer work _____ Thursday.

4 You should return my money _____ tomorrow.

nervous 형 긴장한
volunteer work 자원봉사
Thursday 명 목요일
return 통 돌려주다, 돌아오다

C 다음 영화 상영표를 보고 빈칸에 알맞은 전치사를 쓰시오.

	Tue, May 4	Wed, May 5
10 A.M. – 12 P.M.	*Toy Story*	*Spiderman*
1 P.M. – 3 P.M.	*Toy story*	*Toy Story*
3 P.M. – 5 P.M.	*Inside Out*	*Inside Out*
5 P.M. – 8 P.M.	*Aladdin*	*Aladdin*

1 We can't watch *Spiderman* _____ May 4.

2 *Toy Story* shows _____ *Inside Out*.

3 *Aladdin* shows _____ three hours.

4 We can watch *Inside Out* only _____ the afternoon.

May 명 5월
show 통 상영하다, 보여주다
only 부 오직

D 우리말과 같도록 괄호 안의 말을 활용하여 빈칸에 쓰시오.

1 나는 내년 봄까지 머리를 자르지 않을 것이다. (next spring)

= I will not cut my hair _____ _____ _____ .

2 우리는 주말 전에 시장에 갔다. (the weekend)

= We went to the market _____ _____ _____ .

3 Kyle은 정오쯤에 그들을 만날 것이다. (noon)

= Kyle will meet them _____ _____ .

spring 명 봄
hair 명 머리(털)
market 명 시장

UNIT 03 | 기타 전치사

1 기타 전치사

❶ about(~에 대해)

The story is **about** time travel.

❷ by(~을 타고, ~으로)

Let's visit our grandfather **by** train.

You can contact me **by** phone.

> **TIP** · 「**by**(~을 타고) + 교통수단」: **by** car, **by** bus, **by** subway, **by** train, **by** plane 등
> · 「**by**(~으로) + 통신수단」: **by** phone, **by** mail, **by** fax, **by** text message 등

❸ for(~을 위해)

Ms. Lewis jogs every day **for** her health.

I prepared some snacks **for** my classmates.

❹ to(~에, ~으로, ~에게)

My brother couldn't go **to** school yesterday.

She sent a present **to** her grandchild.

❺ with(~과 함께, ~을 이용해서)

Donna likes reading books **with** her dad.

Mom cut carrots and potatoes **with** a knife.

❻ between A and B(A와 B 사이에)

Please sit **between** *Betty* **and** *me*.

This TV show will be over **between** *10* **and** *10:30*.

❼ from A to B(A에서 B까지)

We took a walk **from** *home* **to** *the park*.

She goes to work **from** *Monday* **to** *Friday*.

 다음 빈칸에 들어갈 알맞은 것을 고르시오.

1 They talked _____ her beautiful voice.

　① about　　　　　　　② by　　　　　　　③ to

2 The café is _____ the bookstore and the grocery store.

　① to　　　　　　　② between　　　　　　　③ from

3 You can climb a mountain more easily _____ this stick.

　① to　　　　　　　② with　　　　　　　③ between

Practice

Answers p.17

A 괄호 안에서 알맞은 것을 고르시오.

1 I went on a trip (by / to) bicycle.

2 She stayed up all night (for / with) the exam.

3 Tell me (to / about) your favorite baseball team.

4 Mario cleaned the garden (for / with) a broom.

5 It takes an hour (from / between) the subway station to the hospital.

go on a trip 여행을 가다
stay up all night 밤을 새우다
exam 몡 시험
garden 몡 정원
broom 몡 빗자루

B 자연스러운 문장이 되도록 알맞게 연결하시오.

1 There was a big tree · · ⓐ for the environment.

2 Joseph saves water · · ⓑ between the school and the bakery.

3 I brought my dog · · ⓒ with his close friend Carol.

4 He had lunch · · ⓓ to the animal hospital.

environment 몡 환경
save 통 절약하다
bakery 몡 빵집
bring 통 데리고 가다
close 혱 친한, 가까운
animal hospital 동물 병원

C 다음 빈칸에 공통으로 들어갈 알맞은 전치사를 <보기>에서 골라 쓰시오.

| <보기> about   for   to   with |

1 ① Her family moved _____ Incheon last month.

 ② Tyler lent the laptop _____ his brother.

2 ① They joined the army _____ the country.

 ② This can of tuna is _____ my cat.

3 ① Rabbits can hear well _____ their big ears.

 ② I went to Taiwan _____ my family.

4 ① She saw a documentary _____ dolphins.

 ② This novel is _____ a famous king of Joseon.

move 통 이사하다
join the army 입대하다
country 몡 국가, 나라
tuna 몡 참치
documentary 몡 다큐멘터리
dolphin 몡 돌고래

D 우리말과 같도록 괄호 안의 말을 활용하여 빈칸에 쓰시오.

1 그 마라톤 코스는 종로에서 여의도까지이다. (Jongno, Yeouido)

 = The marathon course is _____ _____ _____ _____.

2 Bell 선생님은 그의 학생들에게 편지를 썼다. (his students)

 = Mr. Bell wrote letters _____ _____ _____.

3 Rachel은 이메일로 그녀의 독후감을 보냈다. (e-mail)

 = Rachel sent her book report _____ _____.

4 나는 9시와 11시 사이에 매우 바쁘다. (9, 11)

 = I'm very busy _____ _____ _____ _____.

marathon course 마라톤 코스
book report 독후감

전치사 Hackers Grammar Smart Level 1

Writing Exercise

A 우리말과 같도록 괄호 안의 말을 활용하여 문장을 완성하시오.

1 피카소는 20세기에 유명한 예술가였다. (the 20th century)

= Picasso was a famous artist _____.

2 나는 아침 식사 전에 운동할 것이다. (breakfast)

= I will exercise _____.

3 그녀는 우체국 뒤에 그녀의 차를 주차했다. (the post office)

= She parked her car _____.

4 이 뮤지컬은 프랑스 혁명에 대한 것이다. (the French Revolution)

= This musical is _____.

5 내가 나의 여권을 너의 가방 안에 보관해도 되니? (your bag)

= May I keep my passport _____?

6 너는 공연 동안에 말하면 안 된다. (the performance)

= You should not talk _____.

7 저 아이는 젓가락을 이용해서 국수를 먹고 있다. (chopsticks)

= That kid is eating noodles _____.

B 우리말과 같도록 괄호 안의 말을 알맞게 배열하시오.

1 그 말은 울타리 위로 뛰어넘을 수 있다. (over, jump, the fence)

= The horse can _____.

2 Roger는 그의 콘서트에 나를 초대했다. (invited, his concert, to, me)

= Roger _____.

3 나는 Patrick과 Jessica 사이에서 사진을 찍었다. (Jessica, took, and, a picture, Patrick, between)

= I _____.

4 그 형사는 5시쯤에 발자국을 발견했다. (5 o'clock, footprints, around, found)

= The detective _____.

5 너는 추석에 송편을 만들 거니? (Chuseok, make, on, songpyeon)

= Are you going to _____?

6 그는 교회 맞은편에서 그의 여자친구를 기다렸다. (his girlfriend, the church, across from, waited for)

= He _____.

7 수요일부터 금요일까지 특별한 행사가 있다. (Friday, a special event, Wednesday, from, is, to)

= There _____.

C 다음 그림을 보고 <보기>의 전치사와 괄호 안의 말을 한 번씩만 활용하여 문장을 완성하시오.

<보기>	at	in	in front of	next to	to	with

Yesterday, it rained a lot ⓐ_____(the afternoon). I came back home

ⓑ_____(3 o'clock). My mom was reading a book ⓒ_____

(my brother), and my dog was sleeping ⓓ_____(them). My dad was taking a

picture of it ⓔ_____(his camera). There were slippers ⓕ_____

(the door). I put them on because my feet were wet.

D 다음은 박람회의 안내문이다. 알맞은 전치사와 괄호 안의 말을 활용하여 문장을 완성하시오.

Welcome to the Seoul Art Fair!

Opening Hours: Monday (13:00 – 17:00)
　　　　　　　　Tuesday to Sunday (09:30 – 17:00)

- We have a shuttle bus for visitors.
- We will give a handmade bracelet to students.
  Visit the ticket booth and show your student ID card.

---

1 The Seoul Art Fair doesn't open _____. (Monday morning)

2 The Seoul Art Fair opens _____. (Monday, Sunday)

3 Visitors can go to the Seoul Art Fair _____. (shuttle bus)

4 Students can get a handmade bracelet _____. (the ticket booth)

Chapter Test

[1-3] 다음 빈칸에 들어갈 알맞은 것을 고르시오.

1

> Jamie put the tomatoes _____ the refrigerator.

① at   ② for   ③ in
④ to   ⑤ from

2

> The soccer game will start _____ 7 A.M.

① in   ② at   ③ on
④ for   ⑤ during

3

> We planted the tree _____ July 14.

① about   ② during   ③ at
④ in   ⑤ on

서술형

[4-6] 우리말과 같도록 빈칸에 알맞은 전치사를 쓰시오.

4

> 그 아기 근처에 장난감이 있다.

= There is a toy _____ the baby.

5

> 그는 정오쯤에 점심을 먹을 것이다.

= He will have lunch _____ noon.

6

> 나의 여동생은 그녀의 방으로 뛰어가서 침대 아래에 숨었다.

= My sister ran _____ her room and hid _____ the bed.

고난도

[7-8] 다음 빈칸에 공통으로 들어갈 알맞은 것을 고르시오.

7

> • Hand in your homework _____ Monday.
> • I traveled to Canada _____ plane.

① until   ② by   ③ in
④ with   ⑤ before

8

> • This movie is _____ children.
> • Jeffrey practiced his speech _____ 50 minutes.

① to   ② with   ③ about
④ for   ⑤ during

[9-10] 다음 빈칸에 들어갈 말이 나머지 넷과 다른 것을 고르시오.

9

① They will meet _____ my birthday party.
② Fred and his family are _____ home now.
③ I didn't see her _____ school today.
④ Amy was lying _____ the floor.
⑤ Let's buy the ticket _____ the train station.

10

① What did you say _____ the interview?
② Mr. Smith took a bath _____ two hours.
③ What are you going to do _____ your long vacation?
④ Don't talk to each other _____ the exam.
⑤ I was tired _____ the weekend.

서술형 **고난도**

[11-13] 다음 글의 빈칸에 알맞은 전치사를 쓰시오.

11

> The science class started at 9 o'clock, and the history class started at 11 o'clock. We took the science class _____ the history class.

12

> Sarah went to the library to study. She will leave after an hour. She is going to study _____ an hour.

13

> Some students are standing in a line. Amy can see William, but William can't see Amy. William is standing _____ Amy.

서술형

[14-16] 우리말과 같도록 괄호 안의 말을 알맞게 배열하시오.

14

> 그 드레스는 코트와 재킷 사이에 있다. (the coat, the jacket, is, and, between)

= The dress _____ .

15

> 나는 버스 정류장에서 집까지 걸어갔다. (the bus stop, walked, home, to, from)

= I _____ .

16

> 공원 맞은편에 시계탑이 있다. (the park, a clock tower, from, is, across)

= There _____ .

[17-18] 다음 중 밑줄 친 부분이 어법상 어색한 것을 고르시오.

17 ① Mary always writes in her diary <u>at</u> night.
② I usually sleep late <u>in</u> Sunday morning.
③ Greg entered elementary school <u>in</u> 2010.
④ The news program will begin <u>at</u> 5.
⑤ The students will go to the theme park <u>on</u> April 9.

18 ① The book is <u>to</u> animals at the North Pole.
② I got the information <u>by</u> text message.
③ We prepared a gift <u>for</u> Shawn.
④ The clown made a dog <u>with</u> the balloon.
⑤ She gave the medicine <u>to</u> the patient.

19 다음 우리말을 알맞게 영작한 것은?

> 봄 방학은 내일부터 3월 3일까지이다.

① Spring vacation is on tomorrow to March 3.
② Spring vacation is from tomorrow and March 3.
③ Spring vacation is to tomorrow from March 3.
④ Spring vacation is from tomorrow to March 3.
⑤ Spring vacation is between tomorrow to March 3.

20 다음 그림을 보고 빈칸에 알맞은 말을 쓰시오.

(1) The bakery is _____ the supermarket _____ the theater.

(2) The bank is _____ _____ the police station.

(3) The police station is _____ _____ the park.

[21-22] 다음 대화에서 어법상 어색한 부분을 찾아 쓰고 바르게 고쳐 쓰시오.

21

A: Where was your cat? It wasn't on your room or behind the desk.

B: It was under the sofa.

_____ → _____

22

A: What is that in the oven?

B: It is an apple pie. I'm baking it to my new neighbors.

_____ → _____

---

23 다음 중 어법상 바른 것끼리 묶인 것은?

ⓐ Raise your hand over your head.
ⓑ The store is open until 11:30.
ⓒ Ms. Larsen sent me the picture for e-mail.
ⓓ The video is between wild animals.
ⓔ You can do the project with your partner.

① ⓐ, ⓑ, ⓒ 　② ⓐ, ⓑ, ⓔ 　③ ⓐ, ⓓ, ⓔ
④ ⓑ, ⓒ, ⓓ 　⑤ ⓒ, ⓓ, ⓔ

[24-25] 다음 문장에서 어법상 어색한 부분을 찾아 쓰고 바르게 고쳐 쓰시오.

24

Nate found his smartphone next his sister's computer.

_____ → _____

25

I went to the restaurant with subway.

_____ → _____

---

26 다음 글의 밑줄 친 ⓐ~ⓔ 중 어법상 어색한 것을 찾아 기호를 쓰고 바르게 고쳐 쓰시오.

Dear Paul,
Yesterday, I left England ⓐat 10 P.M. I just arrived ⓑon the airport in Germany, and I'm writing this letter ⓒin a beautiful café. There are many interesting places ⓓat Berlin. Next week, I will travel from Germany ⓔto Italy.

(1) _____ → _____
(2) _____ → _____

Chapter

12

접속사

접속사는 단어와 단어, 구와 구, 절과 절을 연결하는 말이다.

UNIT 01 | and, but, or, so

and, but, or는 문법적으로 대등한 단어와 단어, 구와 구, 절과 절을 연결하고, so는 절과 절만 연결한다.

1 **and**(~과, 그리고)

서로 대등한 내용을 연결한다.

Hazel bought *notebooks* **and** *pencils*.
My brother *cleaned his room* **and** *washed the dishes*.

TIP 「**both A and B**」: A와 B 둘 다
We want to travel to **both** *Norway* **and** *Sweden*.

2 **but**(하지만, 그러나)

서로 대조되는 내용을 연결한다.

The girl is *young* **but** *wise*.
I drank two glasses of water, **but** *I'm still thirsty*.

3 **or**(또는, ~이거나, 아니면)

두 가지 이상의 선택 사항을 연결한다.

Susan **or** *George* will be the class president.
She *takes naps* **or** *plays games* on weekends.

TIP 「**either A or B**」: A나 B 둘 중 하나
Please bring **either** *a red pen* **or** *a blue pen*.

4 **so**(그래서, 따라서)

원인을 나타내는 앞의 절과 결과를 나타내는 뒤의 절을 연결한다.

The baby woke up early, **so** *he will be sleepy soon*.
There was a car accident, **so** *we couldn't use the road*.

Smart Check 다음 빈칸에 들어갈 가장 알맞은 것을 고르시오.

1 Ariel had bread _____ milk for lunch.
① and   ② but   ③ so

2 He didn't hurry, _____ he couldn't arrive on time.
① but   ② or   ③ so

3 Ostriches have wings, _____ they can't fly.
① but   ② or   ③ so

Practice

Answers p.18

A 괄호 안에서 가장 알맞은 것을 고르시오.

1 My sister is lovely (and / but) pretty.

2 I have a fever, (so / but) I'm lying on the bed.

3 He likes meat but (hates / to hate) fish.

4 Which vehicle do you want to drive, the truck (and / or) the sports car?

fever 몡 열
lie 통 눕다
vehicle 몡 차량
sports car 스포츠카

B <보기>에서 알맞은 접속사를 한 번씩만 골라 다음 두 문장을 한 문장으로 연결하시오.

| <보기>   and   but   or   so |

1 Kevin may be in the bedroom. Kevin may be in the kitchen.

→ Kevin may be in the bedroom _____ the kitchen.

2 Brenda borrowed a book. Brenda borrowed a magazine.

→ Brenda borrowed a book _____ a magazine.

3 I ordered vanilla flavor. I received chocolate flavor.

→ I ordered vanilla flavor, _____ I received chocolate flavor.

4 His watch was broken. He bought a new one.

→ His watch was broken, _____ he bought a new one.

flavor 몡 맛
receive 통 받다
broken 몡 고장 난

C 자연스러운 문장이 되도록 알맞게 연결하시오.

1 She goes to school by subway   ·

2 Sandra is a fast runner,   ·

3 Mom washed some vegetables   ·

4 Her neighbor was noisy,   ·

· ⓐ and made salad.

· ⓑ so she couldn't sleep well.

· ⓒ or on foot.

· ⓓ but I run faster than her.

runner 몡 주자
noisy 몡 시끄러운

D 우리말과 같도록 괄호 안의 말을 활용하여 빈칸에 쓰시오.

1 그 마술 쇼는 환상적이지만 비쌌다. (fantastic, expensive)

= The magic show was _____ _____ _____.

2 그들은 늦게 일어나서 수업에 늦었다. (be late for)

= They got up late, _____ _____ _____ _____

_____ the class.

3 Evelyn은 기타와 바이올린 둘 다 잘한다. (the guitar, the violin)

= Evelyn is good at _____ _____ _____ _____

_____ _____.

fantastic 몡 환상적인
expensive 몡 비싼
late for ~에 늦은
good at ~을 잘하는

UNIT 02 | when, while, before, after

when, while, before, after는 시간을 나타내는 부사절을 이끈다.

1 when(~할 때)

I wear an apron **when** I cook.
When *Victoria came home,* her cat was sleeping.
  └→ 부사절이 문장 맨 앞에 올 때는 부사절 뒤에 콤마(,)를 쓴다.

2 while(~하는 동안)

While they watch TV, they usually eat snacks.
Nancy fell asleep **while** her mom was making the bed.

3 before(~하기 전에)

Mr. Sanders jogs **before** he goes to work.
Before you send an e-mail, check the address.

4 after(~한 후에)

The students played soccer **after** they did their homework.
After she arrived, we had lunch together.

> **TIP** 시간을 나타내는 부사절에서는 미래시제 대신 현재시제를 쓴다.
> Jack will ask a question *after* the class (~~will end~~, **ends**).

Smart Check 다음 빈칸에 들어갈 가장 알맞은 것을 고르시오.

1 My sister didn't like broccoli _____ she was nine years old.
  ① when   ② before   ③ after

2 _____ you use the ruler, please give it back to me.
  ① When   ② After   ③ While

3 I brush my teeth _____ I go to bed.
  ① before   ② after   ③ while

Practice

Answers p.18

A 괄호 안에서 가장 알맞은 것을 고르시오.

1 We called 119 (before / when) Joseph broke his arm.

2 You should warm up (while / before) you go into the water.

3 (While / After) I was taking a bath, the doorbell rang.

4 I will cross the street after the traffic light (will turn / turns) green.

arm 몡 팔
warm up 준비 운동을 하다
doorbell 몡 초인종
ring 동 울리다
traffic light 신호등

B 우리말과 같도록 빈칸에 알맞은 접속사를 쓰시오.

1 그가 차를 운전하고 있는 동안, 비가 심하게 왔다.

= _____ he was driving a car, it rained heavily.

2 Emily는 그녀의 여행 가방을 싼 후에 잠시 휴식을 취했다.

= Emily took a break _____ she packed her suitcase.

3 너의 방을 떠나기 전에 창문을 닫아라.

= Close the windows _____ you leave your room.

4 나는 초등학생이었을 때 많은 책을 읽었다.

= I read many books _____ I was an elementary school student.

heavily 뷔 심하게
take a break 잠시 휴식을 취하다
pack 동 (짐 등을) 싸다
suitcase 몡 여행 가방

C 다음 빈칸에 가장 알맞은 말을 <보기>에서 한 번씩만 골라 쓰시오.

<보기>	before it gets dark	when he enters a room
	while he was running	after he watched the scary movie

1 Mr. Green knocks on the door _____.

2 My brother should come home _____.

3 He had a nightmare _____.

4 Steve dropped his phone _____.

dark 혱 어두운
enter 동 들어가다
scary 혱 무서운
knock on the door 문을 두드리다
have a nightmare 악몽을 꾸다
drop 동 떨어뜨리다

D 우리말과 같도록 괄호 안의 말을 활용하여 빈칸에 쓰시오.

1 Parker씨는 졸릴 때 커피를 마신다. (be, sleepy)

= Mr. Parker drinks coffee _____ _____ _____ _____.

2 학교가 끝난 후에 보드게임을 하자. (school, finish)

= Let's play a board game _____ _____ _____.

3 나는 Andy가 저녁 식사를 요리하는 동안 식탁을 차렸다. (cook, dinner)

= I set the table _____ _____ _____.

board game 보드게임
set a table 식탁을 차리다

UNIT 03 | because, if, that

1 because(~하기 때문에)

이유를 나타내는 부사절을 이끈다.

I should take this medicine **because** I have a cold.
Because we picked up the trash, the street was clean.

2 if(만약 ~한다면)

조건을 나타내는 부사절을 이끈다.

Take a taxi **if** you're late.
If you get up before 6, you can see the sunrise.

> **TIP** 조건을 나타내는 부사절에서는 미래시제 대신 현재시제를 쓴다.
> *If* it (~~will rain~~, **rains**) tomorrow, he'll stay at home.

3 that(~이라는 것)

that이 이끄는 명사절은 문장 안에서 주어, 목적어, 보어로 쓰인다.

❶ 주어

that절이 주어로 쓰일 때는 주로 주어 자리에 가주어 it을 쓰고 진주어 that절을 뒤로 보낸다.

That the painter is 14 years old is amazing.
= **It** is amazing **that** the painter is 14 years old.

❷ 목적어

that절이 목적어로 쓰일 때는 that을 생략할 수 있다.

I think **(that)** you are a great dancer.

> **TIP** that절을 목적어로 쓰는 동사: **think, believe, know, hope, say, tell, hear 등**
> Charlie **heard** *(that)* his team won the game.

❸ 보어

The fact is **that** Kate lied to her parents.

Smart Check 다음 빈칸에 들어갈 가장 알맞은 것을 고르시오.

1 Hans said _____ he didn't have any money.
① because   ② if   ③ that

2 She got some flowers _____ yesterday was her birthday.
① because   ② if   ③ that

Practice

Answers p.18

A 괄호 안에서 가장 알맞은 것을 고르시오.

1 It is surprising (that / if) Anna wants to be a pianist.

2 Raise your hand (if / because) you know the answer.

3 (Because / That) Donald was hungry, he had two bowls of cereal.

4 I will wear shorts if the weather (will be / is) hot.

surprising 형 놀라운
pianist 명 피아니스트
raise 통 들다
shorts 명 반바지

B 다음 빈칸에 가장 알맞은 접속사를 <보기>에서 골라 쓰시오.

<보기>	because	if	that

1 _____ you need paper, you can use this.

2 The boy cried loudly _____ he lost his toy car.

3 You will get one for free _____ you buy two items.

4 The problem was _____ he didn't bring the key.

loudly 부 큰 소리로
lose 통 잃어버리다
for free 무료로
item 명 물품, 항목

C 밑줄 친 **that**이 이끄는 절의 쓰임을 <보기>에서 골라 그 기호를 쓰시오.

<보기>	ⓐ 주어	ⓑ 목적어	ⓒ 보어

1 It is clear <u>that</u> she stole my wallet. [   ]

2 The doctor said <u>that</u> I should exercise regularly. [   ]

3 The issue is <u>that</u> children use smartphones too much. [   ]

4 They hope <u>that</u> they will be safe from hurricanes. [   ]

clear 형 분명한, 맑은
steal 통 훔치다
regularly 부 규칙적으로
issue 명 문제
safe 형 안전한
hurricane 명 허리케인

D 우리말과 같도록 괄호 안의 말을 활용하여 빈칸에 쓰시오.

1 만약 Carol이 도움이 필요하다면, 우리에게 전화할 것이다. (need, help)

= _____ _____ _____ _____, she will call us.

2 Eric은 그가 운이 좋다고 생각한다. (be, lucky)

= Eric thinks _____ _____ _____ _____.

3 나는 그녀의 주소를 알지 못했기 때문에 그녀에게 편지를 보낼 수 없었다. (know, her address)

= I couldn't send her a letter _____ _____ _____ _____

_____ _____.

lucky 형 운이 좋은
address 명 주소

Writing Exercise

A   우리말과 같도록 괄호 안의 말을 활용하여 문장을 완성하시오.

1   나는 Nicole이나 Emma에게 투표할 것이다. (vote for, Nicole, Emma)

= I will _____ .

2   만약 네가 록 음악을 좋아한다면, 함께 그 콘서트에 가자. (like, rock music)

= _____ , let's go to the concert together.

3   그녀는 수줍음을 많이 타서 낯선 사람들에게 말을 걸지 않는다. (talk to, strangers)

= She is shy, _____ .

4   Samuel은 홍콩으로 여행 갔을 때 많은 망고를 먹었다. (travel to, Hong Kong)

= Samuel ate a lot of mangoes _____ .

5   Ashley는 치통이 있었기 때문에 치과에 갔다. (have, a toothache)

= Ashley went to the dentist _____ .

6   그들은 교실에 들어가기 전에 그들의 신발을 갈아 신는다. (enter, the classroom)

= _____ , they change their shoes.

B   우리말과 같도록 괄호 안의 말을 알맞게 배열하시오.

1   우리는 Rami와 Sami가 쌍둥이라는 것을 알고 있다. (Rami, are, that, and, twins, Sami, know)

= We _____ .

2   나의 삼촌의 차는 낡아 보이지만 잘 작동한다. (old, works, looks, well, it, but)

= My uncle's car _____ , _____ .

3   그는 밥을 먹은 후에 싱크대에 접시를 넣는다. (has, he, dishes, a meal, puts, after, in the sink)

= He _____ .

4   아빠는 약간의 오렌지를 사고 주스를 만드셨다. (and, juice, made, some oranges, bought)

= Dad _____ .

5   Antonio가 그 축구선수를 만났다는 것은 놀랍다. (amazing, the soccer player, is, Antonio, that, met)

= It _____ .

6   나는 책을 읽고 있는 동안 이상한 소리를 들었다. (I, a book, while, a strange sound, was reading, heard)

= I _____ .

C 다음 그림을 보고 빈칸에 알맞은 접속사를 <보기>에서 한 번씩만 골라 쓰시오.

 →  →

<보기>   but   and   so   if   while   because

Daniel and Linda went hiking last weekend. They took hiking sticks ⓐ_____ some water. It was sunny, ⓑ_____ they were excited. ⓒ_____ they were climbing the mountain, it started to rain suddenly. ⓓ_____ it rained too much, they went down the mountain. They were disappointed, ⓔ_____ they decided to go hiking another time. ⓕ_____ the weather is good next weekend, they will try again.

D 다음은 과학 동아리의 홍보 포스터이다. 빈칸에 가장 알맞은 접속사를 <보기>에서 한 번씩만 골라 쓰시오.

<보기>   or   when   so   that   after

<Albert Science Club>

We are looking for new members! You don't have to be good at science, ⓐ_____ don't worry. Every month, we go to a science museum ⓑ_____ do fun science experiments. The science teacher Mr. Simon will help us ⓒ_____ we do experiments. Plus, we give special gifts to all members ⓓ_____ the semester ends. We hope ⓔ_____ you will join our club. Thanks!

Chapter Test

[1-3] 다음 빈칸에 들어갈 가장 알맞은 것을 고르시오.

1

I slept for nine hours, _____ I'm still tired.

① and   ② but   ③ or
④ so   ⑤ when

2

They will eat Korean food _____ Mexican food tomorrow.

① so   ② but   ③ or
④ that   ⑤ while

3

Jamie believes _____ the story is real.

① and   ② because   ③ if
④ so   ⑤ that

서술형

[4-6] 다음 빈칸에 가장 알맞은 접속사를 <보기>에서 한 번씩만 골라 쓰시오.

<보기>	because	if	that

4

My grandparents will be surprised _____ we visit them this weekend.

5

The leaves fell from the tree _____ the wind was so strong.

6

The truth is _____ Jack didn't want to fight with her.

[7-8] 다음 중 어법상 어색한 것을 고르시오.

7
① The soup looked delicious but tasted bad.
② Will you study at this café or that café?
③ The hall was dark and quiet.
④ Thomas has a big and comfortably sofa.
⑤ It was hot, so I turned on the air conditioner.

8
① They baked some cupcakes because today is Frank's birthday.
② Charles will buy a swimsuit before he goes to the beach.
③ I will call you if the package will arrive.
④ After you finish your food, wash the dishes.
⑤ Matt did his homework while his brother was playing computer games.

[9-10] 다음 빈칸에 들어갈 말이 나머지 넷과 <u>다른</u> 것을 고르시오.

9 ① I liked the movie, _____ Steve didn't like it.
② The city is beautiful _____ dangerous.
③ Nancy was hungry, _____ she ate some chocolate.
④ Bears are heavy, _____ they can run fast.
⑤ The weather was cold, _____ he didn't wear a jacket.

10 ① The sky is clear, _____ I'll fly a kite.
② You should either take a test _____ write an essay.
③ The fan didn't work, _____ I opened the window.
④ There were a lot of customers, _____ we waited in line.
⑤ John has a stomachache, _____ he went to the hospital.

11 다음 중 밑줄 친 부분이 문맥상 바른 것을 <u>모두</u> 고르시오.

① I bought the bracelet <u>and</u> the necklace.
② The jeans are pretty <u>or</u> small for me.
③ Fred wrote down the phone number <u>after</u> he forgot it.
④ Hanna looked angry <u>if</u> I broke her cell phone.
⑤ The man is popular <u>because</u> he is smart and funny.

서술형

[12-13] 다음 빈칸에 공통으로 들어갈 가장 알맞은 접속사를 쓰시오.

12
• I heard _____ you moved here. • It is sad _____ our vacation is over.

13
• The farmers have to pick the apples _____ winter comes. • Take off your shoes _____ you enter the room.

서술형

[14-15] 우리말과 같도록 괄호 안의 말을 알맞게 배열하시오.

14
눈이 오고 있어서, Jackie는 야외 수영장을 사용할 수 없었다. (the outdoor swimming pool, Jackie, so, use, couldn't)

= It was snowing, _____
_____ .

15
인터넷이 유용한 정보를 제공한다는 것은 사실이다. (true, is, that, it)

= _____ the Internet provides useful information.

[16-18] 우리말과 같도록 괄호 안의 말을 활용하여 문장을 완성하시오.

16
> Owen은 수학 문제를 푼 후에 그의 답을 검토한다.
> (solve math problems)

= Owen reviews his answers _____

_____ .

17
> 나는 목욕을 할 때 음악을 듣는 것을 좋아한다. (take a bath)

= I like listening to music _____ .

18
> 만약 그 커피가 맛있다면 우리는 약간의 커피콩을 살 것이다. (the coffee, be delicious)

= We will buy some coffee beans _____

_____ .

서술형

[19-20] 다음 대화에서 어법상 어색한 부분을 찾아 쓰고 바르게 고쳐 쓰시오.

19
> A: You should clean the kitchen so do the laundry.
> B: I'll clean the kitchen, then.

_____ → _____

20
> A: Can you take out the cookies from the oven when they will turn brown?
> B: Of course.

_____ → _____

서술형 고난도

21 다음 글의 밑줄 친 ⓐ~ⓔ중 어법상 어색한 것을 찾아 기호를 쓰고 바르게 고쳐 쓰시오.

> This morning, I thought ⓐif I was late for school ⓑbecause my watch said it was 9. I quickly washed my face and ⓒbrushing my teeth. I packed my bag ⓓwhile I ate toast. ⓔBefore I left home, I checked the time again. Shockingly, the watch still said it was 9.

(1) _____ → _____
(2) _____ → _____

고난도

22 다음 중 밑줄 친 부분이 문맥상 바른 것끼리 묶인 것은?

> ⓐ I used your scissors while I lost mine.
> ⓑ You can meet new people because you join the club.
> ⓒ Paul takes the subway when he goes to school.
> ⓓ Let's go running after the sun sets.
> ⓔ There weren't any potatoes, so Harry couldn't make potato soup.

① ⓐ, ⓑ, ⓒ   ② ⓐ, ⓑ, ⓔ   ③ ⓐ, ⓒ, ⓓ
④ ⓑ, ⓓ, ⓔ   ⑤ ⓒ, ⓓ, ⓔ

불규칙 동사 변화표

1. A-A-A형 원형-과거형-과거분사형이 모두 같은 경우

원형	과거형	과거분사형
cost 비용이 들다	cost	cost
hit 치다, 때리다	hit	hit
hurt 다치게 하다	hurt	hurt
let ~하게 하다	let	let

원형	과거형	과거분사형
put 놓다	put	put
read[ri:d] 읽다	read[red]	read[red]
shut 닫다	shut	shut
spread 펼치다	spread	spread

2. A-B-A형 원형-과거분사형이 같은 경우

원형	과거형	과거분사형
become ~이 되다	became	become
come 오다	came	come

원형	과거형	과거분사형
overcome 극복하다	overcame	overcome
run 달리다	ran	run

3. A-B-B형 과거형-과거분사형이 같은 경우

원형	과거형	과거분사형
bring 가져오다	brought	brought
build 짓다, 만들다	built	built
feed 먹이를 주다	fed	fed
feel 느끼다	felt	felt
find 찾다	found	found
get 얻다	got	got(ten)
have 가지다	had	had
hear 듣다	heard	heard
keep 유지하다	kept	kept
lay 놓다, 낳다	laid	laid
lead 이끌다	led	led

원형	과거형	과거분사형
leave 떠나다	left	left
lose 잃다, 지다	lost	lost
make 만들다	made	made
meet 만나다	met	met
send 보내다	sent	sent
sleep 자다	slept	slept
spend 쓰다	spent	spent
tell 말하다	told	told
think 생각하다	thought	thought
understand 이해하다	understood	understood
win 이기다	won	won

4. A-B-C형 원형-과거형-과거분사형이 모두 다른 경우

원형	과거형	과거분사형	원형	과거형	과거분사형
be ~이다, ~하다	was/were	been	hide 숨다	hid	hidden
bear 낳다	bore	born	know 알다	knew	known
begin 시작하다	began	begun	lie 눕다	lay	lain
bite 물다	bit	bitten	mistake 실수하다	mistook	mistaken
blow 불다	blew	blown	ride 타다	rode	ridden
break 깨다	broke	broken	ring 울리다	rang	rung
choose 선택하다	chose	chosen	rise 오르다	rose	risen
do 하다	did	done	see 보다	saw	seen
draw 그리다	drew	drawn	shake 흔들다	shook	shaken
drink 마시다	drank	drunk	show 보여주다	showed	showed shown
drive 운전하다	drove	driven	sing 노래하다	sang	sung
eat 먹다	ate	eaten	sink 가라앉다	sank	sunk sunken
fall 떨어지다, 넘어지다	fell	fallen	sow (씨를) 뿌리다	sowed	sowed sown
fly 날다	flew	flown	speak 말하다	spoke	spoken
forbid 금지하다	forbade	forbidden	steal 훔치다	stole	stolen
forget 잊다	forgot	forgotten	swell 붓다, 부풀다	swelled	swelled swollen
forgive 용서하다	forgave	forgiven	swim 수영하다	swam	swum
freeze 얼다	froze	frozen	take 가지고 가다	took	taken
give 주다	gave	given	throw 던지다	threw	thrown
go 가다	went	gone	wear 입고 있다	wore	worn
grow 자라다	grew	grown	write 쓰다	wrote	written

문법 사항	세부 내용	Starter	Level 1	Level 2	Level 3
be동사	be동사	O	p.14, 16		
	There + be동사	O	p.14		
일반동사	일반동사	O	p.24, 26, 28		
시제	현재시제	O	p.36	O	
	과거시제	O	p.36	O	
	미래시제	O	p.38	O	
	현재진행시제	O	p.40	O	
	과거진행시제		p.40	O	
	현재완료시제			O	O
	과거완료시제				O
	미래완료시제				O
조동사	can	O	p.48	O	O
	may	O	p.48	O	O
	will	O	p.38	O	
	must	O	p.50	O	O
	have to	O	p.50	O	O
	should		p.50	O	O
	would like to			O	
	had better			O	O
	used to			O	O
	would rather				O
	may as well				O
	조동사 + have + p.p.				O
수동태	수동태			O	O
	수동태의 다양한 형태			O	O
	4형식/5형식 문장의 수동태			O	O
	by 이외의 전치사를 쓰는 수동태			O	O
	목적어가 that절인 문장의 수동태				O
	구동사의 수동태				O
부정사	to부정사		p.118, 120	O	O
	부정사를 목적격 보어로 쓰는 동사		p.62		O
	to부정사의 의미상 주어			O	O
	to부정사의 시제, 태				O
	to부정사 구문		p.120	O	O
	독립 부정사				O
동명사	동명사		p.122	O	O
분사	현재분사, 과거분사			O	O
	분사구문			O	O
	주의해야 할 분사구문				O
동사의 종류	주격 보어가 필요한 동사		p.58		
	감각동사	O	p.58	O	
	두 개의 목적어가 필요한 동사(수여동사)	O	p.60	O	
	목적격 보어가 필요한 동사		p.62	O	

문법 사항	세부 내용	Starter	Level 1	Level 2	Level 3
문장의 종류	명령문, 청유문, 감탄문	O	p.70		
	의문사 의문문	O	p.72, 74		
	부정의문문, 선택의문문, 부가의문문		p.76		
명사와 관사	셀 수 있는 명사, 셀 수 없는 명사	O	p.84		
	관사		p.86		
대명사	인칭대명사	O	p.94		
	재귀대명사		p.94	O	
	지시대명사	O	p.96		
	비인칭 주어 it	O	p.96		
	부정대명사		p.98	O	
형용사와 부사	형용사, 부사	O	p.106, 108		
비교구문	원급/비교급/최상급 비교		p.110	O	O
	비교구문을 이용한 표현			O	O
전치사	장소 전치사	O	p.130		
	시간 전치사	O	p.132		
	기타 전치사		p.134		
접속사	등위접속사	O	p.142		
	시간 접속사	O	p.144	O	O
	이유 접속사	O	p.146	O	O
	결과 접속사			O	O
	조건 접속사		p.146	O	O
	양보 접속사			O	O
	that		p.146	O	
	명령문 + and/or		p.70	O	
	상관접속사		p.142	O	O
	간접의문문				O
관계사	관계대명사			O	O
	관계부사			O	O
	주의해야 할 관계사의 쓰임			O	O
	관계사의 계속적 용법				O
	복합관계사				O
가정법	가정법 과거, 가정법 과거완료			O	O
	혼합 가정법				O
	I wish 가정법			O	O
	as if 가정법			O	O
	It's time 가정법				O
	Without[But for] 가정법				O
	if를 생략한 가정법				O
일치와 화법	시제의 일치			O	O
	수의 일치				O
	화법			O	O
특수구문	강조, 도치, 병렬, 부정, 동격, 생략				O

MEMO

MEMO

MEMO

HACKERS
GRAMMAR
SMART 1
LEVEL

ANSWERS

HACKERS

Chapter 01 | be동사

UNIT 01 be동사의 현재형과 과거형

Smart Check p.14

1 ②

Practice p.15

A 1 I'm 2 She's 3 They're
  4 He's 5 You're

B 1 am 2 are 3 is
  4 were 5 was

C 1 was 2 is 3 were
  4 are

D 1 Alex was 2 She is 3 Pancakes are
  4 There were three cats

UNIT 02 be동사의 부정문과 의문문

Smart Check p.16

1 ②

Practice p.17

A 1 Is 2 aren't 3 Were
  4 am not

B 1 We weren't
  2 They're not[They aren't]
  3 It wasn't

C 1 it isn't 2 she was 3 Are they
  4 Were you

D 1 The stars weren't 2 Is he
  3 Was, wasn't, The steak wasn't

Writing Exercise p.18

A 1 He's not[He isn't] in the swimming pool
  2 Were Sam and Julia best friends
  3 His glasses aren't cheap
  4 Was coffee popular in the 1980s
  5 I'm not an elementary school student
  6 Are your sisters in the kitchen

B 1 This documentary is boring
  2 Were you awake
  3 She was not in New York

4 Carrie and I are not in the same class
5 There were three police officers
6 Is that man a movie director

C 1 There was a calendar
  2 It's not[It isn't] a new smartphone
  3 Are they at the subway station
  4 My uncle was a computer programmer
  5 Mr. Cole and Ms. Smith weren't American citizens

D 1 No, it isn't, is empty
  2 No, it wasn't, was rainy
  3 Yes, it was, is on the sofa
  4 Are, in the living room, Yes, they are

Chapter Test p.20

1 ④ 2 ③ 3 ⑤ 4 ② 5 ①

6 was not[wasn't]

7 Sam and Ann are not[aren't] my neighbors

8 Is the weather nice today 9 ② 10 ③

11 ④ 12 ②, ④ 13 ⑤ 14 ④ 15 ⑤

16 The field trip was not[wasn't] interesting

17 Is, is 18 Were, weren't 19 ⑤

20 are 21 There was a newspaper on the table

22 She is not a firefighter 23 ④

1 주어 We는 1인칭 복수이므로 are를 쓴다.

2 주어 Nelly는 3인칭 단수이고 과거를 나타내는 표현(last year)이 있으므로 is의 과거형 was를 쓴다.

3 주어 they는 3인칭 복수이고 과거를 나타내는 표현(yesterday)이 있으므로 Are의 과거형 Were를 쓴다.

4 주어 The room은 3인칭 단수이고 현재를 나타내는 표현(now)이 있으므로 isn't를 쓴다.

5 ①: were ②③④⑤: was

6 Kate는 한 시간 전에 도서관이 아닌 식당에 있었다는 맥락이다. 주어 Kate는 3인칭 단수이므로 was not[wasn't]를 쓴다.

7 be동사의 부정문은 「주어 + be동사 + not」의 형태이며, 줄여 쓸 수 있다.

8 be동사 현재형의 의문문: 「Am/Are/Is + 주어 ~?」

9 주어 I는 1인칭 단수이고 어제 한가했냐는 질문에 대한 긍정의 대답이므로 am의 과거형 was를 쓴다.

10 첫 번째 빈칸: 주어 Mr. Wilson은 3인칭 단수이고 과거를 나타내는 표현(in 2010)이 있으므로 is의 과거형 was를 쓴다. 두 번째 빈칸: 주어 He는 3인칭 단수이고 현재를 나타내는 표현(now)이 있으므로 is를 쓴다.

11 첫 번째 빈칸: 빈칸 뒤에 셀 수 있는 명사의 단수형(a soccer

match)이 있고 과거를 나타내는 표현(last week)이 있으므로 is의 과거형 was를 쓴다.
두 번째 빈칸: 지난주에 있었던 축구 경기가 흥미진진했다는 맥락이다. 주어 It은 3인칭 단수이므로 is의 과거형 was를 쓴다.

12 ② you isn't → you aren't
④ they aren't → they weren't

13 「There + be동사」 뒤에 셀 수 있는 명사의 복수형(fresh carrots)이 왔고 신선한 당근들이 있었다고 했으므로 are의 과거형 were를 쓴다.

14 ④ are → is

15 ⑤ is → are

16 주어 The field trip은 3인칭 단수이므로 was not[wasn't]을 쓴다.

17 첫 번째 빈칸: 주어 breakfast는 3인칭 단수이고 현재를 나타내는 표현(now)이 있으므로 Is를 쓴다.
두 번째 빈칸: 주어 it은 3인칭 단수이고 be동사 현재형의 의문문에 대한 긍정의 대답은 「Yes, 주어 + am/are/is.」의 형태이므로 is를 쓴다.

18 첫 번째 빈칸: 주어 they는 3인칭 복수이고 과거를 나타내는 표현(last night)이 있으므로 Were를 쓴다.
두 번째 빈칸: 주어 they는 3인칭 복수이고 be동사 과거형의 의문문에 대한 부정의 대답은 「No, 주어 + was/were + not.」의 형태이므로 weren't를 쓴다.

19 ① was → were
② were → was
③ was → were
④ were → was

20 「There + be동사」 뒤에 셀 수 있는 명사의 복수형(three dogs)이 왔고 현재를 나타내는 표현(now)이 있으므로 are를 쓴다.

21 a newspaper는 셀 수 있는 명사의 단수형이고 신문이 있었다고 했으므로 There was를 쓴다.

22 주어 She는 3인칭 단수이고 소방관이 아니라고 했으므로 is not를 쓴다.

23 ⓐ is → are
ⓔ are → is(orange juice는 셀 수 없는 명사이다.)

Chapter 02 | 일반동사

UNIT 01 일반동사의 현재형

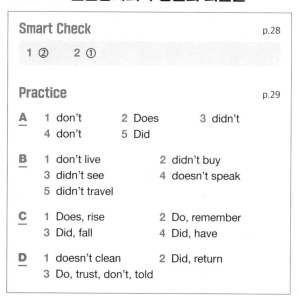

Smart Check   p.24

1 ①   2 ②   3 ③

Practice   p.25

A 1 works   2 solve   3 brushes
     4 do   5 speak

B 1 wears   2 worries   3 has
     4 take   5 teaches

C 1 flies   2 knows   3 walk
     4 listens   5 misses

D 1 I sit   2 He, washes
     3 My cousin stays   4 They plant

UNIT 02 일반동사의 과거형

Smart Check   p.26

1 ③   2 ②

Practice   p.27

A 1 called   2 wrote   3 had
     4 caught   5 finished

B 1 broke   2 read   3 flew
     4 saw   5 went

C 1 found   2 studied   3 swam
     4 cooked   5 visited

D 1 won the medal
     2 woke
     3 brought his friends
     4 left their hometown

UNIT 03 일반동사의 부정문과 의문문

Smart Check   p.28

1 ②   2 ①

Practice   p.29

A 1 don't   2 Does   3 didn't
     4 don't   5 Did

B 1 don't live   2 didn't buy
     3 didn't see   4 doesn't speak
     5 didn't travel

C 1 Does, rise   2 Do, remember
     3 Did, fall   4 Did, have

D 1 doesn't clean   2 Did, return
     3 Do, trust, don't, told

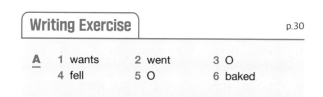

Writing Exercise   p.30

A 1 wants   2 went   3 O
     4 fell   5 O   6 baked

7 misses

B 1 The students did not[didn't] share their ideas,
Did the students share their ideas
2 Janet does not[doesn't] remember his name,
Does Janet remember his name
3 She did not[didn't] make a big mistake, Did
she make a big mistake
4 They do not[don't] play badminton after
school, Do they play badminton after school
5 The soccer team did not[didn't] win the
tournament yesterday, Did the soccer team
win the tournament yesterday
6 Mr. Bean does not[doesn't] enjoy coffee in the
morning, Does Mr. Bean enjoy coffee in the
morning

C 1 My parents did not[didn't] wait
2 Do you know the new teacher
3 I read the story
4 A bear stays
5 We do not[don't] go
6 Did Andrew bring an umbrella
7 This supermarket does not[doesn't] sell
expensive items

D 1 No, he didn't, woke
2 No, he didn't, studied
3 Yes, he did, practiced
4 No, he didn't, ate

Chapter Test
p.32

1 ④ 2 ⑤ 3 ① 4 ④ 5 ⑤
6 they don't 7 she does 8 ④ 9 ⑤
10 ④ 11 ⑤ 12 ②
13 Eugene does not like crabs 14 ④ 15 ④
16 ① 17 ③
18 My brother and I have short hair
19 Martin doesn't[does not] remember Eric
20 They carried the boxes together 21 ②
22 haved → had
23 did not[didn't] read the book
24 studies Korean

1 ④ need – needs

2 ⑤ stop – stopped

3 빈칸 뒤에 동사의 3인칭 단수 현재형(gets)이 있으므로 3인
칭 단수 주어 Jeremy를 쓴다.

4 과거를 나타내는 표현(yesterday)이 있으므로 didn't
meet을 쓴다.

5 주어 he는 3인칭 단수이므로 일반동사 현재형의 의문문은

「Does + 주어 + 동사원형 ~?」의 형태이다.

6 주어 they는 3인칭 복수이므로 일반동사 현재형의 의문문
에 대한 부정의 대답 No, they don't를 쓴다.

7 주어 Nina는 3인칭 단수이므로 일반동사 현재형의 의문문
에 대한 긍정의 대답 Yes, she does를 쓴다.

8 ④ watches → watch

9 ⑤ Does → Did

10 • 주어 Ms. Grant는 3인칭 단수이므로 takes를 쓴다.
• 주어 We는 1인칭 복수이므로 go를 쓴다.

11 • 과거를 나타내는 표현(an hour ago)이 있으므로
brought를 쓴다.
• Bonnie는 러시아가 아닌 이탈리아에 산다는 맥락이다.
주어 Bonnie는 3인칭 단수이므로 doesn't live를 쓴다.

12 ① waited → wait
③ run → runs
④ start → started
⑤ drives → drive

13 주어 Eugene은 3인칭 단수이고 게를 좋아하지 않는다고
했으므로 does not like를 쓴다.

14 일반동사 과거형의 의문문: 「Did + 주어 + 동사원형 ~?」

15 일반동사 과거형의 부정문: 「주어 + did not[didn't] + 동사
원형」

16 일반동사 현재형의 의문문에 대한 긍정의 대답은 「Yes,
주어 + do/does.」, 부정의 대답은 「No, 주어 + don't/
doesn't.」의 형태이다.

17 ③ drinks → drank

18 주어 My brother and I는 1인칭 복수이므로 have를 쓴다.

19 주어 Martin은 3인칭 단수이므로 doesn't[does not]을 쓴
다.

20 동사 carry의 과거형: carried

21 ⓒ Does → Do
ⓔ not met → did not[didn't] meet

22 동사 have의 과거형: had

23 일반동사 과거형의 부정문: 「주어 + did not[didn't] + 동사
원형」

24 주어 James는 3인칭 단수이므로 studies를 쓴다.

Chapter 03 | 시제

UNIT 01 현재시제와 과거시제

Smart Check
p.36

1 ① 2 ② 3 ① 4 ③

Practice
p.37

A 1 ate 2 live 3 died

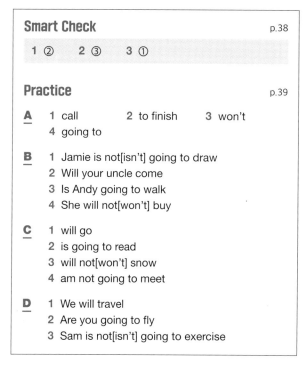

4 bought   **5** goes

B **1** has   **2** won   **3** is
    4 enjoyed

C **1** looks   **2** found   **3** told
    4 dance

D **1** saves   **2** brought   **3** make
    4 hit

UNIT 02 미래시제

Smart Check   p.38

1 ②   **2** ③   **3** ①

Practice   p.39

A **1** call   **2** to finish   **3** won't
    4 going to

B **1** Jamie is not[isn't] going to draw
    2 Will your uncle come
    3 Is Andy going to walk
    4 She will not[won't] buy

C **1** will go
    2 is going to read
    3 will not[won't] snow
    4 am not going to meet

D **1** We will travel
    2 Are you going to fly
    3 Sam is not[isn't] going to exercise

UNIT 03 진행시제

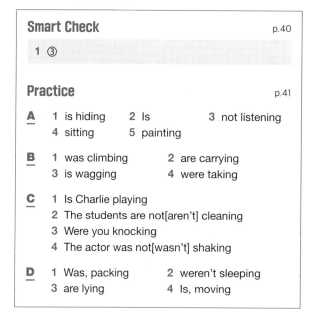

Smart Check   p.40

1 ③

Practice   p.41

A **1** is hiding   **2** Is   **3** not listening
    4 sitting   **5** painting

B **1** was climbing   **2** are carrying
    3 is wagging   **4** were taking

C **1** Is Charlie playing
    2 The students are not[aren't] cleaning
    3 Were you knocking
    4 The actor was not[wasn't] shaking

D **1** Was, packing   **2** weren't sleeping
    3 are lying   **4** Is, moving

Writing Exercise   p.42

A **1** asking   **2** learned
    3 has   **4** O
    5 will not[won't]   **6** O
    7 going to travel

B **1** My sister will take a shower
    2 Did Cindy hear a strange sound
    3 The taxi driver is parking the car
    4 They were not entering the building
    5 He does not cross the street
    6 Mark Zuckerberg started Facebook
    7 I am going to watch my favorite drama
    8 Are you going to buy the sneakers

C **1** I won't[I'm not going to] ride
    2 Justin will[is going to] catch
    3 She wasn't jogging
    4 Alex walks
    5 We are[We're] going
    6 The staff added

D ⓐ am   ⓑ arrived
    ⓒ Are you having   ⓓ played
    ⓔ am enjoying   ⓕ Will you come
    ⓖ am going to return

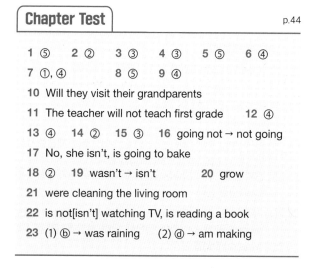

Chapter Test   p.44

1 ⑤   **2** ②   **3** ③   **4** ③   **5** ⑤   **6** ④

7 ①, ④   **8** ⑤   **9** ④

10 Will they visit their grandparents

11 The teacher will not teach first grade   **12** ④

13 ④   **14** ②   **15** ③   **16** going not → not going

17 No, she isn't, is going to bake

18 ②   **19** wasn't → isn't   **20** grow

21 were cleaning the living room

22 is not[isn't] watching TV, is reading a book

23 (1) ⓑ → was raining   (2) ⓓ → am making

---

1 ⑤ hike – hiking

2 주어 They는 3인칭 복수이고 last night이 있으므로 과거시
제 had를 쓴다.

3 주어 Mr. Harris는 3인칭 단수이고 tomorrow가 있으므로
미래시제 will go를 쓴다.

4 주어 Ashley는 3인칭 단수이므로 지금(now) 진행되고 있
는 동작을 나타내는 현재진행시제 is studying을 쓴다.

5 • soon이 있으므로 미래시제 will finish의 will을 쓴다.
    • will이 있는 미래시제의 의문문: 「Will + 주어 + 동사원
형 ~?」

6 ・과거의 특정 시점(yesterday)에 진행되고 있던 동작을 나타내는 과거진행시제 was wearing의 was를 쓴다.
・last weekend가 있으므로 과거시제 was를 쓴다.

7 ① will → won't 또는 No → Yes
④ won't → aren't

8 미래시제 is going to take가 쓰였으므로 과거시제와 주로 함께 쓰이는 부사구 three months ago는 쓸 수 없다.

9 과거시제 watched가 쓰였으므로 미래시제와 주로 함께 쓰이는 부사구 next weekend는 쓸 수 없다.

10 will이 있는 미래시제의 의문문: 「Will + 주어 + 동사원형 ~?」

11 will이 있는 미래시제의 부정문: 「주어 + will not + 동사원형」

12 ④ make → made

13 ④ sells → sell

14 ② is knowing → knows

15 현재진행시제의 부정문: 「주어 + am/are/is + not + V-ing」

16 be going to가 있는 미래시제의 부정문: 「주어 + be동사 + not + going to + 동사원형」

17 미래시제 Is ~ going to swim으로 묻고 있고 일요일이 아닌 토요일에 수영할 것이므로 No, she isn't.를 쓴다. 일요일에는 초콜릿 칩 쿠키를 구울 것이므로 미래시제 is going to bake를 쓴다.

18 ⓐ Are → Were
ⓑ going to 삭제 또는 will → is
ⓓ is → was

19 현재진행시제 Is ~ skating으로 묻고 있고 스케이트를 타고 있는 것이 아닌 휴식을 취하고 있다고 했으므로 No, he isn't.로 대답한다.

20 주어 Bananas는 3인칭 복수이므로 현재시제 grow를 쓴다.

21 주어 They는 3인칭 복수이므로 과거진행시제 were cleaning을 쓴다.

22 첫 번째 빈칸: 주어 She는 3인칭 단수이므로 현재진행시제의 부정형 is not[isn't] watching을 쓴다.
두 번째 빈칸: 주어 She는 3인칭 단수이므로 현재진행시제 is reading을 쓴다.

23 (1) 주어 It은 3인칭 단수이므로 과거의 특정 시점(an hour ago)에 진행되고 있던 동작을 나타내는 과거진행시제 was raining을 쓴다.
(2) 주어 I는 1인칭 단수이므로 지금(now) 진행되고 있는 동작을 나타내는 현재진행시제 am making을 쓴다.

Chapter 04 | 조동사

UNIT 01 can, may

Smart Check
p.48

1 ①

Practice
p.49

A 1 go　2 are able to　3 lift
4 may　5 Is　6 may not

B 1 can have　2 can't jump　3 can speak
4 can't buy

C 1 may turn　2 may not believe
3 may be　4 may not open

D 1 Can[May], watch　2 may rain
3 Can, sing　4 Is, able to make

UNIT 02 must, have to, should

Smart Check
p.50

1 ①　2 ③　3 ②

Practice
p.51

A 1 ⓐ　2 ⓓ　3 ⓑ
4 ⓒ　5 ⓑ

B 1 have to find　2 has to study
3 have to be　4 has to tell

C 1 must not drink
2 don't have to bring
3 doesn't have to drive
4 must not exercise

D 1 don't have to follow
2 must be
3 must not say
4 shouldn't walk

Writing Exercise
p.52

A 1 Anna should not[shouldn't] use
2 The workers must not paint
3 Is he able to post
4 Jackson cannot[can't] explain
5 You may not park
6 Can Ms. Harris take

B 1 Charles should not miss
2 They don't have to send
3 You can plant
4 Students may know
5 Visitors must not eat
6 She is able to bake

C 1 My cousin can[is able to] play
2 Mary doesn't have to wait
3 Dad must be
4 You can[may] do

5 Can you wake
6 Drivers must[have to/should] slow
7 Jacob may be

D 1 Ostriches can run
2 We must not bring
3 May I take
4 Ms. Hill doesn't have to buy

Chapter Test
p.54

1 should　　2 Can　　3 may not　　4 ③
5 ②　　6 ①　　7 ④　　8 ④　　9 are → be
10 may 11 Can 12 don't have to 13 ⑤　14 ②, ④
15 making → make　　16 ③　17 ⑤　18 ③
19 should use not → should not[shouldn't] use
20 ⑤　21 (1) must stop (2) must not take pictures
22 cannot[can't] be a basketball player
23 Visitors have to write their names

---

1 '우리는 잠자리에 들어야 한다. 벌써 오후 11시이다.'라는 의미이므로 should(~해야 한다)를 쓴다.

2 '나를 도와주겠니?'라는 의미이므로 Can(~해주겠니?)을 쓴다.

3 '너는 밖에서 놀면 안 된다. 오늘은 덥다.'라는 의미이므로 may(~해도 된다)의 부정형 may not을 쓴다.

4 must = have to (의무)

5 may = can (허가)

6 ① writes → write

7 '기차는 오전 6시 20분에 떠날 것이다. 나는 내일 일찍 일어나야 한다.'라는 의미이므로 should(~해야 한다)를 쓴다.

8 '우리는 길을 건너면 안 된다. 신호등이 빨간색이다.'라는 의미이므로 must not(~하면 안 된다)을 쓴다.

9 「조동사 + 동사원형」

10 약한 추측(~일지도 모른다)을 나타내는 may를 쓴다.

11 요청(~해주겠니?)을 나타내는 Can을 쓴다.

12 주어 You는 2인칭 단수이므로 불필요(~할 필요가 없다)를 나타내는 don't have to를 쓴다.

13 ⑤ can → can't

14 ① can be able to → can 또는 is able to
③ not must → must not
⑤ listens → listen

15 「조동사 + 동사원형」

16 ③: 강한 추측(~임이 틀림없다)　①②④⑤: 의무(~해야 한다)

17 ⑤: 허가(~해도 된다)　①②③④: 능력·가능(~할 수 있다)

18 • '너는 매일 충분한 물을 마셔야 한다.'라는 의미이므로 must/have to/should(~해야 한다)를 쓴다.

• 'Benji는 전화를 받고 있지 않다. 그는 지금 매우 바쁜 것이 틀림없다.'라는 의미이므로 must(~임이 틀림없다)를 쓴다.

19 should의 부정형: should not[shouldn't]

20 ⓐ is → be
ⓑ has → have

21 (1) 멈춰야 한다는 표지판이므로 must(~해야 한다)를 쓴다.
(2) 사진을 찍으면 안 된다는 표지판이므로 must not(~하면 안 된다)을 쓴다.

22 강한 추측(~임이 틀림없다)을 나타내는 must의 부정 cannot[can't](~일 리가 없다)를 쓴다.

23 주어 Visitors는 3인칭 복수이므로 의무(~해야 한다)를 나타내는 have to를 쓴다.

Chapter 05 | 동사의 종류

UNIT 01 주격 보어가 필요한 동사

Smart Check
p.58

1 ③　　2 ①

Practice
p.59

A 1 salty　　2 warm　　3 good
4 lovely　　5 quiet

B 1 X　　2 like　　3 X
4 like　　5 like

C 1 great　　2 O　　3 bad
4 tastes like　　5 perfect

D 1 tasted strange　　2 looks fresh
3 smells like wood　　4 felt lonely

UNIT 02 두 개의 목적어가 필요한 동사

Smart Check
p.60

1 ②　　2 ①

Practice
p.61

A 1 to　　2 for　　3 of
4 to

B 1 pass　　2 made　　3 wrote
4 lend

C 1 got napkins for us
2 taught science to his nephew
3 told me the rumor

D 1 found the dog for Ms. Wilson
2 read the article to his father
3 sent her a present

UNIT 03 목적격 보어가 필요한 동사

Smart Check p.62

1 ③ 2 ② 3 ② 4 ①

Practice p.63

A 1 sweet   2 to be   3 found
4 to turn   5 to sit

B 1 to be   2 wrong   3 to study

C 1 him a liar   2 to sleep   3 O
4 to run

D 1 expected her grade to be
2 keeps your head safe
3 call a baby dog a puppy
4 want me to become

Writing Exercise p.64

A 1 gave snacks   2 allowed the visitors
3 sounds very good   4 build the children
5 felt hungry   6 found the summer

B 1 smells delicious
2 pass me that spoon
3 made the bakery famous
4 feels like silk
5 teach Japanese to students
6 call the number seven a lucky number
7 advised Brian to exercise
8 will buy a backpack for my sister

C 1 was normal
2 lend me your textbook
3 taste spicy
4 ordered us to stay
5 got the ticket for him

D ⓐ looked beautiful
ⓑ asked my mother to take
ⓒ bring you a souvenir
ⓓ make me happy

Chapter Test p.66

1 became   2 brought   3 sounded
4 ③   5 ③   6 ④   7 ①   8 ④   9 ⑤
10 ③   11 ③   12 ④   13 ⑤
14 the salt and pepper to James
15 a sandcastle for his children   16 ②, ④
17 Did you write an e-mail to Mr. Anderson[Did you write Mr. Anderson an e-mail]
18 ②   19 sound exciting
20 looks friendly   21 to → of
22 I found the glasses for my grandmother
23 She advised us to read many books
24 ⓓ → to call

1 빈칸 뒤에 명사 주격 보어(the class president)가 있으므로 주격 보어가 필요한 동사 became을 쓴다.

2 빈칸 뒤에 간접 목적어(her)와 직접 목적어(the guitar)가 있으므로 수여동사 brought을 쓴다.

3 빈칸 뒤에 형용사 주격 보어(strange)가 있고 '나의 목소리는 오늘 아침에 이상하게 들렸다.'라는 의미이므로 감각동사 sounded를 쓴다.

4 빈칸 뒤에 「직접 목적어(the paper) + to + 간접 목적어(me)」가 있으므로 전치사 to를 쓰는 수여동사 gave를 쓴다. (made, bought, found는 전치사 for를 쓰는 수여동사이고, asked는 전치사 of를 쓰는 수여동사이다.)

5 ③ terribly → terrible

6 ④ for → to

7 (A): 감각동사(looks)의 주격 보어 자리에는 형용사만 오므로 형용사 happy를 쓴다.
(B): 빈칸 뒤에 「직접 목적어(a mouse) + to + 간접 목적어(us)」가 있으므로 전치사 to를 쓰는 수여동사 brought을 쓴다. (got은 전치사 for를 쓰는 수여동사이다.)
(C): 빈칸 뒤에 목적어(her)와 명사 목적격 보어(a famous writer)가 있으므로 목적격 보어로 명사를 쓰는 동사 make를 쓴다.

8 빈칸 뒤에 간접 목적어(us)와 직접 목적어(the letter)가 있으므로 수여동사가 아닌 wanted는 쓸 수 없다.

9 ⑤: for   ①②③④: to

10 ・「tell + 직접 목적어 + to + 간접 목적어」
・「allow + 목적어 + to부정사 목적격 보어」

11 「teach + 간접 목적어 + 직접 목적어」 또는 「teach + 직접 목적어 + to + 간접 목적어」

12 「want + 목적어 + to부정사 목적격 보어」

13 ⑤: 두 개의 목적어가 필요한 수여동사 make
①②③④: 목적격 보어가 필요한 동사 make

14 「pass + 직접 목적어 + to + 간접 목적어」

15 「build + 직접 목적어 + for + 간접 목적어」

16 ① sweetly → sweet

③ sounds like → sounds
⑤ wonderfully → wonderful

17 「write + 직접 목적어 + to + 간접 목적어」 또는 「write + 간 접 목적어 + 직접 목적어」

18 ⓑ her picture us → her picture to us 또는 us her picture
ⓔ to → for

19 「sound + 형용사」: ~하게 들리다

20 「look + 형용사」: ~하게 보이다

21 「ask + 직접 목적어 + of + 간접 목적어」

22 「find + 직접 목적어 + for + 간접 목적어」

23 「advise + 목적어 + to부정사 목적격 보어」

24 「ask + 목적어 + to부정사 목적격 보어」

Chapter 06 | 문장의 종류

UNIT 01 명령문, 청유문, 감탄문

Smart Check   p.70

1 ①

Practice   p.71

A 1 Wash   2 Don't   3 big forest
   4 save   5 How   6 and

B 1 Turn   2 Don't[Do not] lock
   3 Be   4 Don't[Do not] eat

C 1 small that smartphone is
   2 sweet bananas these are
   3 well my brother dances
   4 a careful driver you are

D 1 Let's not waste our time
   2 What a brave boy
   3 Hurry up, or

UNIT 02 의문사 의문문 I

Smart Check   p.72

1 ②   2 ③

Practice   p.73

A 1 Whose   2 Who   3 Who(m)
   4 Who

B 1 Who   2 What   3 makes
   4 Which

C 1 ⓑ   2 ⓓ   3 ⓒ
   4 ⓐ

D 1 Whose wallet
   2 What did you learn
   3 Which do you prefer
   4 Who knows

UNIT 03 의문사 의문문 II

Smart Check   p.74

1 ②

Practice   p.75

A 1 When   2 Where   3 How

B 1 ⓓ   2 ⓔ   3 ⓑ
   4 ⓐ   5 ⓒ

C 1 heavy   2 often   3 much
   4 tall

D 1 How did he get
   2 Why don't you play
   3 Where did Ella travel
   4 How many pens does he have

UNIT 04 부정의문문, 선택의문문, 부가의문문

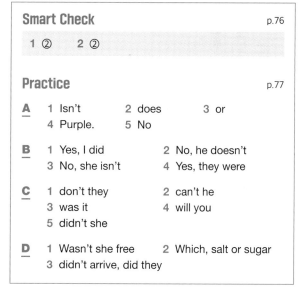

Smart Check   p.76

1 ②   2 ②

Practice   p.77

A 1 Isn't   2 does   3 or
   4 Purple.   5 No

B 1 Yes, I did   2 No, he doesn't
   3 No, she isn't   4 Yes, they were

C 1 don't they   2 can't he
   3 was it   4 will you
   5 didn't she

D 1 Wasn't she free   2 Which, salt or sugar
   3 didn't arrive, did they

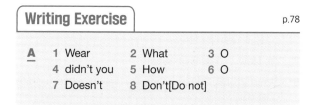

Writing Exercise   p.78

A 1 Wear   2 What   3 O
   4 didn't you   5 How   6 O
   7 Doesn't   8 Don't[Do not]

B 1 Who broke the window
    2 How exciting
    3 Wasn't he tired
    4 How old is that child
    5 Please invite your friends
    6 don't we pack our bags
    7 When did he change his phone number

C 1 What an expensive necklace that is
    2 Let's take a picture
    3 Which season do you like more, summer or winter
    4 Where did Gerald park his car
    5 Stephanie can pass the test, can't she
    6 How often do you brush your teeth

D 1 isn't he, No, he isn't   2 When
    3 How tall   4 What   5 Where
    6 Who

Chapter Test
p.80

1 ①   2 ②   3 ②   4 ②   5 Don't   6 ④
7 ③   8 What big pumpkins   9 How sour
10 No, I didn't   11 ①, ②   12 ④   13 ④
14 Let's go to the gym at 6:30 together
15 Don't[Do not] be rude to other people
16 ③   17 ⑤   18 is → isn't
19 What a beautiful voice she has
20 ⓒ → does he   21 ③
22 Let's not waste money
23 can play the violin, can't he
24 many erasers do you have

1 '그는 나의 영어 선생님이야.'라고 대답했으므로 사람에 대해 물을 때 쓰는 Who(누구)를 쓴다.

2 '그것은 은색이야.'라고 대답했으므로 '무슨, 어떤'이라는 의미의 형용사로 쓰여 명사 앞에서 명사를 꾸밀 수 있는 What을 쓴다.

3 What 감탄문: 「What + (a/an) + 형용사 + 명사 + (주어 + 동사)!」

4 긍정 청유문: 「Let's + 동사원형」

5 • 부정 명령문: 「Don't[Do not] + 동사원형」
  • 일반동사가 있는 부정의문문: 「Don't/Doesn't/Didn't + 주어 + 동사원형 ~?」

6 ④ When(언제)으로 묻고 있으므로 시간이나 날짜에 해당하는 것으로 대답한다.

7 ③: How   ①②④⑤: What

8 What 감탄문: 「What + (a/an) + 형용사 + 명사 + (주어 + 동사)!」

9 How 감탄문: 「How + 형용사/부사 + (주어 + 동사)!」

10 '너는 5월에 부산을 방문하지 않았니?'라는 부정의문문에 5월이 아닌 4월에 부산을 방문했다고 했으므로 No, I didn't.로 대답한다.

11 ③ feeds → feed
  ④ and → or
  ⑤ What → Which

12 부정문 뒤에는 긍정의 부가의문문을 덧붙인다.

13 첫 번째 빈칸: 정해진 범위 안에서의 선택을 묻고 있으므로 Which(어느 것)를 쓴다.
  두 번째 빈칸: 상대방의 선택을 묻는 선택의문문에는 or를 사용한다.

14 긍정 청유문: 「Let's + 동사원형」

15 부정 명령문: 「Don't[Do not] + 동사원형」

16 How(어떻게)로 묻고 있으므로 방법에 해당하는 것으로 대답한다.

17 Why(왜)로 묻고 있으므로 이유에 해당하는 것으로 대답한다.

18 '저 카페는 일요일에 문을 열지 않니?'라는 부정의문문에 일요일이 아닌 월요일부터 토요일까지 문을 연다고 했으므로 No, it isn't로 대답한다.

19 What 감탄문: 「What + (a/an) + 형용사 + 명사 + (주어 + 동사)!」

20 앞 문장의 동사가 일반동사(doesn't eat)이므로 부가의문문의 동사는 does를 쓴다.

21 ⓑ How a → How
  ⓒ did → didn't 또는 sent → didn't send

22 부정 청유문: 「Let's not + 동사원형」

23 첫 번째 빈칸: 바이올린을 연주할 수 있다고 했으므로 조동사 can(~할 수 있다)과 함께 can play the violin을 쓴다.
  두 번째 빈칸: 긍정문 뒤에는 부정의 부가의문문을 덧붙이고, 앞 문장의 동사가 조동사(can)이므로 부가의문문의 동사는 can't를 쓴다. 앞 문장의 주어가 Chris이므로 부가의문문의 주어는 인칭대명사 he를 쓴다.

24 개수를 묻고 있으므로 How many를 쓴다.

Chapter
07 | 명사와 관사

UNIT 01 셀 수 있는 명사와 셀 수 없는 명사

Smart Check
p.84

1 ②

Practice
p.85

A 1 churches   2 cities   3 leaves
    4 dogs   5 men   6 roofs
    7 feet   8 tomatoes   9 sheep

10 boxes

B 1 a tree   **2** pianos   **3** Spain
     4 advice   **5** bread   **6** magazines

C 1 cans of soda   **2** slices of pizza
     3 bottle of water   **4** cups of coffee
     5 pairs of glasses   **6** pieces of paper

D 1 five geese   **2** four bowls of rice
     3 three cherries   **4** Friendship

UNIT 02 관사

Smart Check   p.86

1 ③

Practice   p.87

A 1 The   **2** an   **3** a
     4 the   **5** an

B 1 X   **2** The   **3** X
     4 an   **5** X

C 1 the store   **2** a day   **3** breakfast
     4 The party   **5** school

D 1 a writer   **2** by mail   **3** the recorder
     4 History

Writing Exercise   p.88

A 1 O   **2** stories
     3 a university student
     4 glasses of grape juice
     5 information   **6** O
     7 an hour   **8** O

B 1 play the clarinet
     2 saw seven deer
     3 are five pieces of furniture
     4 Three women were walking
     5 eat dinner
     6 The pencil case was
     7 found an empty seat
     8 packed two pairs of pants

C ⓐ loaves of bread
     ⓑ pairs of socks
     ⓒ bowls of vegetable soup
     ⓓ cup of tea
     ⓔ slices[pieces] of cake

D ⓐ the air conditioner
     ⓑ basketball

ⓒ science
ⓓ the book
ⓔ a year

Chapter Test   p.90

1 ③   **2** ⑤   **3** ②   **4** ⑤   **5** ①   **6** ⑤
7 ④   **8** ①   **9** ②   **10** ③   **11** ④   **12** the
13 advice   **14** Geese   **15** the flute
16 a watermelon **17** a pair of socks
18 school, bus   **19** ⑤   **20** ⑤   **21** ⑤
22 a phone → phone   **23** the bed → bed
24 (1) soups → soup   (2) strawberrys → strawberries
25 ⑤   **26** (1) ⓑ → a week   (2) ⓔ → the violin

1 ③ wolf – wolves

2 ⑤ butterfly – butterflies

3 빈칸 앞에 부정관사 a가 있으므로 셀 수 있는 명사의 단수형 cup을 쓴다. 셀 수 없는 명사 paint와 salt 앞에는 a(n)을 붙일 수 없다.

4 단위명사 loaf와 함께 쓰는 명사 bread를 쓴다.

5 빈칸 앞에 복수동사 are가 있으므로 셀 수 있는 명사의 단수형 woman은 쓸 수 없다.

6 ⑤: an   ①②③④: a

7 ① glasses of water → glass of water
     ② slice of cheese → slices of cheese
     ③ cans of paints → cans of paint
     ⑤ bowls of cereals → bowl of cereal

8 ① the basketball → basketball

9 주어진 문장과 ②: '~마다(per)'를 나타낼 때 쓰는 a
     ①: 정해지지 않은 막연한 하나를 가리킬 때 쓰는 a
     ③④⑤: '하나의(one)'를 나타낼 때 쓰는 a

10 첫 번째 빈칸: 'Carol은 목걸이 한 개를 가지고 있다'라는 의미이고 빈칸 뒤에 첫소리가 자음으로 발음되는 단어(necklace)가 있으므로 '하나의(one)'를 나타낼 때 쓰는 부정관사 a를 쓴다.
     두 번째 빈칸: 앞에서 언급된 명사(a necklace)가 반복될 때는 정관사 the를 쓴다.

11 첫 번째 빈칸: 장소의 고유한 이름을 나타내는 명사(London) 앞에는 a(n)을 붙일 수 없다.
     두 번째 빈칸: 식사 이름(dinner) 앞에는 관사를 쓰지 않는다.

12 • 정황상 서로 알고 있는 것(window)을 말할 때는 정관사 the를 쓴다.
     • 유일한 것(sun)을 말할 때는 정관사 the를 쓴다.

13 셀 수 없는 명사(advice)는 앞에 a(n)을 붙일 수 없고 복수형으로도 쓸 수 없으므로 advice를 쓴다.

14 빈칸 뒤에 복수동사 were가 있으므로 명사 Goose의 복수형 Geese를 쓴다.

15 악기 이름(flute) 앞에는 정관사 the를 쓴다.

16 '하나의(one)'를 나타내고 watermelon의 첫소리는 자음으로 발음되므로 a watermelon을 쓴다.

17 한 쌍이 짝을 이루는 명사(socks)는 단위명사 pair를 활용하여 수량을 나타낸다.

18 첫 번째 빈칸: 장소나 건물(school)이 본래의 목적(공부)으로 쓰일 때는 관사를 쓰지 않는다.
두 번째 빈칸: 「by + 교통수단(bus)」에는 관사를 쓰지 않는다.

19 ⑤ a → an

20 구(next to the hospital)의 수식을 받는 명사(building) 앞에는 정관사 the를 쓴다.

21 ⓐ Moon → The moon
ⓒ mouses → mice

22 「by + 통신수단(phone)」에는 관사를 쓰지 않는다.

23 장소(bed)가 본래의 목적(잠)으로 쓰일 때는 관사를 쓰지 않는다.

24 (1) 셀 수 없는 명사(soup)의 복수형은 단위명사(bowl)에 -(e)s를 붙여 만든다.
(2) 명사 strawberry의 복수형은 strawberries이다.

25 ⑤ the breakfast → breakfast

26 (1) week의 첫소리는 자음으로 발음되므로 부정관사 a를 쓴다.
(2) 악기 이름(violin) 앞에는 정관사 the를 쓴다.

Chapter 08 | 대명사

UNIT 01 인칭대명사

Smart Check p.94

1 ②

Practice p.95

A　1 He　　2 her　　3 its
　　　4 them　　5 us　　6 They

B　1 it　　2 He　　3 their
　　　4 mine　　5 herself　　6 theirs

C　1 X　　2 O　　3 X
　　　4 O　　5 X

D　1 your old picture
　　　2 me a pencil
　　　3 her homework herself

UNIT 02 this, that, it

Smart Check p.96

1 ②　　2 ③　　3 ②

Practice p.97

A　1 This　　2 these　　3 It
　　　4 Those

B　1 It is[It's] January 5
　　　2 It was snowy
　　　3 It is[It's] 7 kilometers

C　1 it　　2 This　　3 those
　　　4 that　　5 These

D　1 It was cold
　　　2 She bought those paintings
　　　3 This accident hurt many people

UNIT 03 one, some, any

Smart Check p.98

1 ①　　2 ②　　3 ②　　4 ③

Practice p.99

A　1 some　　2 It　　3 one
　　　4 any　　5 ones

B　1 one　　2 it　　3 them
　　　4 ones

C　1 some　　2 any　　3 some
　　　4 any　　5 some

D　1 some museums　　2 scary one
　　　3 any food　　　　4 small ones

Writing Exercise p.100

A　1 it　　2 those　　3 These
　　　4 that　　5 some　　6 one
　　　7 any　　8 ones

B　1 It is very cold
　　　2 Logan's tumbler
　　　3 these peaches
　　　4 introduced herself
　　　5 some information
　　　6 didn't eat yours
　　　7 black one

<u>C</u> 1 Those rabbits look lovely
    2 Our uncle will read us a book
    3 Mason doesn't listen to any advice
    4 Ms. Moore gave them some chances
    5 Her school uniform is that yellow one
    6 Matthew didn't finish his
    7 My neighbor lent this to me
    8 Joanna knows herself very well

<u>D</u> ⓐ our   ⓑ their   ⓒ myself
    ⓓ him   ⓔ himself   ⓕ his
    ⓖ They   ⓗ us

Chapter Test

p.102

1 ②   2 ④   3 ②   4 theirs 5 himself
6 ③   7 ①   8 ③   9 ③   10 It   11 ④
12 ④   13 ⑤   14 ④   15 ③   16 ②
17 herself   18 ③   19 Some children
20 It was December 31
21 (1) ⓑ → one   (2) ⓓ → some   22 These → This
23 some oranges → any oranges   24 Ones → They

1　빈칸 뒤에 복수명사(vegetables)가 있으므로 지시형용사 These를 쓴다.

2　'책상 위에 약간의 책이 있었다.'라는 의미의 긍정문이므로 some을 쓴다.

3　앞에서 언급된 명사(jacket)와 같은 종류의 불특정한 대상을 가리키고 빈칸 앞에 부정관사 a가 있으므로 one을 쓴다.

4　'그들의 것'이라는 의미의 소유대명사 theirs를 쓴다.

5　주어 Charles는 인칭대명사 He로 바꿔 쓸 수 있으므로 '~ 자신, 직접'이라는 의미의 재귀대명사 himself를 쓴다.

6　③ That → It

7　① These → This

8　빈칸 앞에 단수동사(Is)가 있고 멀리 있는 사람(your brother)을 가리키고 있으므로 지시대명사 that을 쓴다.

9　전치사 for의 목적어가 주어 I와 같은 대상이므로 재귀대명사 myself를 쓴다.

10　첫 번째 빈칸: '여기는 너무 어두워.'라는 의미이므로 명암을 나타내는 비인칭 주어 It을 쓴다.
　　두 번째 빈칸: 앞에서 언급된 특정한 단수명사 the white button을 가리키고 있으므로 인칭대명사 It을 쓴다.

11　① This → It
　　② any → some
　　③ my → mine
　　⑤ This → These

12　첫 번째 빈칸: '그것은 너의 것이니?'라는 의미이므로 소유대명사 yours를 쓴다.

두 번째 빈칸: '그는 어제 그의 펜을 잃어버렸어.'라는 의미이므로 소유격 인칭대명사 his를 쓴다.

13　⑤: 인칭대명사 it   주어진 문장과 ①②③④: 비인칭 주어 it

14　④ have some → have any

15　③ that → those

16　②: ones   ①③④⑤: one

17　• 동사 saw의 목적어가 주어 Ms. Smith와 같은 대상이므로 재귀대명사 herself를 쓴다.
　　• '나의 할머니는 이것을 직접 만드셨다.'라는 의미이므로 재귀대명사 herself를 쓴다.

18　ⓑ him → his
　　ⓒ Jenna → Jenna's

19　긍정문에서 '약간(의), 조금(의), 몇몇(의)'를 의미하는 Some을 쓴다.

20　날짜를 나타내는 비인칭 주어 It을 쓴다.

21　(1) 앞에서 언급된 명사(bookshelf)와 같은 종류의 불특정한 대상을 가리키고 부정관사 a가 있으므로 one을 쓴다.
　　(2) '나는 약간의 쿠키를 구웠어.'라는 의미의 긍정문이므로 some을 쓴다.

22　단수명사(knife) 앞에는 지시형용사 This를 쓴다.

23　'접시 위에 오렌지가 전혀 없어.'라는 의미의 부정문이므로 any를 쓴다.

24　앞에서 언급된 특정한 복수명사 some sunflowers를 가리키고 문장의 주어 역할을 하고 있으므로 주격 인칭대명사 They를 쓴다.

Chapter 09 형용사/부사와 비교구문

UNIT 01 형용사

Smart Check

p.106

1 ②

Practice

p.107

<u>A</u> 1 spots   2 someone   3 books
    4 anybody

<u>B</u> 1 lovely   2 little   3 angry
    4 something new

<u>C</u> 1 ① much   ② many
    2 ① a little   ② a few
    3 ① Few   ② little

<u>D</u> 1 something cool   2 a lot of vegetables
    3 was nervous

UNIT 02 부사

Smart Check
p.108

1 ③

Practice
p.109

A 1 shines 2 gently
3 my brother entered the army
4 delicious

B 1 are usually 2 Luckily 3 highly

C 1 usually goes swimming
2 seldom reads a book
3 always walks to school
4 never drinks coffee

D 1 worked really 2 drives, fast
3 will never forget

UNIT 03 원급/비교급/최상급 비교

Smart Check
p.110

1 ③

Practice
p.111

A 1 stronger, strongest
2 nicer, nicest
3 prettier, prettiest
4 more quickly, most quickly
5 less, least
6 more difficult, most difficult
7 thinner, thinnest

B 1 hard 2 coldest
3 cleaner 4 more famous
5 biggest

C 1 as heavy as 2 lighter than
3 the cheapest 4 more expensive than

D 1 the oldest 2 as tall as
3 more delicious than

Writing Exercise
p.112

A 1 O 2 noisy
3 healthier 4 O
5 sometimes eats 6 worst
7 O 8 A few

B 1 little juice 2 usually leaves
3 jump high 4 anything wrong

---

5 as well as 6 will never buy
7 few coins
8 the most exciting performance

C 1 It seldom rains
2 His doll is much cuter than mine
3 She saves a little money
4 Linda reads a weekly newspaper
5 Math is the most difficult of all subjects
6 Lots of tourists took pictures

D 1 as close as
2 the cheapest
3 more expensive than
4 the most popular

Chapter Test
p.114

1 ③ 2 ② 3 ③ 4 ① 5 ③ 6 ①
7 ② 8 as heavy as 9 the highest
10 more important than 11 ④ 12 ⑤
13 as tall as 14 the hottest city 15 ②
16 ④ 17 ③
18 Russia is much bigger than India
19 You should not touch anything dangerous
20 a few → a little 21 most → the most
22 ③
23 (1) uses never → never uses (2) hard → harder
24 (1) ⓒ → something strange (2) ⓔ → Actually

1 ③ good – well

2 ② many – more – most

3 빈칸 뒤에 명사(cat)가 있으므로 동사, 형용사, 다른 부사, 문장 전체를 꾸미는 부사 wildly는 쓸 수 없다.

4 빈칸 뒤에 비교급(taller)이 있으므로 원급을 강조하는 very는 쓸 수 없다.

5 ① quiet → quietly
② quick → quickly
④ brightly → bright
⑤ strong → strongly

6 빈도부사(often)는 일반동사(goes) 앞에 온다.

7 빈도부사(always)는 조동사(will) 뒤에 온다.

8 「as + 형용사의 원급 + as」 '…만큼 ~한'

9 「the + 형용사의 최상급」 '가장 ~한'

10 「형용사의 비교급 + than」 '…보다 더 ~한'

11 '…만큼 ~하게'라는 의미의 「as + 부사의 원급 + as」를 쓴다.

12 '가장 ~한'이라는 의미의 「the + 형용사의 최상급」을 쓴다. 형용사 short의 최상급은 shortest이다.

13 Julia는 Hanna와 키가 같으므로 「as + 형용사의 원급 + as」를 쓴다.

14 서울이 세 도시 중에서 가장 더우므로 「the + 형용사의 최상급」을 쓴다.

15 ① much → many[a lot of/lots of]
③ angry → angrier
④ exciting anything → anything exciting
⑤ few → little

16 • 동사(moved)를 꾸미는 부사 carefully를 쓴다.
• 주어(The new curtain)를 보충 설명하는 형용사 nice 를 쓴다.

17 • 'Burns씨는 이 노래를 매우 추천했다.'라는 의미이므로 부사 highly(매우, 대단히)를 쓴다.
• '새들이 하늘 높이 날고 있다.'라는 의미이므로 부사 high (높게, 높이)를 쓴다.

18 '…보다 더 ~한'이라는 의미의 「형용사의 비교급 + than」을 쓰고, 비교급을 강조하는 much는 비교급 앞에 쓴다.

19 -thing으로 끝나는 대명사(anything)를 꾸밀 때는 형용사 (dangerous)가 대명사 뒤에 온다.

20 milk는 셀 수 없는 명사이므로 a little을 쓴다.

21 「the + 형용사의 최상급」 '가장 ~한'

22 ⓑ thickest → thick
ⓓ many → much[a lot of/lots of]

23 (1) 빈도부사(never)는 일반동사(uses) 앞에 온다.
(2) '…보다 더 ~하게'라는 의미의 「부사의 비교급 + than」을 쓴다. 부사 hard의 비교급은 harder이다.

24 (1) -thing으로 끝나는 대명사(something)를 꾸밀 때는 형용사(strange)가 대명사 뒤에 온다.
(2) 문장 전체(nobody lives in that house)를 꾸미는 부사 Actually를 쓴다.

Chapter 10 | to부정사와 동명사

UNIT 01 to부정사의 명사적 용법

Smart Check p.118

1 ①

Practice p.119

A 1 ⓐ 2 ⓒ 3 ⓑ
4 ⓐ 5 ⓑ

B 1 to keep   2 to wear
3 to exercise 4 to meet

C 1 It is scary to walk alone at night
2 It is healthy to eat slowly
3 It is comfortable to sleep in this bed

D 1 to save   2 promised to help
3 where to cut 4 It, to arrive

UNIT 02 to부정사의 형용사적/부사적 용법

Smart Check p.120

1 ③ 2 ②

Practice p.121

A 1 to cut   2 to say   3 to wash

B 1 ⓑ   2 ⓐ   3 ⓒ
4 ⓐ

C 1 to ask   2 to see
3 in order to talk

D 1 to learn
2 many paintings to see
3 smart enough to understand

UNIT 03 동명사의 쓰임

Smart Check p.122

1 ③

Practice p.123

A 1 ⓓ   2 ⓑ   3 ⓐ
4 ⓒ   5 ⓑ

B 1 coming   2 O   3 talking
4 smoking

C 1 using   2 biting   3 brushing
4 playing

D 1 avoid ordering
2 feel like walking
3 Wearing seat belts is
4 were busy chasing

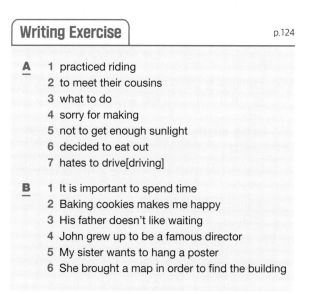

Writing Exercise p.124

A 1 practiced riding
2 to meet their cousins
3 what to do
4 sorry for making
5 not to get enough sunlight
6 decided to eat out
7 hates to drive[driving]

B 1 It is important to spend time
2 Baking cookies makes me happy
3 His father doesn't like waiting
4 John grew up to be a famous director
5 My sister wants to hang a poster
6 She brought a map in order to find the building

7 Nicole knows something wonderful to see

C
1 needs a new violin to play
2 was glad to see her favorite actor
3 promised to cook dinner
4 were busy preparing
5 learned how to solve the problem
6 is to arrive[arriving]

D
1 hopes to help   2 likes to take[taking]
3 enjoys teaching   4 plans to make

Chapter Test

p.126

1 ④   2 ⑤   3 ②   4 to write → writing
5 hearing → hear   6 to   7 ③   8 ③
9 ②   10 ③, ⑤   11 ①   12 ④   13 ⑤
14 to see the bird   15 where to put this box
16 was busy painting the wall
17 am afraid of taking an elevator   18 ④
19 It is important to keep promises
20 George found something warm to wear   21 ④
22 (1) to visit when → when to visit
   (2) checking → to check
23 ②   24 I was happy to meet my old teacher
25 ⓓ → thinking

1 need는 to부정사를 목적어로 쓰는 동사이므로 to wake를 쓴다.

2 stop은 동명사를 목적어로 쓰는 동사이므로 playing을 쓴다.

3 to부정사(to exercise)가 주어로 쓰일 때는 주로 주어 자리에 가주어 it을 쓰고 진주어 to부정사(구)를 뒤로 보낸다.

4 finish는 동명사를 목적어로 쓰는 동사이므로 writing을 쓴다.

5 '그들은 그 소식을 들어서 화가 났었다.'라는 의미의 감정의 원인을 나타내는 to부정사이므로 「to + 동사원형」의 형태로 쓴다.

6 • 'James는 볼 영화를 골랐다.'라는 의미로 명사(a movie)를 뒤에서 꾸미는 형용사적 용법의 to부정사이므로 to를 쓴다.
• 목적을 나타내는 to부정사의 to 대신 in order to를 쓸 수 있다.

7 • want는 to부정사를 목적어로 쓰는 동사이므로 to visit을 쓴다.
• enjoy는 동명사를 목적어로 쓰는 동사이므로 walking을 쓴다.

8 ③: 보어   ①②④⑤: 주어

9 ②: 보어   ①③④⑤: 목적어

10 begin은 to부정사와 동명사를 모두 목적어로 쓰는 동사이므로 to write와 writing을 쓴다.

11 ① how make → how to make

12 주어진 문장과 ④: 명사적 용법(목적어)
①⑤: 부사적 용법(목적)
②: 부사적 용법(감정의 원인)
③: 부사적 용법(결과)

13 주어진 문장과 ⑤: 부사적 용법(목적)
①②③④: 형용사적 용법

14 목적을 나타내는 부사적 용법의 to부정사를 쓴다.

15 「where + to부정사」 '어디에(서)/어디로 ~할지'

16 「be busy + V-ing」 '~하느라 바쁘다'

17 전치사(of)의 목적어로 쓰이는 동명사를 쓴다.

18 ① to sell not → not to sell
② get → to get
③ solve → solving
⑤ sharing → to share

19 to부정사(to keep)가 주어로 쓰일 때는 주로 주어 자리에 가주어 it을 쓰고 진주어 to부정사(구)를 뒤로 보낸다.

20 -thing으로 끝나는 대명사(something)를 형용사(warm)와 to부정사(to wear)가 동시에 꾸밀 때는 「-thing + 형용사 + to부정사」의 형태로 쓴다.

21 두 번째 문장은 첫 번째 문장에 대한 목적이므로 목적을 나타내는 부사적 용법의 to부정사를 쓴다. 목적의 의미를 강조하기 위해 to 대신 in order to를 쓸 수 있다.

22 (1) 「when + to부정사」 '언제 ~할지'
(2) need는 to부정사를 목적어로 쓰는 동사이므로 to check을 쓴다.

23 ⓑ edit → to edit[editing]
ⓓ to running → to run[running]

24 두 번째 문장은 첫 번째 문장의 감정(happy)에 대한 원인이므로 감정의 원인을 나타내는 부사적 용법의 to부정사를 쓴다.

25 keep은 동명사를 목적어로 쓰는 동사이므로 thinking을 쓴다.

Chapter 11 | 전치사

UNIT 01 장소를 나타내는 전치사

Smart Check
p.130

1 ②   2 ③   3 ③

Practice
p.131

A
1 in   2 on   3 at
4 on   5 at   6 in

B 1 in　　　2 under　　　3 across from
　4 at

C 1 next to　　2 on　　　3 behind

D 1 on the envelope
　2 over the lake
　3 in front of your seat
　4 at the airport

UNIT 02 시간을 나타내는 전치사

Smart Check　　　　　　　　p.132

1 ①

Practice　　　　　　　　　　p.133

A 1 at　　　　2 in　　　　3 on

B 1 for　　　2 during　　　3 on
　4 by

C 1 on　　　2 before　　　3 for
　4 in

D 1 until next spring
　2 before the weekend
　3 around noon

UNIT 03 기타 전치사

Smart Check　　　　　　　　p.134

1 ①　　　2 ②　　　3 ②

Practice　　　　　　　　　　p.135

A 1 by　　　2 for　　　3 about
　4 with　　5 from

B 1 ⓑ　　　2 ⓐ　　　3 ⓓ
　4 ⓒ

C 1 to　　　2 for　　　3 with
　4 about

D 1 from Jongno to Yeouido
　2 to his students
　3 by e-mail
　4 between 9 and 11

Writing Exercise　　　　　　p.136

A 1 in the 20th century
　2 before breakfast

---

　3 behind the post office
　4 about the French Revolution
　5 in your bag
　6 during the performance
　7 with chopsticks

B 1 jump over the fence
　2 invited me to his concert
　3 took a picture between Patrick and Jessica
　4 found footprints around 5 o'clock
　5 make songpyeon on Chuseok
　6 waited for his girlfriend across from the church
　7 is a special event from Wednesday to Friday

C ⓐ in the afternoon
　ⓑ at 3 o'clock
　ⓒ to my brother
　ⓓ next to them
　ⓔ with his camera
　ⓕ in front of the door

D 1 on Monday morning
　2 from Monday to Sunday
　3 by shuttle bus
　4 at the ticket booth

Chapter Test　　　　　　　　p.138

1 ③　　2 ②　　3 ⑤　　4 near　5 around
6 to, under　　7 ②　　8 ④　　9 ④　　10 ②
11 before　　12 for　　　　13 in front of
14 is between the coat and the jacket
15 walked from the bus stop to home
16 is a clock tower across from the park
17 ②　　18 ①　　19 ④
20 (1) between, and　(2) next to　(3) across from
21 on → in　　22 to → for　　23 ②
24 next → next to　　25 with → by
26 (1) ⓑ → at　(2) ⓓ → in

1　공간(the refrigerator)의 내부를 나타낼 때는 전치사 in(~ 안에, ~에)을 쓴다.

2　시각(7 A.M.)을 나타낼 때는 전치사 at(~에)을 쓴다.

3　날짜(July 14)를 나타낼 때는 전치사 on(~에)을 쓴다.

4　'~ 근처에'라는 의미의 전치사 near를 쓴다.

5　'~쯤'이라는 의미의 전치사 around를 쓴다.

6　첫 번째 빈칸: '~에, ~으로, ~에게'라는 의미의 전치사 to를 쓴다.
　두 번째 빈칸: '~ 아래에'라는 의미의 전치사 under를 쓴다.

7　• '너의 숙제를 월요일까지 제출해라.'라는 의미이고 숙제를 제출하는 것은 월요일까지 완료되는 것이므로 전치사

by(~까지)를 쓴다.
- '나는 비행기를 타고 캐나다로 여행 갔다.'라는 의미이므로 전치사 by(~을 타고, ~으로)를 쓴다.

8 • '이 영화는 아이들을 위한 것이다.'라는 의미이므로 전치사 for(~을 위해)를 쓴다.
- 'Jeffrey는 50분 동안 그의 연설을 연습했다.'라는 의미이고 50 minutes는 숫자를 포함한 기간 표현이므로 전치사 for(~ 동안)를 쓴다.

9 ④: on ①②③⑤: at

10 ②: for ①③④⑤: during

11 과학 수업은 9시에 시작했고 역사 수업은 11시에 시작했다고 했으므로 '우리는 역사 수업 전에 과학 수업을 들었다.'라는 문장을 만드는 전치사 before(~ 전에)를 쓴다.

12 Sarah는 공부하기 위해 도서관에 갔고 한 시간 후에 떠날 것이라고 했으므로 빈칸 뒤의 숫자를 포함한 기간 표현(an hour)과 함께 '그녀는 한 시간 동안 공부할 것이다.'라는 문장을 만드는 전치사 for(~ 동안)를 쓴다.

13 몇몇 학생들이 일렬로 나란히 서 있고 Amy는 William을 볼 수 있지만 William은 Amy를 볼 수 없다고 했으므로 'William은 Amy 앞에 서 있다.'라는 문장을 만드는 전치사 in front of(~ 앞에)를 쓴다.

14 'A와 B 사이에'라는 의미의 전치사 between A and B를 쓴다.

15 'A에서 B까지'라는 의미의 전치사 from A to B를 쓴다.

16 '~ 맞은편에'라는 의미의 전치사 across from을 쓴다.

17 ② in → on

18 ① to → about

19 'A에서 B까지'라는 의미의 전치사 from A to B를 쓴다.

20 (1) 빵집은 슈퍼마켓과 극장 사이에 있으므로 전치사 between A and B(A와 B 사이에)를 쓴다.
(2) 은행은 경찰서 옆에 있으므로 전치사 next to(~ 옆에)를 쓴다.
(3) 경찰서는 공원 맞은편에 있으므로 전치사 across from(~ 맞은편에)을 쓴다.

21 공간(your room)의 내부를 나타낼 때는 전치사 in(~ 안에, ~에)을 쓴다.

22 '나는 나의 새 이웃들을 위해 그것을 굽고 있어.'라는 의미이므로 전치사 for(~을 위해)를 쓴다.

23 ⓒ for → by
ⓓ between → about

24 'Nate는 그의 누나의 컴퓨터 옆에서 그의 스마트폰을 찾았다.'라는 의미이므로 전치사 next to(~ 옆에)를 쓴다.

25 '나는 지하철을 타고 그 식당에 갔다.'라는 의미이므로 전치사 by(~을 타고, ~으로)를 쓴다.

26 (1) 하나의 지점(the airport)을 나타낼 때는 전치사 at(~에, ~에서)을 쓴다.
(2) 비교적 넓은 장소(Berlin)를 나타낼 때는 전치사 in(~ 안에, ~에)을 쓴다.

UNIT 01 and, but, or, so

Smart Check p.142

1 ① 2 ③ 3 ①

Practice p.143

A 1 and 2 so 3 hates
4 or

B 1 or 2 and 3 but
4 so

C 1 ⓒ 2 ⓓ 3 ⓐ
4 ⓑ

D 1 fantastic but expensive
2 so they were late for
3 both the guitar and the violin

UNIT 02 when, while, before, after

Smart Check p.144

1 ① 2 ② 3 ①

Practice p.145

A 1 when 2 before 3 While
4 turns

B 1 While 2 after 3 before
4 when

C 1 when he enters a room
2 before it gets dark
3 after he watched the scary movie
4 while he was running

D 1 when he is sleepy
2 after school finishes
3 while Andy cooked dinner

UNIT 03 because, if, that

Smart Check p.146

1 ③ 2 ①

Practice p.147

A 1 that 2 if 3 Because
4 is

B 1 If 2 because 3 if
4 that

C 1 ⓐ 2 ⓑ 3 ⓒ
4 ⓑ

D 1 If Carol needs help
2 that he is lucky
3 because I didn't know her address

Writing Exercise

A 1 vote for Nicole or Emma
2 If you like rock music
3 so she doesn't talk to strangers
4 when he traveled to Hong Kong
5 because she had a toothache
6 Before they enter the classroom

B 1 know that Rami and Sami are twins
2 looks old, but it works well
3 puts dishes in the sink after he has a meal
4 bought some oranges and made juice
5 is amazing that Antonio met the soccer player
6 heard a strange sound while I was reading a book

C ⓐ and   ⓑ so   ⓒ While
ⓓ Because   ⓔ but   ⓕ If

D ⓐ so   ⓑ or   ⓒ when
ⓓ after   ⓔ that

Chapter Test

1 ② 2 ③ 3 ⑤ 4 if 5 because
6 that 7 ④ 8 ③ 9 ③ 10 ② 11 ①, ⑤
12 that 13 before
14 so Jackie couldn't use the outdoor swimming pool
15 It is true that
16 after he solves math problems
17 when I take a bath
18 if the coffee is delicious
19 so → or   20 will turn → turn
21 (1) ⓐ → that (2) ⓒ → brushed   22 ⑤

1 '나는 9시간 동안 잤지만, 아직 피곤하다.'라는 의미이므로 but(하지만, 그러나)을 쓴다.

2 '그들은 내일 한국 음식이나 멕시코 음식을 먹을 것이다.'라는 의미이므로 or(또는, ~이거나, 아니면)를 쓴다.

3 'Jamie는 그 이야기가 진짜라고 생각한다.'라는 의미이고

빈칸 앞에 that절을 목적어로 쓰는 동사(believes)가 있으므로 that(~이라는 것)을 쓴다.

4 '만약 우리가 이번 주말에 그들을 방문한다면 나의 조부모님들은 놀라실 것이다.'라는 의미이므로 if(만약 ~한다면)를 쓴다.

5 '바람이 아주 강했기 때문에 나뭇잎들이 나무에서 떨어졌다.'라는 의미이므로 because(~하기 때문에)를 쓴다.

6 '사실은 Jack이 그녀와 싸우고 싶지 않았다는 것이다.'라는 의미이고 빈칸 뒤의 절(Jack didn't want to fight with her)이 주어(The truth)를 보충 설명하는 보어이므로 that(~이라는 것)을 쓴다.

7 ④ comfortably → comfortable

8 ③ will arrive → arrives

9 ③: so ①②④⑤: but

10 ②: or ①③④⑤: so

11 ② or → but
③ after → before
④ if → because

12 • '나는 당신이 여기로 이사했다는 것을 들었다.'라는 의미이고 빈칸 앞에 that절을 목적어로 쓰는 동사(heard)가 있으므로 that(~이라는 것)을 쓴다.
• '우리의 방학이 끝났다는 것은 슬프다.'라는 의미이고 빈칸 앞에 가주어 It이 있고 빈칸 뒤의 절(our vacation is over)이 진주어이므로 that(~이라는 것)을 쓴다.

13 • '그 농부들은 겨울이 오기 전에 사과를 따야 한다.'라는 의미이므로 before(~하기 전에)를 쓴다.
• '방에 들어가기 전에 너의 신발을 벗어라.'라는 의미이므로 before(~하기 전에)를 쓴다.

14 '그래서, 따라서'라는 의미의 so로 절과 절을 연결한다.

15 that절이 주어로 쓰일 때는 주로 주어 자리에 가주어 it을 쓰고 진주어 that절을 뒤로 보낸다.

16 '~한 후에'라는 의미의 after를 쓴다.

17 '~할 때'라는 의미의 when을 쓴다.

18 '만약 ~한다면'이라는 의미의 if를 쓴다. 조건을 나타내는 부사절(if ~ delicious)에서는 미래시제 대신 현재시제를 쓰고 주어 the coffee는 3인칭 단수이므로 is를 쓴다.

19 '너는 부엌을 청소하거나 빨래를 해야 해.'라는 의미이므로 or(또는, ~이거나, 아니면)를 쓴다.

20 시간을 나타내는 부사절(when ~ brown)에서는 미래시제 대신 현재시제를 쓰고 주어 they는 3인칭 복수이므로 turn을 쓴다.

21 (1) '나는 학교에 늦었다고 생각했다'라는 의미이고 thought은 that절을 목적어로 쓰는 동사이므로 that(~이라는 것)을 쓴다.
(2) '나는 빠르게 세수를 하고 이를 닦았다.'라는 의미이고 and는 문법적으로 대등한 단어와 단어, 구와 구, 절과 절을 연결하므로 washed와 대등한 brushed를 쓴다.

22 ⓐ while → because
ⓑ because → if

Chapter 12 접속사 **19**

Chapter 01 be동사

UNIT 01 be동사의 현재형과 과거형

p.2

A 1 She's   2 They're   3 was
    4 am   5 were   6 are

B 1 is   2 O   3 was
    4 were

C 1 is   2 was   3 are
    4 were, are   5 was

D 1 The weather is hot
    2 I was at the theme park
    3 There were five frogs
    4 Ms. Chen was a Chinese teacher

UNIT 02 be동사의 부정문과 의문문

p.3

A 1 They're not[They aren't]   2 Is she
    3 I wasn't   4 Were the birds

B 1 Are, I'm not   2 Was, it wasn't
    3 Are, they are   4 Is, he isn't

C 1 am not   2 O
    3 wasn't[was not]   4 O

D 1 Was Jake late
    2 Chris and I are not[aren't] good
    3 Are you a drummer
    4 This sweater was not[wasn't] in the store

Chapter Test +

p.4

1 ②   2 ③   3 ④

4 My English textbook is not[isn't] very thick

5 Were they absent from school on Monday

6 ②   7 ④   8 ④   9 ②

10 There were four cars in the parking lot

11 The weather wasn't[was not] cold last winter

12 was   13 are   14 was, was, am

15 ③   16 Was, wasn't   17 Are, are

18 ④, ⑤   19 ③

20 am full, is hungry

21 was not[wasn't] in London

22 Are you and your brother

23 There are dishes in the sink

---

1 • 주어 Tina는 3인칭 단수이므로 is를 쓴다.
   • 주어 Some bananas는 3인칭 복수이므로 are를 쓴다.

2 • 빈칸 뒤에 셀 수 있는 명사의 단수형(a coat)이 있으므로 is를 쓴다.
   • 주어 My grandparents는 3인칭 복수이고 과거를 나타내는 표현(last week)이 있으므로 are의 과거형 were를 쓴다.

3 • 주어 the thief는 3인칭 단수이고 과거를 나타내는 표현(yesterday)이 있으므로 Is의 과거형 Was를 쓴다.
   • 주어 Your new jeans는 3인칭 복수이므로 aren't를 쓴다.

4 be동사의 부정문은 「주어 + be동사 + not」의 형태이며, 줄여 쓸 수 있다.

5 be동사 과거형의 의문문: 「Was/Were + 주어 ~?」

6 be동사 과거형의 의문문에 대한 긍정의 대답은 「Yes, 주어 + was/were.」, 부정의 대답은 「No, 주어 + was/were + not.」의 형태이다.

7 ① are → is
   ② were → was
   ③ was → were
   ⑤ is → are

8 「There + be동사」 뒤에 셀 수 있는 명사의 단수형(a big basketball game)이 왔고 어제 경기가 있었다고 했으므로 is의 과거형 was를 쓴다.

9 주어 The bank는 3인칭 단수이고 경찰서 옆에 있지 않다고 했으므로 isn't를 쓴다.

10 「There + be동사」 뒤에 셀 수 있는 명사의 복수형(four cars)이 왔으므로 were를 쓴다.

11 주어 The weather는 3인칭 단수이고 과거를 나타내는 표현(last winter)이 있으므로 wasn't[was not]을 쓴다.

12 Ronald는 지금 키가 170센티미터이고 작년에는 160센티미터였다는 맥락이다. 주어 Ronald는 3인칭 단수이므로 was를 쓴다.

13 마당에 나무 한 그루가 있고 약간의 꽃들도 있다는 맥락이다. 빈칸 뒤에 셀 수 있는 명사의 복수형(some flowers)이 있으므로 are를 쓴다.

14 첫 번째 빈칸: 주어 Yesterday는 3인칭 단수이고 과거를 나타내는 표현이므로 was를 쓴다.
두 번째 빈칸: 주어 I는 1인칭 단수이고 과거를 나타내는 표현(yesterday)이 있으므로 was를 쓴다.
세 번째 빈칸: 주어 I는 1인칭 단수이고 현재를 나타내는 표현(Now)이 있으므로 am을 쓴다.

15 ③ Is → Was

16 첫 번째 빈칸: 주어 it은 3인칭 단수이고 과거를 나타내는 표현(last weekend)이 있으므로 Was를 쓴다.
두 번째 빈칸: 주어 it은 3인칭 단수이고 be동사 과거형의 의문문에 대한 부정의 대답은 「No, 주어 + was/were + not.」이므로 wasn't를 쓴다.

17 첫 번째 빈칸: Jamie와 Alice가 지금(now) 같은 병원에서 일한다고 대답했으므로 그들이 간호사냐고 질문하는 맥락이다. 주어 Jamie and Alice는 3인칭 복수이므로 Are를 쓴다.
두 번째 빈칸: 주어 they는 3인칭 복수이고 be동사 현재형

의 의문문에 대한 긍정의 대답은 「Yes, 주어 + am/are/is.」 이므로 are를 쓴다.

18 ④ wasn't → weren't[were not]
　⑤ Were → Was

19 ③: Are[Were]　①②④⑤: is[was] 또는 Is[Was]

20 첫 번째 빈칸: 주어 I는 1인칭 단수이고 배부르다고 했으므로 am을 쓴다.
두 번째 빈칸: 주어 Jane은 3인칭 단수이고 배고프다고 했으므로 is를 쓴다.

21 주어 Ms. Taylor는 3인칭 단수이고 런던에 있지 않았다고 했으므로 was not[wasn't]를 쓴다.

22 주어 you and your brother는 2인칭 복수이고 쌍둥이냐고 질문했으므로 Are를 쓴다.

23 dishes는 셀 수 있는 명사의 복수형이고 접시들이 있다고 했으므로 There are를 쓴다.

Chapter 02 일반동사

UNIT 01 일반동사의 현재형

p.7

A 1 fixes　2 love　3 carries
　4 has

B 1 looks　2 cries　3 live
　4 practices　5 eat

C 1 O　2 plays　3 teaches
　4 O

D 1 They wear seat belts
　2 Emily goes
　3 My mother buys a magazine
　4 This club helps poor people

UNIT 02 일반동사의 과거형

p.8

A 1 began　2 lives　3 fell
　4 cut

B 1 arrived　2 tied　3 caught
　4 became　5 joined

C 1 did　2 told　3 O
　4 visited　5 O

D 1 Lenna bought a new cell phone
　2 Students learned
　3 Mr. Clark drank too much coffee

UNIT 03 일반동사의 부정문과 의문문

p.9

A 1 Does　2 didn't　3 sing
　4 don't　5 Did

B 1 Did, clean, he didn't
　2 Do, like, I do
　3 Did, brush, she did
　4 Do, live, they don't

C 1 O　2 didn't　3 O
　4 spend

D 1 Does your dog bark
　2 Did he run
　3 My friends did not forget my birthday
　4 Baseball players do not kick the ball

Chapter Test +

p.10

1 ①　2 ③, ④　3 ④　4 ②　5 ②
6 ③　7 ④　8 she did　9 he doesn't
10 they didn't　11 ③　12 ④
13 Kelly does not write
14 Did you break the vase
15 Kevin told an interesting story to us
16 Penguins don't[do not] fly in the sky
17 Do they speak Spanish in Mexico
18 ②　19 (1) ⓐ → bought　(2) ⓓ → didn't go
20 ③　21 does not[doesn't] keep secrets
22 teaches math
23 read a newspaper, did her homework
24 did not[didn't] open
25 won the final game

---

1 ① say - says

2 ③ keep - kept
　④ cost - cost

3 빈칸 뒤에 동사의 3인칭 단수 현재형(jogs)이 있으므로 3인칭 단수 주어 My dad를 쓴다.

4 Shore씨는 그의 여동생이 아닌 남동생과 함께 산다는 맥락이다. 주어 He는 3인칭 단수이므로 lives를 쓴다.

5 • 주어 I는 1인칭 단수이므로 wash를 쓴다.
　• 주어 Bart는 3인칭 단수이므로 rides를 쓴다.

6 • 과거를 나타내는 표현(yesterday)이 있으므로 went를 쓴다.
　• 주어 My parents는 3인칭 복수이므로 take를 쓴다.

7 일반동사 과거형의 부정문: 「주어 + did not[didn't] + 동사원형」

8 일반동사 과거형의 의문문에 대한 긍정의 대답: 「Yes, 주어 + did.」

9 주어 Thomas는 3인칭 단수이므로 일반동사 현재형의 의문문에 대한 부정의 대답 No, he doesn't를 쓴다.

10 일반동사 과거형의 의문문에 대한 부정의 대답: 「No, 주어 + didn't.」

11 ① want → wants
② checks → checked
④ bakes → baked
⑤ lives → live

12 ① doesn't → don't
② Do → Did
③ don't → doesn't
⑤ don't → didn't

13 일반동사 현재형의 부정문: 「주어 + do/does not + 동사원형」

14 일반동사 과거형의 의문문: 「Did + 주어 + 동사원형 ~?」

15 동사 tell의 과거형: told

16 주어 Penguins는 3인칭 복수이므로 don't[do not]을 쓴다.

17 일반동사 현재형의 의문문: 「Do/Does + 주어 + 동사원형 ~?」

18 ② does → did

19 (1) 동사 buy의 과거형: bought
(2) 어제 일찍 잠자리에 들지 않아서 오늘 아침에 늦게 일어났다는 맥락이므로 didn't go를 쓴다.

20 ⓐ enjoied → enjoyed
ⓓ not caught → did not[didn't] catch
ⓔ Does → Do

21 주어 Collin은 3인칭 단수이므로 일반동사 현재형의 부정문은 「주어 + does not[doesn't] + 동사원형」의 형태이다.

22 주어 Ms. Smith는 3인칭 단수이므로 teaches를 쓴다.

23 첫 번째 빈칸: 동사 read의 과거형 read를 쓴다.
두 번째 빈칸: 동사 do의 과거형 did를 쓴다.

24 일반동사 과거형의 부정문: 「주어 + did not[didn't] + 동사원형」

25 동사 win의 과거형 won을 쓴다.

Chapter 03 시제

UNIT 01 현재시제와 과거시제

p.13

A 1 visited   2 have   3 learned
4 met   5 is

B 1 walked   2 turns   3 invited
4 need

C 1 chatted   2 O   3 ended
4 lives

D 1 The bus leaves   2 Mr. Diaz started
3 My sister comes   4 I watched

UNIT 02 미래시제

p.14

A 1 take   2 Is   3 going
4 not going   5 won't

B 1 Are they going to eat
2 Will you be
3 Paul is going to practice
4 She won't[will not] clean

C 1 am going to leave
2 won't open
3 Is, going to help

D 1 Will Susan stay
2 The president will take an airplane
3 He is not going to make cupcakes

UNIT 03 진행시제

p.15

A 1 tying   2 Were   3 chasing
4 am not   5 was, is

B 1 The elephant is swimming
2 They weren't[were not] playing
3 Was he having

C 1 Is your brother cooking
2 The athletes were waiting
3 I am not[I'm not] feeding

D 1 The singers are not singing
2 He is cutting
3 The alarm was not ringing

Chapter Test +

p.16

1 ④   2 ④   3 ②   4 ③   5 ③   6 ⑤
7 ⑤   8 ③   9 ②   10 ③   11 ⑤   12 ①
13 ②   14 ⑤   15 Are you going to watch a movie
16 won't → isn't   17 meeting → meet
18 ⓒ → will not[won't] come   19 ③
20 changes   21 will not[won't] go camping
22 were lying, was digging a hole
23 bought the coat, is selling it

1 ④ run – running

2 ④ die – dying

3 주어 She는 3인칭 단수이고 매일 버스가 아닌 지하철을 타고 학교에 간다는 현재의 습관이나 반복되는 일을 나타내고 있으므로 현재시제 goes를 쓴다.

4 in 1879이 있으므로 과거시제 invented를 쓴다.

5 • 주어 Ms. Ford는 3인칭 단수이므로 지금(now) 진행되고 있는 동작을 나타내는 현재진행시제 is buying을 쓴다.
   • last night이 있으므로 과거시제 talked를 쓴다.

6 • next week이 있으므로 미래시제 will play를 쓴다.
   • 과거의 특정 시점(30 minutes ago)에 진행되고 있던 동작을 나타내는 과거진행시제 was looking을 쓴다.

7 과거진행시제 was blowing을 쓴다.

8 미래시제 will go가 쓰였으므로 과거시제와 주로 함께 쓰이는 부사구 last year는 쓸 수 없다.

9 ① be → is
   ③ study → studied[were studying]
   ④ going to 삭제 또는 will → am
   ⑤ was → is

10 ③ I wasn't → I'm not

11 ⑤ is washing → was washing

12 ① going wear → going to wear

13 • 주어 The painter는 3인칭 단수이고 빈칸 뒤에 동사의 V-ing형(drawing)이 있으므로 「be동사 + V-ing」 형태의 진행시제를 만드는 be동사 is나 was를 쓴다.
   • 주어 Cathy는 3인칭 단수이고 last year가 있으므로 과거시제 was를 쓴다.

14 • 빈칸 뒤에 동사원형(become)이 있으므로 「will + 동사원형」 형태의 미래시제를 만드는 will을 쓴다.
   • will이 있는 미래시제의 의문문: 「Will + 주어 + 동사원형 ~?」

15 주어 you는 2인칭 단수이므로 be going to가 있는 미래시제의 의문문 Are you going to watch ~?를 쓴다.

16 현재진행시제 Is ~ baking으로 묻고 있고 케이크가 아닌 파이를 굽고 있다고 했으므로 No, she isn't.로 대답한다.

17 be going to가 있는 미래시제의 의문문: 「be동사 + 주어 + going to + 동사원형 ~?」

18 will이 있는 미래시제의 부정문: 「주어 + will not[won't] + 동사원형」

19 ⓐ is knowing → knows
   ⓓ go → going
   ⓔ goes → went

20 주어 The weather는 3인칭 단수이므로 현재시제 changes를 쓴다.

21 will이 있는 미래시제의 부정문: 「주어 + will not[won't] + 동사원형」

22 첫 번째 빈칸: 주어 The children은 3인칭 복수이므로 과거진행시제 were lying을 쓴다.
   두 번째 빈칸: 주어 the dog은 3인칭 단수이므로 과거진행시제 was digging을 쓴다.

23 첫 번째 빈칸: 과거시제 bought를 쓴다.

두 번째 빈칸: 주어 He는 3인칭 단수이므로 지금(now) 진행되고 있는 동작을 나타내는 현재진행시제 is selling을 쓴다.

Chapter 04 조동사

UNIT 01 can, may

p.19

A 1 may   2 Can   3 sleep
   4 may

B 1 ⓐ   2 ⓒ   3 ⓓ
   4 ⓑ

C 1 Can Marley fix
   2 You may not skip
   3 Jerry and I are not[aren't] able to win
   4 Airplanes could not[couldn't] fly

D 1 Can[May] I use
   2 Tom is able to travel
   3 They could hear

UNIT 02 must, have to, should

p.20

A 1 must change   2 don't have to
   3 O   4 must not eat
   5 O

B 1 should   2 can't
   3 should   4 must
   5 don't have to

C 1 must[have to] buy   2 must be
   3 don't have to hurry   4 must not run

D 1 Ella has to take
   2 John cannot[can't] be
   3 They shouldn't smoke
   4 She doesn't have to help

Chapter Test ✛

p.21

1 ①   2 ④   3 ⑤   4 be not → not be

5 has → have   6 doesn't have to

7 should not   8 Could   9 ④

10 may not like   11 don't have to worry

12 Does he have to buy a train ticket

13 Bats are able to fly   14 ②   15 ①   16 ⑤

17 ④   18 ②   19 ④

20 (1) must not[should not/shouldn't] turn right

(2) must not[should not/shouldn't] feed the birds

21 You must not throw out the trash on the street

22 (1) ⓒ → must be   (2) ⓓ → Can[Could] you bring

1　'나를 위해 이 오이들을 썰어주겠니?'라는 의미이므로 Can(~해주겠니?)을 쓴다.

2　'드라이아이스는 위험하다. 너는 그것을 만지면 안 된다.'라는 의미이므로 must not(~하면 안 된다)을 쓴다.

3　can = be able to(능력·가능)

4　may의 부정형: may not

5　주어 George and Diana는 3인칭 복수이므로 have to를 쓴다.

6　'그녀는 오늘 밤에 요리할 필요가 없다. 그녀는 피자를 주문할 것이다.'라는 의미이므로 doesn't have to(~할 필요가 없다)를 쓴다.

7　'우리는 도서관에서 큰 소리로 이야기하면 안 된다.'라는 의미이므로 should(~해야 한다)의 부정형 should not을 쓴다.

8　'저에게 약간의 돈을 빌려주시겠어요?'라는 의미이므로 can(~해주겠니?)보다 정중한 요청을 나타내는 Could를 쓴다.

9　④ No, you may not. → Yes, you may.

10　약한 추측(~일지도 모른다)을 나타내는 may의 부정형 may not을 쓴다.

11　주어 They는 3인칭 복수이므로 불필요(~할 필요가 없다)를 나타내는 don't have to를 쓴다.

12　의무(~해야 한다)를 나타내는 have to를 쓴다.

13　주어 Bats는 3인칭 복수이므로 능력·가능(~할 수 있다)을 나타내는 are able to를 쓴다.

14　②: 약한 추측(~일지도 모른다)
①③④⑤: 허가(~해도 된다)

15　①: 강한 추측(~임이 틀림없다)
②③④⑤: 의무(~해야 한다)

16　⑤ must not walks → must not walk

17　④ don't have to take → doesn't have to take

18　ⓒ plays → play
ⓔ have → has

19　• '너는 거짓말하면 안 된다.'라는 의미이므로 must not (~하면 안 된다)의 must나, should(~해야 한다)의 부정형 should not의 should를 쓴다.
• 'Richard는 오늘 결석했다. 그는 매우 아픈 것이 틀림없다.'라는 의미이므로 must(~임이 틀림없다)를 쓴다.

20　각각 우회전하면 안 된다는 표지판과 새들에게 먹이를 주면 안 된다는 표지판이므로 must not(~하면 안 된다)이나, should(~해야 한다)의 부정형 should not[shouldn't]를 쓴다.

21　must의 부정형: must not

22　(1) 「조동사 + 동사원형」
(2) '저에게 약간의 물을 가져다주시겠어요?'라는 의미이므로 Can(~해주겠니?)이나, can보다 정중한 요청을 나타내는 Could를 쓴다.

Chapter 05 동사의 종류

UNIT 01 주격 보어가 필요한 동사

p.24

A 1 sounded　2 healthy　3 famous
4 looks like

B 1 look tight　　　　2 tastes spicy
3 smells like cherries　4 sounds familiar

C 1 This chocolate tastes like mint
2 The forest turns green
3 Fried chicken smells delicious
4 That sheep looks like cotton candy

D 1 feels comfortable
2 smelled like an old place
3 look young

UNIT 02 두 개의 목적어가 필요한 동사

p.25

A 1 to me　　2 for　　3 us the menu
4 found　　5 a pen to Todd

B 1 a watch to him　　2 Alice some biscuits
3 a ring for their mom　4 a favor of his brother

C 1 taught my cousin the alphabet
2 built a small garden for his family
3 wrote her boss an e-mail
4 read a fairy tale to me

D 1 showed a trick to us
2 passed the towel to him
3 tell them the truth
4 cooked a special dish for her

UNIT 03 목적격 보어가 필요한 동사

p.26

A 1 poor　　2 to enter　　3 found
4 to pass

B 1 to run　　2 warm　　3 darling
4 to read

C
  1 ask her to be
  2 found eggplants delicious
  3 made him a famous director

D
  1 told his son to drink
  2 wanted me to do
  3 found Kate pretty

Chapter Test +
p.27

1 ②   2 ④   3 ③   4 ①   5 ④   6 ⑤
7 ④   8 to   9 ①, ⑤ 10 ④   11 ⑤
12 safely → safe   13 the message to them
14 some questions of Sarah
15 wash → to wash   16 ①, ②
17 smells delicious
18 asked me to make the bed
19 (1) ⓑ → for   (2) ⓒ → to be
20 Eric showed us his painting
21 Can you keep the window open
22 My sister cooked pasta for them
23 Mom allowed me to play games   24 ④

1 빈칸 뒤에 「직접 목적어(the salt) + to + 간접 목적어(his father)」가 있으므로 전치사 to를 쓰는 수여동사 passed를 쓴다. (found, made, bought는 전치사 for를 쓰는 수여동사이고, asked는 전치사 of를 쓰는 수여동사이다.)

2 「expect + 목적어 + to부정사 목적격 보어」

3 ③: to ①②④⑤: for

4 (A): 빈칸 뒤에 명사 주격 보어(a doctor)가 있으므로 주격 보어 자리에 명사나 형용사가 오는 동사 became을 쓴다.
  (B): 빈칸 뒤에 간접 목적어(me)와 직접 목적어(the dance)가 있으므로 수여동사 show를 쓴다.
  (C): 감각동사(tastes)의 주격 보어 자리에는 형용사만 오므로 형용사 great을 쓴다.

5 • 빈칸 뒤에 간접 목적어(me)와 직접 목적어(a sweater)가 있으므로 수여동사 gave, made, sent를 쓴다.
  • 빈칸 뒤에 목적어(Paul)와 형용사 목적격 보어(tired)가 있으므로 목적격 보어로 형용사를 쓰는 동사 made를 쓴다.

6 ⑤ looks → looks like

7 ④ a map his friend → a map to his friend 또는 his friend a map

8 • 「ask + 목적어 + to부정사 목적격 보어」
  • 「tell + 직접 목적어 + to + 간접 목적어」

9 「find + 간접 목적어 + 직접 목적어」 또는 「find + 직접 목적어 + for + 간접 목적어」

10 주어진 문장과 ④: 주어 + 동사 + 간접 목적어 + 직접 목적어
  ①, ⑤: 주어 + 동사 + 목적어 + 목적격 보어
  ②: 주어 + 동사 + 직접 목적어 + for + 간접 목적어
  ③: 주어 + 동사 + 주격 보어

11 ⑤: 목적격 보어가 필요한 동사 make
  ①②③④: 두 개의 목적어가 필요한 수여동사 make

12 keep은 목적격 보어로 형용사를 쓰는 동사이므로 형용사 safe를 쓴다.

13 「send + 직접 목적어 + to + 간접 목적어」

14 「ask + 직접 목적어 + of + 간접 목적어」

15 「tell + 목적어 + to부정사 목적격 보어」

16 ③ angrily → angry
  ④ some tricks the dog → some tricks to the dog 또는 the dog some tricks
  ⑤ pay → to pay

17 「smell + 형용사」: ~한 냄새가 나다

18 「ask + 목적어 + to부정사 목적격 보어」

19 (1) 「make + 직접 목적어 + for + 간접 목적어」
  (2) 「want + 목적어 + to부정사 목적격 보어」

20 「show + 간접 목적어 + 직접 목적어」

21 「keep + 목적어 + 형용사 목적격 보어」

22 「cook + 직접 목적어 + for + 간접 목적어」

23 「allow + 목적어 + to부정사 목적격 보어」

24 ⓑ sadly → sad
  ⓒ a cupcake Irene → a cupcake for Irene 또는 Irene a cupcake
  ⓔ differently → different

Chapter 06 문장의 종류

UNIT 01 명령문, 청유문, 감탄문

p.30

A
  1 leave   2 the concert was
  3 and   4 What   5 Let's not

B
  1 Take a taxi
  2 What a colorful sunset (it is)
  3 Don't[Do not] break the rules
  4 How friendly (my neighbors are)

C
  1 Let's not worry
  2 What a smart girl Linda is
  3 Do not use a smartphone

D
  1 How wonderfully
  2 Let's finish our homework
  3 Please drive fast, or

UNIT 02 의문사 의문문 I

A p.31
1 Whom 2 Whose 3 What
4 Which

B
1 Whose house has
2 What do, want
3 Who(m) does, like

C
1 Who sent this package
2 What kind of books does he read
3 Which season do you prefer

D
1 Whose dog barked
2 What did your brother make
3 Which does Mary usually wear

UNIT 03 의문사 의문문 II

A p.32
1 When 2 How 3 Why
4 Where

B
1 long 2 far 3 old
4 many

C
1 When will, wake 2 Where did, see
3 How much is 4 Why does, look

D
1 Where does Ms. Lopez work
2 How does Brook know
3 Why don't we take
4 How heavy is your new laptop

UNIT 04 부정의문문, 선택의문문, 부가의문문

A p.33
1 or 2 Wasn't 3 didn't
4 didn't

B
1 didn't they, they didn't
2 can she, she can
3 weren't you, we weren't

C
1 Didn't Annie come
2 Will you watch, or
3 Isn't he planting
4 Which does Albert like, or

D
1 Let's not exercise, shall we
2 Police officers didn't visit your house, did they
3 Which do you play more, baseball or basketball

Chapter Test ✚
p.34

1 ① 2 ② 3 ③ 4 ⑤ 5 ④
6 How friendly 7 What a fantastic novel
8 ③ 9 ⑤ 10 ③, ⑤ 11 ① 12 ②
13 What musical instrument do you like
14 What a difficult puzzle this is
15 Don't walk on the grass 16 isn't → won't
17 does → did 18 Yes → No
19 Let's not turn off the air conditioner
20 won the game, didn't they
21 Why don't you go camping
22 Why don't we travel around the world 23 ④
24 (1) ⓐ → What (2) ⓔ → Which 25 How 26 or

1 'Rebecca가 그것을 썼어.'라고 대답했으므로 사람에 대해 물을 때 쓰는 Who(누구)를 쓴다.

2 긍정 청유문: 「Let's + 동사원형」

3 '그것은 오후 12시에 떠나.'라고 대답했고 빈칸 뒤에 time이 있으므로 시간을 물을 때 쓰는 What time(몇 시에)의 What 을 쓴다.

4 • 정해진 범위 안에서의 선택을 묻고 있으므로 Which(어느 것)를 쓴다.
  • 빈칸 뒤에 명사 bicycle이 있으므로 형용사로 쓰여 명사 앞에서 명사를 꾸밀 수 있는 Whose(누구의)를 쓴다.

5 ④ not do → don't[do not]

6 How 감탄문: 「How + 형용사/부사 + (주어 + 동사)!」

7 What 감탄문: 「What + (a/an) + 형용사 + 명사 + (주어 + 동사)!」

8 '나는 어젯밤에 그것을 봤어.'라고 대답했으므로 시간이나 날짜를 물을 때 쓰는 When(언제)을 쓴다.

9 무게를 묻고 있으므로 How heavy를 쓴다.

10 ① bothers → bother
  ② Not let's → Let's not
  ④ and → or

11 ①: How ②③④⑤: What

12 ② How often으로 묻고 있으므로 빈도에 해당하는 것으로 대답한다.

13 What은 '무슨, 어떤'이라는 의미의 형용사로 쓰여 명사 (musical instrument) 앞에서 명사를 꾸밀 수 있다.

14 What 감탄문: 「What + (a/an) + 형용사 + 명사 + (주어 + 동사)!」

15 부정 명령문: 「Don't[Do not] + 동사원형」

16 긍정문 뒤에는 부정의 부가의문문을 덧붙이고, 앞 문장의 동사가 조동사(will)이므로 부가의문문의 동사는 won't를 쓴다.

17 부정문 뒤에는 긍정의 부가의문문을 덧붙이고, 앞 문장의 동사가 일반동사 과거형의 부정형(didn't fight)이므로 부가의

문문의 동사는 did를 쓴다.

18 '너는 새 휴대폰이 필요하지 않니?'라는 부정의문문에 지난 주에 새것을 사서 필요하지 않다고 대답하는 맥락이므로 No, I don't.로 대답한다.

19 부정 청유문: 「Let's not + 동사원형」

20 첫 번째 빈칸: 경기를 이겼다고 했으므로 won the game을 쓴다.
두 번째 빈칸: 긍정문 뒤에는 부정의 부가의문문을 덧붙이고, 앞 문장의 동사가 일반동사의 과거형(won)이므로 부가의문문의 동사는 didn't를 쓴다. 앞 문장의 주어가 They이므로 부가의문문의 주어는 인칭대명사 they를 쓴다.

21 「Why don't you + 동사원형 ~?」: (너는) ~하는 게 어때?

22 「Why don't we + 동사원형 ~?」: (우리) ~하지 않겠니?

23 ⓐ How a → How
ⓓ will we → will you

24 (1) What 감탄문: 「What + (a/an) + 형용사 + 명사 + (주어 + 동사)!」
(2) 정해진 범위 안에서의 선택을 묻고 있으므로 Which(어느 것)를 쓴다.

25 • How 감탄문: 「How + 형용사/부사 + (주어 + 동사)!」
• 'Brown씨는 키가 얼마나 크니?'라는 의미이므로 높이나 키를 묻는 How tall의 How를 쓴다.

26 • '너의 코트를 입어라, 그렇지 않으면 너는 추울 것이다.'라는 의미이므로 「명령문 + or ~」(…해라, 그렇지 않으면 ~)의 or를 쓴다.
• 상대방의 선택을 묻는 선택의문문에는 or를 사용한다.

Chapter 07 명사와 관사

UNIT 01 셀 수 있는 명사와 셀 수 없는 명사

p.37

A
| 1 Love | 2 a doll | 3 sand |
| 4 Knives | 5 Seoul | |

B
| 1 dishes | 2 O | 3 babies |
| 4 bottle of orange juice | | 5 O |

C
1 slice of cheese
2 pairs of shoes
3 bowls of corn soup
4 glasses of milk

D
1 are nine oxen
2 moved four pieces of furniture
3 needs advice
4 used three cans of blue paint

UNIT 02 관사

p.38

A
| 1 the | 2 a | 3 X |
| 4 a | 5 an, the | |

B
| 1 O | 2 The table | 3 taxi |
| 4 O | 5 an hour | |

C
| 1 science | 2 the park |
| 3 text message | 4 a day |

D
1 open the door
2 worked with an engineer
3 play tennis

Chapter Test ✚

p.39

1 ⑤ 2 ④ 3 a 4 X 5 the 6 ③, ④

7 ①, ③ 8 ④ 9 the 10 ③ 11 ④ 12 ①

13 ④ 14 cans of soda 15 the airplane, the sky

16 the hockey → hockey 17 the month → a month

18 ⑤ 19 a help → help

20 The children, a piece of paper

21 a notebook, The notebook

22 History, the history 23 ① 24 ②, ⑤

25 (1) an → a (2) tomato → tomatoes

---

1 ⑤ window – windows

2 ④ tooth – teeth

3 '모퉁이에 경찰관 한 명이 있다.'라는 의미이므로 '하나의 (one)'를 나타낼 때 쓰는 부정관사 a를 쓴다.

4 식사 이름(lunch) 앞에는 관사를 쓰지 않는다.

5 유일한 것(world)을 말할 때는 정관사 the를 쓴다.

6 단위명사 slice나 piece와 함께 쓰는 cake와 cheese pizza는 쓸 수 없다.

7 빈칸 뒤에 복수동사 are가 있으므로 셀 수 없는 명사 Salt와 Chocolate milk는 쓸 수 없다.

8 셀 수 없는 명사(water)의 복수형은 단위명사(glass)에 -(e)s를 붙여 만든다.

9 • 정황상 서로 알고 있는 것(hamburger)을 말할 때는 정관사 the를 쓴다.
• 구(on the list)의 수식을 받는 명사(songs) 앞에는 정관사 the를 쓴다.

10 주어진 문장과 ③: '~마다(per)'를 나타낼 때 쓰는 a
①⑤: '하나의(one)'를 나타낼 때 쓰는 a
②④: 정해지지 않은 막연한 하나를 가리킬 때 쓰는 a

11 ① loaves of breads → loaves of bread
② slice of cheeses → slices of cheese
③ pieces of furniture → piece of furniture
⑤ pair of scissors → pairs of scissors

12 ① fishes → fish

13 ④ the yoga → yoga

14 셀 수 없는 명사(soda)의 복수형은 단위명사(can)에 -(e)s 를 붙여 만든다.

15 첫 번째 빈칸: 구(in the sky)의 수식을 받는 명사(airplane) 앞에는 정관사 the를 쓴다.
두 번째 빈칸: 유일한 것(sky)을 말할 때는 정관사 the를 쓴다.

16 운동 이름(hockey) 앞에는 관사를 쓰지 않는다.

17 '너는 한 달에 한 번 그 수조를 청소해야 한다.'라는 의미이고 month의 첫소리는 자음으로 발음되므로 '~마다(per)'를 나타낼 때 쓰는 부정관사 a를 쓴다.

18 ⑤: 셀 수 있는 명사 ①②③④: 셀 수 없는 명사

19 셀 수 없는 명사(help)는 앞에 a(n)을 붙일 수 없고 복수형으로도 쓸 수 없다.

20 첫 번째 빈칸: 명사 child의 복수형은 children이고, 구(in the classroom)의 수식을 받는 명사(children) 앞에는 정관사 the를 쓴다.
두 번째 빈칸: 셀 수 없는 명사 paper는 단위명사 piece를 활용하여 수량을 나타낸다.

21 첫 번째 빈칸: '하나의(one)'를 나타내고 notebook의 첫소리는 자음으로 발음되므로 a notebook을 쓴다.
두 번째 빈칸: 앞에서 언급된 명사(a notebook)가 반복될 때는 정관사 the를 쓴다.

22 첫 번째 빈칸: 과목 이름(history) 앞에는 관사를 쓰지 않는다.
두 번째 빈칸: 구(of Seoul)의 수식을 받는 명사(history) 앞에는 정관사 the를 쓴다.

23 ⓓ a empty box → an empty box
ⓔ guitar → the guitar

24 ① café → a café
③ piece of breads → pieces of bread
④ green teas → cups of green tea

25 (1) week의 첫소리는 자음으로 발음되므로 부정관사 a를 쓴다.
(2) 명사 tomato의 복수형은 tomatoes이다.

Chapter 08 대명사

UNIT 01 인칭대명사

p.42

A 1 you 2 himself 3 Its
　　4 We 5 my, hers

B 1 It 2 us 3 your
　　4 himself 5 them

C 1 know ourselves
　　2 was upset with herself

---

3 called themselves

D 1 Your textbook is in his backpack
　　2 I looked at myself
　　3 Amy showed her house to him

UNIT 02 this, that, it

p.43

A 1 This 2 those 3 It
　　4 these 5 It 6 that

B 1 ⓐ 2 ⓑ 3 ⓑ
　　4 ⓐ

C 1 that 2 O 3 This
　　4 it 5 O

D 1 It was November
　　2 These are not[aren't] my toys
　　3 Those students played soccer

UNIT 03 one, some, any

p.44

A 1 some 2 one 3 them
　　4 ones 5 any

B 1 ones 2 some 3 any
　　4 one

C 1 O 2 it 3 O
　　4 ones 5 one

D 1 does not[doesn't] have any money
　　2 added some salt
　　3 write new ones

Chapter Test ✚

p.45

1 ④ 2 ③ 3 ④ 4 ③ 5 ③ 6 ②

7 ③ 8 ⑤ 9 ① 10 These buildings

11 were proud of ourselves

12 It is Wednesday 13 some pepper 14 It

15 one 16 ones 17 ③ 18 it 19 it → one

20 ③ 21 (1) ⓐ → some (2) ⓒ → them

22 hers → her 23 These → This

24 some → any 25 herself 26 ①

---

1 '그녀는 우리에게 저녁 식사를 요리해줬다.'라는 의미이므로 목적격 인칭대명사 us를 쓴다.

2 '그것들은 너의 것이니?'라는 의미이므로 소유대명사 yours

3
- 'Jason은 그 눈사람을 직접 만들었다.'라는 의미이므로 재귀대명사 himself를 쓴다.
- 빈칸 뒤에 단수명사(man)가 있으므로 지시형용사 This 를 쓴다.

4
- '너는 차를 좀 원하니?'라는 의미의 권유를 나타내는 의문 문이므로 some을 쓴다.
- '오후 세 시이다.'라는 의미이므로 시간을 나타내는 비인 칭 주어 It을 쓴다.

5 앞에서 언급된 명사(notebook)와 같은 종류의 불특정한 대 상을 가리키는 one을 쓴다.

6 'Mary는 그 시험에 대해 질문이 전혀 없었다.'라는 의미의 부정문이므로 any를 쓴다.

7 ③ that → those

8 ⑤ any → some

9 ①: 비인칭 주어 it   ②③④⑤: 인칭대명사 it

10 '이 ~'라는 의미의 지시형용사 These를 쓴다.

11 전치사 of의 목적어가 주어 We와 같은 대상이므로 재귀대 명사 ourselves를 쓴다.

12 요일을 나타내는 비인칭 주어 It을 쓴다.

13 긍정문에서 '약간(의), 조금(의), 몇몇(의)'를 의미하는 some 을 쓴다.

14 앞에서 언급된 특정한 단수명사 the article을 가리키는 인 칭대명사 It을 쓴다.

15 앞에서 언급된 명사(bicycle)와 같은 종류의 불특정한 대상 을 가리키고 빈칸 앞에 부정관사 a가 있으므로 one을 쓴다.

16 앞에서 언급된 복수명사(socks)와 같은 종류의 불특정한 대상을 가리키는 ones를 쓴다.

17 ③ themselves → them

18
- '어제는 며칠이었니?'라는 의미이므로 날짜를 나타내는 비인칭 주어 it을 쓴다.
- 앞에서 언급된 특정한 단수명사 this sweater를 가리키 고 있으므로 인칭대명사 it을 쓴다.

19 앞에서 언급된 명사(raincoat)와 같은 종류의 불특정한 대 상을 가리키고 부정관사 a가 있으므로 one을 쓴다.

20 ③: 주어나 목적어를 강조할 때 쓰는 재귀대명사는 생략할 수 있다.
①②④⑤: 동사나 전치사의 목적어가 주어와 같은 대상일 때 목적어로 쓰는 재귀대명사는 생략할 수 없다.

21 (1) '냉장고 안에 약간의 배와 사과가 있어.'라는 의미의 긍정 문이므로 some을 쓴다.
(2) 앞에서 언급된 특정한 복수명사 some pears and apples를 가리키고 동사 bought의 목적어 역할을 하 고 있으므로 목적격 인칭대명사 them을 쓴다.

22 'Mandy는 그녀의 생일 파티에 우리를 초대했다.'라는 의미 이므로 소유격 인칭대명사 her를 쓴다.

23 단수명사(book) 앞에는 지시형용사 This를 쓴다.

24 '우리는 정글에서 호랑이를 전혀 보지 못했다.'라는 의미의 부정문이므로 any를 쓴다.

25 '~ 자신, 직접'이라는 의미의 재귀대명사 herself를 쓴다.

26 ⓓ This → It
ⓔ some → any

UNIT 01 형용사

p.48

A
1 a few
2 tight
3 much
4 anyone smart
5 Lots of

B
1 interesting pictures
2 O
3 nice
4 O

C
1 much work
2 a few coins
3 many empty seats
4 little information

D
1 They told the surprising news
2 Thomas made a few mistakes
3 Ms. Wilson likes someone diligent
4 A lot of students are studying

UNIT 02 부사

p.49

A
1 well
2 late
3 often goes
4 Interestingly

B
1 hard
2 highly
3 high
4 hardly

C
1 seldom leaves
2 is usually
3 will never change

D
1 This pillow feels really soft
2 His uncle drives very carefully
3 They sometimes enjoy a vacation

UNIT 03 원급/비교급/최상급 비교

p.50

A
1 big
2 more wisely
3 much
4 nicest

B
1 as hot as
2 more slowly than
3 higher than

C
1 best
2 tastier
3 most dangerous
4 faster

D
1 The music is much louder than his voice
2 This soup smells as salty as seawater
3 Susan is the most important player

Chapter Test +

p.51

1 ④   2 ②   3 ③   4 ④   5 ③

6 Africa is much hotter than Europe

7 We can often see the stars

8 more interesting than   9 the happiest

10 something special   11 ②   12 ⑤   13 ①

14 ⑤   15 ⑤   16 ④   17 the longest

18 as old as   19 ③   20 ④   21 bad → worse

22 highly → high 23 ③   24 better → best

25 light → lighter 26 ④   27 ⓒ → strong

---

1 ④ easy – easily

2 ② helpful – more helpful – most helpful

3 빈칸 뒤에 명사(language)가 있으므로 동사, 형용사, 다른 부사, 문장 전체를 꾸미는 부사 beautifully는 쓸 수 없다.

4 빈칸 뒤에 셀 수 있는 명사의 복수형(tomatoes)이 있으므로 셀 수 없는 명사와 함께 쓰는 a little은 쓸 수 없다.

5 빈칸 뒤에 비교급(harder)이 있으므로 원급을 강조하는 very는 쓸 수 없다.

6 '…보다 더 ~한'이라는 의미의 「형용사의 비교급 + than」을 쓰고, 비교급을 강조하는 much는 비교급 앞에 쓴다.

7 빈도부사(often)는 조동사(can) 뒤에 온다.

8 「형용사의 비교급 + than」 '…보다 더 ~한'

9 「the + 형용사의 최상급」 '가장 ~한'

10 -thing으로 끝나는 대명사(something)를 꾸밀 때는 형용사(special)가 대명사 뒤에 온다.

11 ① good → well
③ a few → a little
④ Surprising → Surprisingly
⑤ lately(최근에) → late(늦게)

12 ⑤ Few → Little

13 • '그 바이올리니스트는 매우 열심히 연습했다.'라는 의미이므로 부사 hard(열심히)를 쓴다.
• '그 수학 시험은 매우 어려웠다.'라는 의미이므로 형용사 hard(어려운, 단단한)를 쓴다.

14 • 동사(showed)를 꾸미는 부사 kindly를 쓴다.
• 'Johnson씨는 그 다이아몬드를 면밀히 살폈다.'라는 의미이므로 부사 closely(면밀히)를 쓴다.

15 '가장 ~한'이라는 의미의 「the + 형용사의 최상급」을 쓴다. 형용사 large의 최상급은 largest이다.

16 '…보다 더 ~하게'라는 의미의 「부사의 비교급 + than」을 쓰고, 비교급을 강조하는 much를 비교급 앞에 쓴다. 부사 fast의 비교급은 faster이다.

17 낙동강이 세 강 중에서 가장 기므로 형용사 long을 활용하여 「the + 형용사의 최상급」인 the longest를 쓴다.

18 Jeremy와 Kate는 Bill과 나이가 같으므로 형용사 old를 활용하여 「as + 형용사의 원급 + as」인 as old as를 쓴다.

19 빈도부사(always)는 일반동사(rises) 앞에 온다.

20 -thing으로 끝나는 대명사(something)를 꾸밀 때는 형용사(mysterious)가 대명사 뒤에 온다.

21 '…보다 더 ~한'이라는 의미의 「형용사의 비교급 + than」을 쓴다. 형용사 bad의 비교급은 worse이다.

22 '그 풍선은 하늘 높이 떠 있었다.'라는 의미이므로 부사 high(높게, 높이)를 쓴다. 부사 highly는 '매우, 대단히'라는 의미이다.

23 ① more warm → warmer
② most funny → funniest
④ brighter → bright 또는 as brighter as → brighter than
⑤ A little → A few

24 '가장 ~한'이라는 의미의 「the + 형용사의 최상급」을 쓴다. 형용사 good의 최상급은 best이다.

25 '…보다 더 ~한'이라는 의미의 「형용사의 비교급 + than」을 쓴다. 형용사 light의 비교급은 lighter이다.

26 ⓐ sadly → sad
ⓒ much → many (How many는 개수를 물을 때 쓰는 표현이다.)

27 주어(They)를 보충 설명하는 형용사 strong을 쓴다.

Chapter 10 to부정사와 동명사

UNIT 01 to부정사의 명사적 용법

p.54

A 1 to take   2 to see   3 not to lie
4 is

B 1 ⓑ   2 ⓒ   3 ⓐ
4 ⓑ

C 1 It is dangerous to stay
2 I'm planning what to do
3 Josh wanted to work

D 1 hopes to get a perfect score
2 is exciting to ride a horse
3 decided to leave his hometown
4 is to help poor children

UNIT 02 to부정사의 형용사적/부사적 용법

p.55

A 1 to see   2 O   3 to do
4 O

B 1 to study music
2 some magazines to read
3 to be a soccer player

4 to receive the gift

C
1 (in order) to travel around the world
2 to see her brother on TV
3 to lose the game
4 (in order) to apologize to her

D
1 is excited to win first prize
2 needs someone to work with
3 are too small to read

UNIT 03 동명사의 쓰임

p.56

A 1 is   2 getting   3 fixing

B
1 writing[to write]   2 uploading
3 growing[to grow]   4 Checking[To check]

C
1 are worth trying   2 avoid making
3 not getting up   4 Stop talking

D
1 I thank you for inviting
2 Bob's wish is becoming[to become]
3 Saving[To save] energy is

Chapter Test +

p.57

1 ⑤   2 ④   3 ④   4 ⑤   5 ③   6 ④
7 ⑤   8 ④   9 ③   10 plant → to plant
11 eat → eating   12 This → It   13 ②
14 someone diligent to help
15 love to spend[spending]   16 happy to travel
17 too angry to calm down   18 ③
19 He was busy fixing his chair
20 It is dangerous to play
21 I don't know what to prepare
22 I thanked him for finding   23 ④
24 going → to go
25 (1) ⓒ → to be   (2) ⓓ → dancing

1 mind는 동명사를 목적어로 쓰는 동사이므로 waiting을 쓴다.

2 decide는 to부정사를 목적어로 쓰는 동사이므로 to eat을 쓴다.

3 ④: 보어   ①②③⑤: 목적어

4 ⑤: 주어   ①②③④: 목적어

5 • want는 to부정사를 목적어로 쓰는 동사이므로 to see를 쓴다.
• 'Anna는 너에게 어디에서 Bart를 만날지 말해줄 것이다.' 라는 의미이므로 '어디에(서)/어디로 ~할지'라는 의미의

「where + to부정사」를 쓴다.

6 • 전치사(about)의 목적어로 쓰이는 동명사 having을 쓴다.
• avoid는 동명사를 목적어로 쓰는 동사이므로 drinking을 쓴다.

7 • '헬멧 없이 자전거를 타는 것은 안전하지 않다.'라는 의미이고 주어 자리에 가주어 It이 있으므로 진주어 to부정사 to ride를 쓴다.
• keep은 동명사를 목적어로 쓰는 동사이므로 swimming을 쓴다.

8 주어진 문장과 ④: 부사적 용법(목적)
①: 명사적 용법(목적어)
②⑤: 형용사적 용법
③: 명사적 용법(주어)

9 주어진 문장과 ③: 형용사적 용법
①: 명사적 용법(주어)
②: 명사적 용법(보어)
④: 부사적 용법(목적)
⑤: 명사적 용법(목적어)

10 '엄마는 정원에 심을 약간의 꽃을 사셨다.'라는 의미로 명사 (some flowers)를 뒤에서 꾸미는 형용사적 용법의 to부정사이므로 「to + 동사원형」의 형태로 쓴다.

11 finish는 동명사를 목적어로 쓰는 동사이므로 eating을 쓴다.

12 to부정사(to recycle)가 주어로 쓰일 때는 주로 주어 자리에 가주어 it을 쓰고 진주어 to부정사(구)를 뒤로 보낸다.

13 ① to watch anything interesting
→ anything interesting to watch
③ to loses → to lose
④ reach → to reach
⑤ to playing → to play[playing]

14 -one으로 끝나는 대명사(someone)를 형용사(diligent)와 to부정사(to help)가 동시에 꾸밀 때는 「-one + 형용사 + to부정사」의 형태로 쓴다.

15 love는 to부정사와 동명사를 모두 목적어로 쓰는 동사이므로 to spend나 spending을 쓴다.

16 감정 형용사(happy)에 대한 원인을 나타내는 부사적 용법의 to부정사를 쓴다.

17 「too + 형용사 + to부정사」 '…하기에 너무 ~한'

18 ③ what wear → what to wear

19 「be busy + V-ing」 '~하느라 바쁘다'

20 to부정사(to play)가 주어로 쓰일 때는 주로 주어 자리에 가주어 it을 쓰고 진주어 to부정사(구)를 뒤로 보낸다.

21 「what + to부정사」 '무엇을 ~할지'

22 「thank … for + V-ing」 '~한 것에 대해 …에게 감사해하다'

23 ⓐ to bring → bringing
ⓓ were → was

24 want는 to부정사를 목적어로 쓰는 동사이므로 to go를 쓴다.

25 (1) '그는 자라서 선생님이 되었다'라는 의미의 결과를 나타내는 to부정사이므로 「to + 동사원형」의 형태로 쓴다.

(2) give up은 동명사를 목적어로 쓰는 동사이므로 dancing을 쓴다.

Chapter 11 전치사

UNIT 01 장소를 나타내는 전치사

p.60

A 1 in   2 on   3 at

B 1 over   2 on   3 in
    4 in front of

C 1 a house across from the river
    2 their babies in a pouch
    3 the key under the chair

D 1 played basketball at school
    2 was a fire near the mountain
    3 is next to the hospital

UNIT 02 시간을 나타내는 전치사

p.61

A 1 at   2 in   3 on
    4 in

B 1 ① during   ② for
    2 ① by   ② until

C 1 in 2020   2 around 4 o'clock
    3 after dinner

D 1 sleep for 14 hours
    2 hang the national flag on March 1
    3 opens the door before sunrise

UNIT 03 기타 전치사

p.62

A 1 to   2 with   3 between

B 1 for   2 by   3 with
    4 about

C 1 to the tourists   2 with paper
    3 about air pollution

D 1 studied from 9 A.M. to 3 P.M.
    2 sent the document by fax
    3 practiced hard for the speech contest

Chapter Test ✚

p.63

1 ③   2 ⑤   3 ①   4 ⑤   5 ②   6 for

7 around, with   8 in front of, on   9 ③   10 ④

11 jogged from their house to the river

12 is a chair between the tree and the table

13 sit next to you   14 in → on

15 during → for   16 ⑤   17 ④   18 under

19 after   20 ①, ③   21 ②

22 from, to   23 across from

24 by, between, and   25 about → with

1 • 하나의 지점(the corner of the street)을 나타낼 때는 전치사 at(~에, ~에서)을 쓴다.
  • '너는 30분 동안 그것을 끓여야 한다.'라는 의미이고 30 minutes는 숫자를 포함한 기간 표현이므로 전치사 for (~동안)를 쓴다.

2 • 표면(the sofa)에 접촉한 상태를 나타낼 때는 전치사 on(~ 위에, ~에)을 쓴다.
  • '빵과 치즈 사이에 햄 한 조각이 있다.'라는 의미이므로 전치사 between A and B(A와 B 사이에)를 쓴다.

3 • '우리는 우리의 계획에 대해 이야기했다.'라는 의미이므로 전치사 about(~에 대해)을 쓴다.
  • 비교적 넓은 장소(LA)를 나타낼 때는 전치사 in(~ 안에, ~에)을 쓴다.

4 • '너는 배를 타고 제주도로 여행 갈 수 있다.'라는 의미이므로 전치사 by(~을 타고, ~으로)를 쓴다.
  • '그 가게는 자정까지 문을 연다.'라는 의미이고 문을 여는 것은 자정까지 계속되는 것이므로 전치사 until(~까지)을 쓴다.

5 ②: on   ①③④⑤: in

6 '~을 위해'라는 의미의 전치사 for를 쓴다.

7 첫 번째 빈칸: '~쯤'이라는 의미의 전치사 around를 쓴다.
두 번째 빈칸: '~과 함께, ~을 이용해서'라는 의미의 전치사 with를 쓴다.

8 첫 번째 빈칸: '~ 앞에'라는 의미의 전치사 in front of를 쓴다.
두 번째 빈칸: 요일(Sunday)을 나타낼 때는 전치사 on (~에)을 쓴다.

9 • 비교적 좁은 장소(the police station)를 나타낼 때는 전치사 at(~에, ~에서)을 쓴다.
  • 시점(noon)을 나타낼 때는 전치사 at(~에)을 쓴다.

10 • '나는 다음 주까지 포스터를 만들 것이다.'라는 의미이고 포스터를 만드는 것은 다음 주까지 완료되는 것이므로 전치사 by(~까지)를 쓴다.
  • 'Dorothy는 전화로 피자를 주문했다.'라는 의미이므로 전치사 by(~을 타고, ~으로)를 쓴다.

11 'A에서 B까지'라는 의미의 전치사 from A to B를 쓴다.

12 'A와 B 사이에'라는 의미의 전치사 between A and B를 쓴다.

---

13 '~ 옆에'라는 의미의 전치사 next to를 쓴다.

14 기념일(her birthday)을 나타낼 때는 전치사 on(~에)을 쓴다.

15 '3분 동안 너의 몸을 움직이지 마라.'라는 의미이고 three minutes는 숫자를 포함한 기간 표현이므로 전치사 for(~ 동안)를 쓴다.

16 ⑤ across → across from

17 ④ at → in

18 Christina와 나는 같은 아파트 건물에 살고 나는 1층, 그녀는 2층에 산다고 했으므로 '나의 아파트는 그녀의 것 아래에 있다.'라는 문장을 만드는 전치사 under(~ 아래에)를 쓴다.

19 나의 가족은 7시에 저녁을 먹을 것이고 영화 '작은 아씨들'은 8시 30분에 시작할 것이라고 했으므로 '우리는 저녁 식사 후에 그 영화를 볼 것이다.'라는 문장을 만드는 전치사 after(~ 후에)를 쓴다.

20 ② about → with
④ by → for
⑤ for → about

21 ⓒ under → over
ⓔ at → in

22 Barney's 사과 축제는 11월 10일부터 11월 12일까지이므로 전치사 from A to B(A와 B 사이에)를 쓴다.

23 Barney 공원은 도서관 맞은편에 있으므로 전치사 across from(~ 맞은편에)을 쓴다.

24 첫 번째 빈칸: Barney's 사과 축제가 열리는 Barney 공원 근처에 버스 정류장이 있으므로 전치사 by(~을 타고, ~으로)를 쓴다.
두 번째 빈칸: 버스 정류장은 도서관과 소방서 사이에 있으므로 전치사 between A and B(A와 B 사이에)를 쓴다.

25 '나는 매일 Hanna와 함께 학교에 가.'라는 의미이므로 전치사 with(~과 함께, ~을 이용해서)를 쓴다.

Chapter 12 접속사

UNIT 01 and, but, or, so

p.66

A 1 so 2 and 3 kind
4 but

B 1 but Adam likes it
2 so I gave it some water
3 a fork or chopsticks
4 and went jogging

C 1 but she failed the exam
2 a doctor or a nurse
3 so it can run fast

D 1 so I couldn't walk well
2 both English and Spanish
3 either Friday or Saturday

UNIT 02 when, while, before, after

p.67

A 1 When 2 finishes 3 before
4 while

B 1 Before 2 when 3 after

C 1 While I was sleeping
2 when he drinks juice
3 After she fell down the stairs

D 1 after he exercised
2 before her dad arrives
3 when he was a university student

UNIT 03 because, if, that

p.68

A 1 that 2 because 3 is
4 that 5 If

B 1 ⓒ 2 ⓑ 3 ⓐ
4 ⓓ

C 1 (that) people will love this song
2 Because his mother lost her wallet
3 If the weather is nice

D 1 if you have a headache
2 that Amy hates him
3 Because I liked its design
4 If he doesn't make trouble

Chapter Test ✚ p.69

1 ② 2 ⑤ 3 ② 4 ⑤ 5 ② 6 ③
7 after 8 so 9 ②, ③, ⑤ 10 ① 11 ②
12 ④
13 When he rides a bike, he will wear a helmet
14 before she gets on the plane
15 but my test score was bad 16 If it snows
17 I heard (that) 18 ③ 19 ④ 20 or → and
21 ⓔ → that

---

1 • 'Megan은 아침으로 계란과 베이컨을 먹었다.'라는 의미이므로 and(~과, 그리고)를 쓴다.
• '너는 캠핑하러 가고 싶니, 아니면 낚시하러 가고 싶니?'라는 의미이므로 or(또는, ~이거나, 아니면)를 쓴다.

2 • '나는 어렸을 때 나의 할머니와 함께 살았다.'라는 의미이므로 When(~할 때)을 쓴다.
• 'Allen은 너무 졸렸기 때문에 낮잠을 잤다.'라는 의미이므로 because(~하기 때문에)를 쓴다.

3 • '저 자전거는 좋아 보이지만, 나는 그것을 원하지 않는다.' 라는 의미이므로 but(하지만, 그러나)을 쓴다.
   • '만약 네가 택시를 탄다면, 너는 늦지 않을 것이다.'라는 의 미이므로 If(만약 ~한다면)를 쓴다.

4 ⑤ will return → return

5 ②: but   ①③④⑤: so

6 ③: if   ①②④⑤: that

7 '물이 끓은 후에 그것들을 넣어.'라는 의미이므로 after(~한 후에)를 쓴다.

8 '그는 감기에 걸려서 집에 머물렀어.'라는 의미이므로 so(그 래서, 따라서)를 쓴다.

9 ① and → or 또는 either → both
   ④ will be → are

10 ① → after ('너는 머리를 감은 후에 그것을 말려야 한다.')

11 • '나는 바다에서 수영하는 동안 물고기 몇 마리를 봤다.'라 는 의미이므로 while(~하는 동안)을 쓴다.
   • 'Brandon은 그의 방을 청소하는 동안 라디오를 들었다.' 라는 의미이므로 while(~하는 동안)을 쓴다.

12 • '좋은 소식은 우리가 특별 할인을 받을 수 있다는 것이 다.'라는 의미이고 빈칸 뒤의 절(we can get a special discount)이 주어(The good news)를 보충 설명하는 보 어이므로 that(~이라는 것)을 쓴다.
   • 'Jake는 그 아이들이 길을 건너고 있었다고 말했다.'라는 의미이고 빈칸 앞에 that절을 목적어로 쓰는 동사(said) 가 있으므로 that(~이라는 것)을 쓴다.

13 '그는 자전거를 탈 때 헬멧을 쓸 것이다.'라는 의미이다. 시간 을 나타내는 부사절(When ~ bike)에서는 미래시제 대신 현 재시제를 쓰고 주어 he는 3인칭 단수이므로 rides를 쓴다. 부사절이 문장 맨 앞에 올 때는 부사절 뒤에 콤마(,)를 쓴다.

14 '~하기 전에'라는 의미의 before를 쓴다. 시간을 나타내는 부사절(before ~ plane)에서는 미래시제 대신 현재시제를 쓰고 주어 she는 3인칭 단수이므로 gets를 쓴다.

15 '하지만, 그러나'라는 의미의 but을 쓴다.

16 '만약 ~한다면'이라는 의미의 If를 쓴다.

17 '~이라는 것'이라는 의미의 that을 쓴다. that절이 문장 안에 서 목적어로 쓰일 때는 that을 생략할 수 있다.

18 「either A or B」 'A나 B 둘 중 하나'

19 ⓐ if → that
   ⓓ that → if

20 '나는 피곤하고 걱정돼'라는 의미이므로 and(~과, 그리고)를 쓴다.

21 '나는 그녀가 나의 친구가 아니라는 것을 알았다'라는 의미 이고 knew는 that절을 목적어로 쓰는 동사이므로 that(~이 라는 것)을 쓴다.

MEMO

MEMO

| 해커스 중고등 교재 MAP | 나에게 맞는 교재 선택!

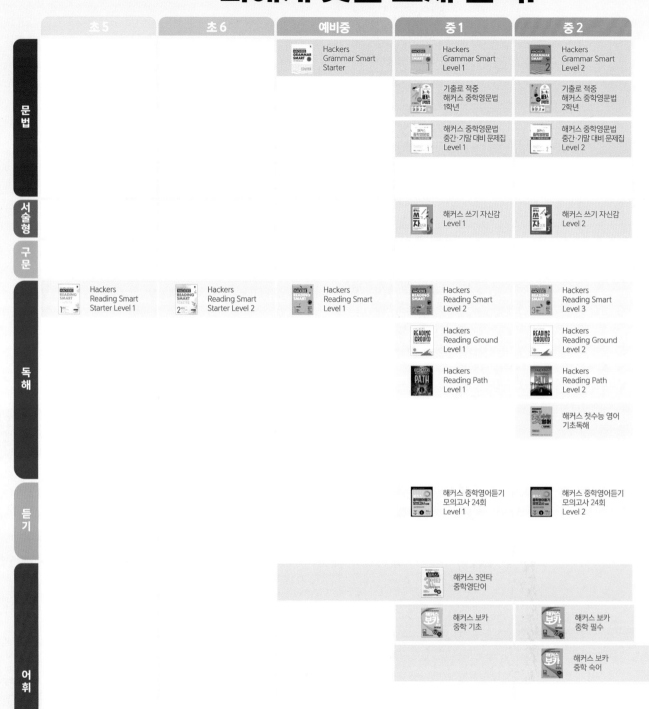

	초5	초6	예비중	중1	중2
문법			Hackers Grammar Smart Starter	Hackers Grammar Smart Level 1	Hackers Grammar Smart Level 2
				기출로 적중 해커스 중학영문법 1학년	기출로 적중 해커스 중학영문법 2학년
				해커스 중학영문법 중간·기말 대비 문제집 Level 1	해커스 중학영문법 중간·기말 대비 문제집 Level 2
서술형				해커스 쓰기 자신감 Level 1	해커스 쓰기 자신감 Level 2
구문					
독해	Hackers Reading Smart Starter Level 1	Hackers Reading Smart Starter Level 2	Hackers Reading Smart Level 1	Hackers Reading Smart Level 2	Hackers Reading Smart Level 3
				Hackers Reading Ground Level 1	Hackers Reading Ground Level 2
				Hackers Reading Path Level 1	Hackers Reading Path Level 2
				해커스 첫수능 영어 기초독해	
듣기				해커스 중학영어듣기 모의고사 24회 Level 1	해커스 중학영어듣기 모의고사 24회 Level 2
어휘				해커스 3연타 중학영단어	
				해커스 보카 중학 기초	해커스 보카 중학 필수
				해커스 보카 중학 숙어	

	READING	LISTENING	VOCA
토플	HACKERS APEX READING for the TOEFL iBT Basic/Intermediate/Advanced/Expert	HACKERS APEX LISTENING for the TOEFL iBT Basic/Intermediate/Advanced/Expert	HACKERS APEX VOCA for the TOEFL iBT HACKERS VOCABULARY

Smart, Useful, and Essential Grammar

HACKERS
GRAMMAR
SMART

1

LEVEL 1

초판 4쇄 발행 2023년 8월 7일
초판 1쇄 발행 2022년 1월 3일

지은이	해커스 어학연구소
펴낸곳	㈜해커스 어학연구소
펴낸이	해커스 어학연구소 출판팀

주소	서울특별시 서초구 강남대로61길 23 ㈜해커스 어학연구소
고객센터	02-537-5000
교재 관련 문의	publishing@hackers.com
	해커스북 사이트(HackersBook.com) 고객센터 Q&A 게시판
동영상강의	star.Hackers.com

ISBN	978-89-6542-455-0 (53740)
Serial Number	01-04-01

중고등영어 1위,
해커스북 HackersBook.com

· 깊은 이해로 이끄는 **예문/문제 해석**
· 불규칙 동사의 확실한 암기를 돕는 **불규칙 동사 테스트**
· 학습한 단어의 암기 여부를 쉽게 점검할 수 있는 **단어 리스트 및 단어 테스트**
· 교재의 단어를 언제 어디서나 들으면서 외우는 **단어암기 MP3**
· 서술형 시험을 완벽하게 대비할 수 있는 **영작/해석 워크시트**

한경비즈니스 선정 2020 한국품질만족도 교육(온·오프라인 중·고등영어) 부문 1위

HACKERS

GRAMMAR SMART

1
LEVEL

WORKBOOK

HACKERS
GRAMMAR
SMART 1

LEVEL

WORKBOOK

UNIT 01 be동사의 현재형과 과거형

Answers p.20

A 괄호 안에서 알맞은 것을 고르시오.

1 (She's / She'm) a great dancer.

2 (They's / They're) so lovely.

3 There (was / were) an old hospital on the hill.

4 I (am / was) angry at my brother now.

5 You (are / were) the best actor yesterday.

6 The toys (is / are) in the living room.

B 밑줄 친 부분이 어법상 맞으면 O를 쓰고, 틀리면 바르게 고쳐 쓰시오.

1 The girl are my cousin.   → _____

2 There is a tiger in this forest.   → _____

3 He were a winner last year.   → _____

4 We is in the laboratory yesterday. → _____

C 다음 빈칸에 알맞은 be동사를 쓰시오.

1 There _____ an airport in Incheon. It is big.

2 My grandfather _____ in Vietnam 30 years ago.

3 Tom and Jolly _____ nine years old this year.

4 They _____ at home an hour ago. They _____ at school now.

5 Sophia _____ the leader of the book club in 2017.

D 우리말과 같도록 괄호 안의 말과 be동사를 활용하여 문장을 완성하시오.

1 여름에는 날씨가 덥다. (the weather, hot)
= _____ in summer.

2 나는 지난 주말에 테마파크에 있었다. (I, at the theme park)
= _____ last weekend.

3 연못에 개구리 다섯 마리가 있었다. (there, five frogs)
= _____ in the pond.

4 Chen씨는 2년 전에 중국어 선생님이었다. (Ms. Chen, a Chinese teacher)
= _____ two years ago.

Answers p.20

A 다음 문장을 괄호 안의 지시대로 바꿔 쓰시오. (단, 부정문에서는 줄임말을 쓰시오.)

1 They are French musicians. (부정문으로)   → _____ French musicians.

2 She is a news reporter. (의문문으로)   → _____ a news reporter?

3 I was busy with homework. (부정문으로)   → _____ busy with homework.

4 The birds were in the nest. (의문문으로)   → _____ in the nest?

B 다음 빈칸에 알맞은 말을 넣어 대화를 완성하시오.

1 A: _____ you Ms. Scott?
   B: No, _____ _____. She is over there.

2 A: _____ the pencil on the desk?
   B: No, _____ _____. It was in my bag.

3 A: _____ they twins?
   B: Yes, _____ _____. Their birthdays are the same.

4 A: _____ Lucas your favorite soccer player?
   B: No, _____ _____. My favorite soccer player is Sonny.

C 밑줄 친 부분이 어법상 맞으면 O를 쓰고, 틀리면 바르게 고쳐 쓰시오.

1 I wasn't upset now.   → _____

2 That car isn't new. It is very old.   → _____

3 Lenna isn't in Japan last week.   → _____

4 Were your shoes clean two days ago?   → _____

D 우리말과 같도록 괄호 안의 말과 be동사를 활용하여 문장을 완성하시오.

1 Jake는 어제 그 콘서트에 늦었니? (Jake, late)
   = _____ for the concert yesterday?

2 Chris와 나는 체스를 잘하지 못한다. (Chris and I, good)
   = _____ at chess.

3 너는 너의 밴드에서 드럼 연주자니? (you, a drummer)
   = _____ in your band?

4 이 스웨터는 지난주에 가게에 없었다. (this sweater, in the store)
   = _____ last week.

Chapter Test +

[1-3] 다음 빈칸에 들어갈 말이 순서대로 짝지어진 것을 고르시오.

1

> • Tina _____ interested in golf.
> • Some bananas _____ on the table.

① is – is   ② is – are
③ are – is   ④ are – are
⑤ is – am

2

> • There _____ a coat in the closet.
> • My grandparents _____ in Europe last week.

① is – is   ② is – are
③ is – were   ④ are – are
⑤ are – were

3

> • _____ the thief in your room yesterday?
> • Your new jeans _____ short.

① Is – isn't   ② Is – aren't
③ Was – isn't   ④ Was – aren't
⑤ Were – isn't

서술형

[4-5] 다음 문장을 괄호 안의 지시대로 바꿔 쓰시오.

4

> My English textbook is very thick. (부정문으로)
> → _____ .

5

> They were absent from school on Monday. (의문문으로)
> → _____ ?

6 다음 질문에 대한 대답으로 알맞은 것은?

> A: Was the piano lesson fun?
> B: _____

① Yes, it is.   ② Yes, it was.
③ Yes, it wasn't.   ④ No, it isn't.
⑤ No, it was.

7 다음 중 밑줄 친 부분이 어법상 바른 것은?

① The package <u>are</u> 25 kilograms.
② There <u>were</u> a sock on the bed.
③ Many ants <u>was</u> under the rock.
④ There <u>are</u> some balloons in the sky.
⑤ Jerry and Ben <u>is</u> with their friends.

[8-9] 다음 우리말을 알맞게 영작한 것을 고르시오.

8

| 어제 큰 농구 경기가 있었다. |

① There be a big basketball game yesterday.
② There is a big basketball game yesterday.
③ There are a big basketball game yesterday.
④ There was a big basketball game yesterday.
⑤ There were a big basketball game yesterday.

9

| 그 은행은 경찰서 옆에 있지 않다. |

① The bank is next to the police station.
② The bank isn't next to the police station.
③ The bank aren't next to the police station.
④ The bank was next to the police station.
⑤ The bank wasn't next to the police station.

서술형
[10-11] 다음 문장에서 <u>틀린</u> 부분을 바르게 고쳐 완전한 문장을 쓰시오.

10

| There was four cars in the parking lot.
→ _____. |

11

| The weather aren't cold last winter.
→ _____. |

서술형 고난도
[12-14] be동사를 활용하여 다음 글의 빈칸에 알맞은 말을 쓰시오.

12

| Ronald _____ 160 centimeters tall last year. He is 170 centimeters tall now. |

13

| There is a tree in the yard. There _____ some flowers in the yard, too. |

14

| Yesterday _____ December 31. Today is January 1. I _____ thirteen years old yesterday. Now, I _____ fourteen years old. |

15 다음 중 어법상 <u>어색한</u> 것은?

① The towels weren't wet five minutes ago.
② Was Tony at the library on Tuesday?
③ Is Henry sick yesterday?
④ My neighbors were noisy last night.
⑤ Mr. and Mrs. Nicholas are from Germany.

[16-17] be동사를 활용하여 다음 대화의 빈칸에 알맞은 말을 쓰시오.

16
A: _____ it rainy in Busan last weekend?
B: No, it _____. It was sunny.

17
A: _____ Jamie and Alice nurses?
B: Yes, they _____. They work at the same hospital now.

18 다음 중 어법상 <u>어색한</u> 것을 <u>모두</u> 고르시오.

① These scientists are very famous.
② Her sister isn't healthy.
③ There is a ladybug on the window.
④ The students wasn't in the classroom.
⑤ Were the watermelon cool and sweet?

19 다음 빈칸에 들어갈 말이 나머지 넷과 <u>다른</u> 것은?

① There _____ a toothbrush in the glass.
② Miranda _____ an excellent painter.
③ _____ you proud of your parents?
④ _____ the necklace silver?
⑤ The dog _____ not in the bathroom.

[20-22] 우리말과 같도록 괄호 안의 말을 활용하여 문장을 완성하시오.

20
나는 배부르지만, Jane은 배고프다. (full, hungry)

= I _____, but Jane _____.

21
Taylor씨는 지난주에 런던에 있지 않았다. (in London)

= Ms. Taylor _____
last week.

22
너와 너의 형은 쌍둥이니? (you and your brother)

= _____ twins?

23 우리말과 같도록 주어진 <조건>에 맞게 영작하시오.

싱크대 안에 접시들이 있다.

<조건>   1. dishes, in the sink를 활용하시오.
         2. 6단어로 쓰시오.

= _____.

Chapter 02 일반동사

UNIT 01 일반동사의 현재형

Answers p.21

A 괄호 안에서 알맞은 것을 고르시오.

1 Ms. White (fixes / fixies) cars well.

2 They (love / loves) fast food very much.

3 Jim (carrys / carries) a tumbler every day.

4 The teacher (has / haves) special gifts for students.

B <보기>에서 알맞은 동사를 한 번씩만 골라 현재형으로 바꿔 빈칸에 쓰시오.

<보기>	cry	practice	look	eat	live

1 This tomato _____ fresh and delicious.

2 The cat _____ loudly at night.

3 Blue whales _____ in many oceans.

4 She _____ the violin for the contest.

5 We usually _____ lunch together at school.

C 밑줄 친 부분이 어법상 맞으면 O를 쓰고, 틀리면 바르게 고쳐 쓰시오.

1 He <u>posts</u> pictures on his blog.　　　　→ _____

2 Nicole <u>plaies</u> computer games on weekends.　→ _____

3 Mr. Harris <u>teachs</u> art at a high school.　　→ _____

4 I <u>need</u> a new pencil case.　　　　　→ _____

D 우리말과 같도록 괄호 안의 말을 활용하여 문장을 완성하시오.

1 그들은 차 안에서 안전벨트를 맨다. (they, wear, seat belts)

= _____ in the car.

2 Emily는 주말마다 소풍을 간다. (Emily, go)

= _____ on a picnic every weekend.

3 나의 어머니는 일주일에 한 번 잡지를 사신다. (my mother, buy, a magazine)

= _____ once a week.

4 이 동아리는 토요일마다 가난한 사람들을 돕는다. (this club, help, poor people)

= _____ on Saturdays.

A   괄호 안에서 알맞은 것을 고르시오.

1 The Korean War (began / beginned) in 1950.

2 Matilda (lives / lived) in Australia now.

3 The leaves (fall / fell) so fast last autumn.

4 My roommate (cutted / cut) his hair two weeks ago.

B   <보기>에서 알맞은 동사를 한 번씩만 골라 과거형으로 바꿔 빈칸에 쓰시오.

<보기>   join   arrive   become   tie   catch

1 The bus _____ late today.

2 She _____ her shoelaces.

3 That dog _____ the thief last night.

4 The man _____ a dentist ten years ago.

5 My friend and I _____ the basketball team together.

C   밑줄 친 부분이 어법상 맞으면 O를 쓰고, 틀리면 바르게 고쳐 쓰시오.

1 They <u>do</u> the laundry three days ago.   → _____

2 He <u>told</u> the news to me yesterday.   → _____

3 The chef <u>added</u> onions to the soup an hour ago. → _____

4 Ariana <u>visits</u> the concert hall in 2018.   → _____

5 The customer <u>sent</u> an e-mail last Friday.   → _____

D   우리말과 같도록 괄호 안의 말을 활용하여 문장을 완성하시오.

1 Lenna는 지난달에 새 휴대폰을 샀다. (Lenna, buy, a new cell phone)

= _____ last month.

2 학생들은 과학 수업에서 공룡에 대해 배웠다. (students, learn)

= _____ about dinosaurs in science class.

3 Clark씨는 오늘 아침에 너무 많은 커피를 마셨다. (Mr. Clark, drink, too much coffee)

= _____ this morning.

A 괄호 안에서 알맞은 것을 고르시오.

1 (Do / Does) she take the bus to work?

2 I (don't / didn't) close the window last night.

3 Isaac didn't (sing / sang) a song at the festival.

4 They (don't / doesn't) know the answer for the quiz.

5 (Does / Did) Charlie wipe the blackboard five minutes ago?

B 괄호 안의 동사를 활용하여 대화를 완성하시오.

1 A: _____ Paul _____ the kitchen yesterday? (clean)

　　B: No, _____ _____.

2 A: _____ you _____ swimming? (like)

　　B: Yes, _____ _____. I'm a good swimmer.

3 A: _____ Charlotte _____ her teeth this morning? (brush)

　　B: Yes, _____ _____. I saw her in the bathroom.

4 A: _____ they _____ in Seoul? (live)

　　B: No, _____ _____. They live in New York.

C 밑줄 친 부분이 어법상 맞으면 O를 쓰고, 틀리면 바르게 고쳐 쓰시오.

1 Mina didn't like the actor last year.　　　　→ _____

2 I don't go to the hospital yesterday.　　　　→ _____

3 Do Tina and Lola have some money now?　　　→ _____

4 Does she spends time with her family on holidays? → _____

D 우리말과 같도록 괄호 안의 말을 알맞게 배열하시오.

1 너의 개는 낯선 사람들에게 짖니? (your dog, does, bark)

　　= _____ at strangers?

2 그는 1분 전에 계단을 달려 내려갔니? (he, run, did)

　　= _____ down the stairs a minute ago?

3 나의 친구들은 나의 생일을 잊지 않았다. (not, my birthday, did, my friends, forget)

　　= _____.

4 야구 선수들은 공을 발로 차지 않는다. (do, the ball, kick, baseball players, not)

　　= _____.

Chapter Test +

Answers p.21

1 다음 중 동사의 3인칭 단수 현재형이 <u>잘못된</u> 것은?

① say – saies ② laugh – laughs

③ do – does ④ miss – misses

⑤ arrive – arrives

2 다음 중 동사의 과거형이 <u>잘못된</u> 것을 <u>모두</u> 고르시오.

① hope – hoped ② marry – married

③ keep – keeped ④ cost – costed

⑤ drop – dropped

[3-4] 다음 빈칸에 들어갈 알맞은 것을 고르시오.

3

_____ jogs at the park on Mondays.

① They ② I ③ You

④ My dad ⑤ Ann and Josh

4

Mr. Shore doesn't live with his sister. He _____ with his brother.

① live ② lives ③ lived

④ don't live ⑤ didn't live

[5-6] 다음 빈칸에 들어갈 말이 순서대로 짝지어진 것을 고르시오.

5

• I _____ my face every morning.
• Bart _____ a skateboard very well.

① wash – ride ② wash – rides

③ washes – ride ④ washes – rides

⑤ washs – ride

6

• She _____ to the beach yesterday.
• My parents _____ vitamins every day.

① go – take ② goes – take

③ went – take ④ goes – takes

⑤ went – takes

7 다음 우리말을 알맞게 영작한 것은?

Nate는 지난 금요일에 개를 산책시키지 않았다.

① Nate walked the dog last Friday.

② Nate doesn't walk the dog last Friday.

③ Nate don't walk the dog last Friday.

④ Nate didn't walk the dog last Friday.

⑤ Nate didn't walked the dog last Friday.

서술형

[8-10] 다음 빈칸에 알맞은 말을 넣어 질문에 대한 대답을 완성하시오.

8
A: Did she lock the door last night?
B: Yes, _____ _____ .

9
A: Does Thomas play tennis?
B: No, _____ _____ .

10
A: Did Paul and Carol find the shop?
B: No, _____ _____ .

[11-12] 다음 중 어법상 바른 것을 고르시오.

11 ① Jack want that backpack.
② My father checks his car yesterday.
③ We study English every day.
④ Ms. Nelson bakes the cookies an hour ago.
⑤ These ducks lives in the pond.

12 ① I doesn't watch scary movies.
② Do they visit the museum last Wednesday?
③ Fred don't know my name.
④ Do you have toothpaste and a toothbrush?
⑤ The neighbors don't make a noise last night.

서술형

[13-14] 우리말과 같도록 괄호 안의 말을 알맞게 배열하시오.

13
Kelly는 그녀의 일기를 쓰지 않는다. (not, does, write, Kelly)

= _____ in her diary.

14
너는 어제 그 꽃병을 깼니? (the vase, break, you, did)

= _____ yesterday?

서술형

[15-17] 다음 문장에서 틀린 부분을 바르게 고쳐 완전한 문장을 쓰시오.

15
Kevin told an interesting story to us.
→ _____ .

16
Penguins doesn't fly in the sky.
→ _____ .

17
Do they speaks Spanish in Mexico?
→ _____ ?

18 다음 중 자연스럽지 <u>않은</u> 대화는?

① A: Do you exercise at the gym?
　B: Yes, I do.
② A: Did she run in the hall?
　B: Yes, she does.
③ A: Does Billy walk home?
　B: No, he doesn't. He takes the subway.
④ A: Did I miss the class?
　B: No, you didn't.
⑤ A: Do they like Japanese food?
　B: No, they don't. They like Chinese food.

서술형　고난도

19 다음 글의 밑줄 친 ⓐ~ⓔ 중 어법상 어색한 것을 찾아 기호를 쓰고 바르게 고쳐 쓰시오.

> Yesterday, Michael ⓐ<u>buyed</u> a smartphone.
> He ⓑ<u>talked</u> on the phone with his friends.
> And he ⓒ<u>played</u> mobile games all night. He
> ⓓ<u>doesn't go</u> to bed early, so he ⓔ<u>woke</u> up
> late this morning.

(1) _____ → _____
(2) _____ → _____

고난도

20 다음 중 어법상 <u>어색한</u> 것끼리 묶인 것은?

> ⓐ We enjoied our time at the festival.
> ⓑ Did your brother cook dinner yesterday?
> ⓒ Owen put some salt in his soup.
> ⓓ Ashley not caught the baseball.
> ⓔ Does the dolphins live in the river?

① ⓐ, ⓑ, ⓒ　　② ⓐ, ⓑ, ⓓ　　③ ⓐ, ⓓ, ⓔ
④ ⓑ, ⓒ, ⓔ　　⑤ ⓒ, ⓓ, ⓔ

서술형

[21-25] 우리말과 같도록 괄호 안의 말을 활용하여 문장을 완성하시오.

21
> Collin은 비밀을 잘 지키지 않는다. (keep secrets)

= Collin _____ well.

22
> Smith 선생님은 수학을 가르치신다. (teach math)

= Ms. Smith _____ .

23
> 나의 아버지는 오후에 신문을 읽으셨다. 나의 여동생은 그녀의 숙제를 했다. (read a newspaper, do her homework)

= My father _____ in the afternoon. My sister _____ .

24
> 학교 도서관은 지난 토요일에 문을 열지 않았다. (open)

= The school library _____ last Saturday.

25
> 그 축구팀은 2년 전에 결승전을 이겼다. (win the final game)

= The soccer team _____ two years ago.

Chapter 03 시제

UNIT 01   현재시제와 과거시제

Answers p.22

A   괄호 안에서 알맞은 것을 고르시오.

1   I (visit / visited) the bank yesterday.

2   Birds (have / had) wings and feathers.

3   The students (learn / learned) taekwondo last week.

4   Helen Keller (meets / met) Ms. Sullivan in 1887.

5   The tulip (is / was) the national flower of the Netherlands.

B   <보기>의 동사를 한 번씩만 활용하여 빈칸에 쓰시오.

| <보기>   turn   invite   need   walk |

1   Neil Armstrong _____ on the Moon in 1969.

2   Rain _____ to snow at 0℃.

3   Harry _____ me to his birthday party two weeks ago.

4   We _____ new musical instruments now.

C   밑줄 친 부분이 어법상 맞으면 O를 쓰고, 틀리면 바르게 고쳐 쓰시오.

1   The girls chat about the drama yesterday.   → _____

2   Bears sleep for several months in winter.   → _____

3   The Korean War ends in 1953.   → _____

4   Katherine is my neighbor. She lived next to my house.   → _____

D   우리말과 같도록 괄호 안의 말을 활용하여 문장을 완성하시오.

1   그 버스는 매일 6시에 떠난다. (the bus, leave)

= _____ at 6 every day.

2   Diaz씨는 작년에 그의 첫 번째 사업을 시작했다. (Mr. Diaz, start)

= _____ his first business last year.

3   나의 누나는 금요일마다 집에 늦게 온다. (my sister, come)

= _____ home late on Fridays.

4   나는 3일 전에 그 만화 영화를 봤다. (I, watch)

= _____ the animation three days ago.

A 괄호 안에서 알맞은 것을 고르시오.

1 Tim and Tina will (taking / take) a walk after lunch.

2 (Is / Will) Daniel going to change his mind?

3 I'm (go / going) to be with you this weekend.

4 The teacher is (not going / going not) to tell the story to us.

5 Janet (isn't / won't) go to church tomorrow.

B 다음 문장을 괄호 안의 말을 활용하여 미래시제로 바꿔 쓰시오.

1 Do they eat out on weekends? (be going to)

→ _____ out this weekend?

2 Are you free now? (will)

→ _____ free next week?

3 Paul practices yoga every morning. (be going to)

→ _____ yoga tomorrow.

4 She doesn't clean her room every day. (will)

→ _____ her room tonight.

C 우리말과 같도록 괄호 안의 동사를 활용하여 빈칸에 쓰시오.

1 나는 이번 일요일에 런던으로 떠날 것이다. (leave)

= I _____ _____ _____ _____ for London this Sunday.

2 그 서점은 다음 주말에 문을 열지 않을 것이다. (open)

= The bookstore _____ _____ next weekend.

3 Helen은 내일 그녀의 어머니를 도울 거니? (help)

= _____ Helen _____ _____ _____ her mother tomorrow?

D 우리말과 같도록 괄호 안의 말을 알맞게 배열하시오.

1 Susan은 그 시험을 위해 밤을 샐 거니? (will, stay, Susan)

= _____ up all night for the exam?

2 대통령은 오늘 오후에 비행기를 탈 것이다. (the president, take, will, an airplane)

= _____ this afternoon.

3 그는 나의 생일에 컵케이크를 만들지 않을 것이다. (is, he, cupcakes, not, make, going to)

= _____ on my birthday.

UNIT 03 진행시제

A 괄호 안에서 알맞은 것을 고르시오.

1 Is she (tying / tie) the ribbon?

2 (Did / Were) Luke and Anna washing their hands?

3 A police officer was (chasing / chaseing) a thief.

4 I (don't / am not) talking to Gary.

5 It (is / was) snowing yesterday, but it (is / was) raining now.

B 다음 문장을 진행시제로 바꿔 쓰시오.

1 The elephant swims in the lake.

→ _____ in the lake.

2 They didn't play soccer last night.

→ _____ soccer last night.

3 Did he have a good time yesterday?

→ _____ a good time yesterday?

C 우리말과 같도록 괄호 안의 말을 활용하여 문장을 완성하시오.

1 너의 형은 지금 아침 식사를 요리하고 있니? (your brother, cook)

= _____ breakfast now?

2 그 운동선수들은 신호를 기다리고 있었다. (the athletes, wait)

= _____ for the signal.

3 나는 오리들에게 먹이를 주고 있지 않다. (I, feed)

= _____ the ducks.

D 우리말과 같도록 괄호 안의 말을 알맞게 배열하시오.

1 그 가수들은 무대 위에서 노래하고 있지 않다. (singing, are, the singers, not)

= _____ on the stage.

2 그는 도끼를 이용해서 나무를 베고 있다. (is, he, cutting)

= _____ trees with an ax.

3 알람은 오늘 아침에 울리고 있지 않았다. (was, the alarm, ringing, not)

= _____ this morning.

[1-2] 다음 중 동사의 V-ing형이 잘못된 것을 고르시오.

1 ① smile – smiling   ② eat – eating
   ③ visit – visiting   ④ run – runing
   ⑤ stay – staying

2 ① be – being   ② sleep – sleeping
   ③ close – closing   ④ die – dieing
   ⑤ plan – planning

[3-4] 다음 빈칸에 들어갈 알맞은 것을 고르시오.

3
| Karen doesn't go to school by bus. She _____ to school by subway every day. |

   ① go   ② goes
   ③ went   ④ will go
   ⑤ is going to go

4
| Thomas Edison _____ the light bulb in 1879. |

   ① invent   ② invents
   ③ invented   ④ will invent
   ⑤ is going to invent

[5-6] 다음 빈칸에 들어갈 말이 순서대로 짝지어진 것을 고르시오.

5
| • Ms. Ford _____ some fruit now. |
| • Alan and I _____ on the phone last night. |

   ① buy – talked   ② is buying – talk
   ③ is buying – talked   ④ was buying – talk
   ⑤ was buying – talking

6
| • They _____ tennis next week. |
| • My dad _____ for the key 30 minutes ago. |

   ① played – looks   ② played – is looking
   ③ played – was looking   ④ will play – is looking
   ⑤ will play – was looking

7 다음 우리말을 알맞게 영작한 것은?

| 아침에 바람이 불고 있었다. |

   ① The wind blows in the morning.
   ② The wind will blow in the morning.
   ③ The wind is going to blow in the morning.
   ④ The wind is blowing in the morning.
   ⑤ The wind was blowing in the morning.

8 다음 빈칸에 들어갈 말로 어색한 것은?

> Jake will go to a concert _____ .

① next week
② tomorrow
③ last year
④ tonight
⑤ soon

9 다음 중 어법상 바른 것은?

① Beth be going to exercise at the gym.
② Mike is riding a bike on the street.
③ We study English last night.
④ I will going to take a train to Busan.
⑤ The song was very popular now.

10 다음 중 자연스럽지 않은 대화는?

① A: Were they eating hotdogs?
　 B: No, they weren't.
② A: Are you going to join the book club?
　 B: Yes, I am.
③ A: Are you boiling the eggs?
　 B: No, I wasn't.
④ A: Will Johnny travel to Europe this year?
　 B: Yes, he will. He is planning a long trip.
⑤ A: Is the teacher writing on the board?
　 B: No, she isn't. She is reading a book.

[11-12] 다음 중 밑줄 친 부분이 어법상 어색한 것을 고르시오.

11 ① I was having an apple for breakfast.
② Are they moving the chairs?
③ The leaves were falling from the tree.
④ Laura and I aren't playing a board game.
⑤ Ms. Riley is washing her car yesterday.

12 ① Is Jane going wear a new shirt?
② The students weren't preparing for the test.
③ Will he make some tea?
④ The cat was hiding under the bed.
⑤ Matt and I are not taking the same class.

[13-14] 다음 빈칸에 공통으로 들어갈 알맞은 것을 고르시오.

13
> • The painter _____ drawing a tiger.
> • Cathy _____ in elementary school last year.

① is
② was
③ are
④ were
⑤ will

14
> • Amy _____ become a great musician.
> • _____ the movie start at 5:30?

① is
② do
③ are
④ were
⑤ will

서술형 고난도
15 우리말과 같도록 주어진 <조건>에 맞게 문장을 완성하시오.

> 너는 오늘 밤에 영화를 볼 거니?

> <조건>　1. watch, a movie를 활용하시오.
> 　　　　2. 7단어로 쓰시오.

= _____ tonight?

[16-17] 다음 대화에서 어법상 어색한 부분을 찾아 쓰고 바르게 고쳐 쓰시오.

16
> *A*: Is Martha baking a cake now?
> *B*: No, she won't. She is baking a pie.

_____ → _____

17
> *A*: Are you going to meeting Erica at the shopping mall?
> *B*: Yes, I am. I am going to buy a hat, and she will buy shoes.

_____ → _____

18 다음 글의 밑줄 친 ⓐ~ⓔ 중 어법상 어색한 것을 찾아 기호를 쓰고 바르게 고쳐 쓰시오.

> Tomorrow, my family ⓐis going to go to a park. My dad ⓑwill fly a kite with me. Sadly, my sister ⓒnot will come with us because she ⓓis going to take a huge test tomorrow. But we ⓔwill have dinner together.

_____ → _____

19 다음 중 어법상 어색한 것끼리 묶인 것은?

> ⓐ He is knowing about the surprise party.
> ⓑ They were walking to school yesterday.
> ⓒ The library won't open next Friday.
> ⓓ Is Tom go to read the newspaper?
> ⓔ My grandfather goes to China in 2001.

① ⓐ, ⓑ, ⓒ   ② ⓐ, ⓑ, ⓓ   ③ ⓐ, ⓓ, ⓔ
④ ⓑ, ⓒ, ⓔ   ⑤ ⓒ, ⓓ, ⓔ

[20-23] 우리말과 같도록 괄호 안의 말을 활용하여 문장을 완성하시오.

20
> 날씨는 매일 바뀐다. (change)

= The weather _____ every day.

21
> 우리는 이번 주말에 캠핑하러 가지 않을 것이다. (will, go camping)

= We _____
this weekend.

22
> 아이들은 잔디 위에 누워있었고, 개는 땅에 구멍을 파고 있었다. (lie, dig a hole)

= The children _____ on the
grass, and the dog _____ in
the ground.

23
> Anderson씨는 지난겨울에 그 코트를 샀다. 그는 지금 그것을 팔고 있다. (buy the coat, sell it)

= Mr. Anderson _____ last
winter. He _____ now.

UNIT 01 can, may

Answers p.23

A 괄호 안에서 가장 알맞은 것을 고르시오.

1 The article (mays / may) not be true.

2 (Can / Be able to) you pass the exam?

3 Daisy couldn't (sleep / slept) yesterday.

4 Bruce wears glasses. He (may / may not) have bad eyesight.

B 밑줄 친 부분의 의미를 <보기>에서 골라 그 기호를 쓰시오.

<보기>   ⓐ ~할 수 있다   ⓑ ~해도 된다   ⓒ ~해주겠니?   ⓓ ~일지도 모른다

1 Monkeys <u>can</u> climb trees well.   [   ]

2 <u>Can</u> you hold my backpack for a minute?   [   ]

3 Jessie <u>may</u> be awake already.   [   ]

4 <u>May</u> I borrow your pencil?   [   ]

C 다음 문장을 괄호 안의 지시대로 바꿔 쓰시오.

1 Marley can fix this machine. (의문문으로)

→ _____ this machine?

2 You may skip lunch today. (부정문으로)

→ _____ lunch today.

3 Jerry and I are able to win this game. (부정문으로)

→ _____ this game.

4 Airplanes could fly high in the 1930s. (부정문으로)

→ _____ high in the 1930s.

D 우리말과 같도록 괄호 안의 동사를 활용하여 빈칸에 쓰시오.

1 내가 너의 컴퓨터를 사용해도 되니? (use)

= _____ _____ _____ your computer?

2 Tom은 혼자서 여행할 수 있다. (travel)

= _____ _____ _____ _____ alone.

3 그들은 어젯밤에 시끄러운 소리를 들을 수 있었다. (hear)

= _____ _____ _____ a loud noise last night.

UNIT 02 must, have to, should

A 밑줄 친 부분이 어법상 맞으면 O를 쓰고, 틀리면 바르게 고쳐 쓰시오.

1 My sister <u>must changes</u> her bad habits.　　　→ _____

2 Peter and Janet <u>doesn't have to</u> do the laundry.　→ _____

3 Henry <u>has to</u> do his best.　　　　　　　　　→ _____

4 They <u>not must eat</u> too many candy bars.　　　→ _____

5 You <u>shouldn't touch</u> the pictures in the gallery.　→ _____

B 괄호 안에서 가장 알맞은 것을 고르시오.

1 She (should / must not) use the stairs. The elevator is broken.

2 This book (must / can't) be boring. The writer is very famous.

3 My brother wakes up late. He (should / shouldn't) set an alarm.

4 That animal has a brown body with black stripes. It (must / must not) be a squirrel.

5 Summer vacation began yesterday. Students (shouldn't / don't have to) go to school.

C must 또는 have to와 괄호 안의 동사를 활용하여 문장을 완성하시오.

1 I _____ a gift for Alex. Today is his birthday. (buy)

2 Ms. Gray lives in a big house. She _____ rich. (be)

3 We have enough time. We _____. (hurry)

4 You _____ around the pool. The floor is slippery. (run)

D 우리말과 같도록 괄호 안의 동사를 활용하여 빈칸에 쓰시오.

1 Ella는 그 버스를 타야 한다. (take)

= _____ _____ _____ _____ the bus.

2 John은 영국에서 왔을 리가 없다. (be)

= _____ _____ _____ from England.

3 그들은 공공장소에서 담배를 피우면 안 된다. (smoke)

= _____ _____ _____ in public places.

4 그녀는 그녀의 남동생을 도와줄 필요가 없다. (help)

= _____ _____ _____ _____ her brother.

[1-2] 다음 빈칸에 들어갈 가장 알맞은 것을 고르시오.

1

| _____ you chop these cucumbers for me? |

① Can   ② May   ③ Must
④ Should   ⑤ Have to

2

| Dry ice is dangerous. You _____ touch it. |

① can   ② may   ③ should
④ must not   ⑤ don't have to

3 다음 밑줄 친 부분과 바꿔 쓸 수 있는 것은?

| Elephants <u>can't</u> jump. They are too heavy. |

① shouldn't   ② may not
③ must not   ④ don't have to
⑤ aren't able to

서술형
[4-5] 다음 문장에서 어법상 어색한 부분을 찾아 쓰고 바르게 고쳐 쓰시오.

4

| It may be not sunny tomorrow. |

_____ → _____

5

| George and Diana has to look after their little brother. |

_____ → _____

서술형
[6-8] 다음 빈칸에 가장 알맞은 말을 <보기>에서 한 번씩만 골라 쓰시오.

| <보기>   could   doesn't have to   should not |

6

| She _____ cook tonight. She will order pizza. |

7

| We _____ talk loudly in the library. |

8

| _____ you lend some money to me? |

9 다음 중 자연스럽지 <u>않은</u> 대화는?

   ① A: Can I use the bathroom?

     B: Yes, you can. It's next to the bedroom.

   ② A: Do you have to go to the dentist?

     B: Yes. I have a toothache.

   ③ A: Is Jason in Korea now?

     B: He can't be in Korea now. He called me from New York last night.

   ④ A: May I come into your office?

     B: No, you may not. Please come in.

   ⑤ A: Must I go there tomorrow?

     B: No, you don't have to.

서술형

[10-11] 우리말과 같도록 괄호 안의 말을 활용하여 문장을 완성하시오.

10
> Amy는 그 TV 쇼를 좋아하지 않을지도 모른다. (like)

= Amy _____ the TV show.

11
> 그들은 나에 대해 걱정할 필요가 없다. (worry)

= They _____ about me.

서술형

12 우리말과 같도록 괄호 안의 말을 알맞게 배열하시오.

> 그는 기차표를 사야 하니? (have, buy, he, does, to, a train ticket)

= _____?

서술형

13 우리말과 같도록 주어진 <조건>에 맞게 문장을 완성하시오.

> 박쥐들은 어둠 속에서 날 수 있다.

> <조건>   1. bats, fly를 활용하시오.
>   2. 5단어로 쓰시오.

= _____ in the dark.

[14-15] 다음 중 밑줄 친 부분의 의미가 나머지 넷과 <u>다른</u> 것을 고르시오.

14 ① You <u>may</u> enter the building.

   ② This movie <u>may</u> be interesting.

   ③ <u>May</u> I drink this orange juice?

   ④ We <u>may</u> take pictures here.

   ⑤ You <u>may</u> try on these jeans.

15 ① Mr. Nelson <u>must</u> be a doctor.

   ② They <u>must</u> arrive at school on time.

   ③ We <u>must</u> wear life jackets on the boat.

   ④ You <u>must</u> come home before 10 P.M.

   ⑤ She <u>must</u> finish her report by Monday.

[16-17] 다음 중 밑줄 친 부분이 어법상 <u>어색한</u> 것을 고르시오.

16 ① Mr. Smith <u>can dance</u> very well.
② Do I <u>have to send</u> this letter?
③ Cindy <u>should apologize</u> to her roommate.
④ <u>May</u> I <u>ask</u> a question about the concert?
⑤ They <u>must not walks</u> on the grass.

17 ① You <u>may play</u> computer games.
② <u>Can</u> we <u>visit</u> your house today?
③ The man <u>must be</u> very shy.
④ Wendy <u>don't have to take</u> the test.
⑤ You <u>should not drop</u> your phone in the water.

18 다음 중 어법상 바른 것끼리 묶인 것은?

ⓐ This book can't be helpful to us.
ⓑ You should brush your hair now.
ⓒ Eric cannot plays the violin.
ⓓ May I pay with a credit card?
ⓔ The child have to go to bed early.

① ⓐ, ⓑ, ⓒ　　② ⓐ, ⓑ, ⓓ　　③ ⓐ, ⓓ, ⓔ
④ ⓑ, ⓒ, ⓔ　　⑤ ⓒ, ⓓ, ⓔ

19 다음 빈칸에 공통으로 들어갈 가장 알맞은 것은?

• You _____ not tell a lie.
• Richard is absent today. He _____ be very sick.

① does　　② have to　　③ can
④ must　　⑤ should

서술형 **고난도**

20 다음 표지판을 보고 알맞은 조동사와 괄호 안의 말을 활용하여 문장을 완성하시오.

(1)　　　　　　　　　　(2)

(1) You _____
here. (turn right)
(2) You _____
at the park. (feed the birds)

서술형

21 다음 문장에서 틀린 부분을 바르게 고쳐 완전한 문장을 쓰시오.

You must throw not out the trash on the street.

→ _____
_____.

서술형 **고난도**

22 다음 대화의 밑줄 친 ⓐ~ⓔ 중 어법상 <u>어색한</u> 것을 찾아 기호를 쓰고 바르게 고쳐 쓰시오.

A: ⓐ<u>May I take</u> your order, sir?
B: ⓑ<u>Could you give</u> me more time? My
friends ⓒ<u>must is</u> late.
A: Of course.
B: Thank you. ⓓ<u>May you bring</u> me some
water? It ⓔ<u>doesn't have to be</u> cold.
A: Sure.

(1) _____ → _____
(2) _____ → _____

UNIT 01 주격 보어가 필요한 동사

A 괄호 안에서 알맞은 것을 고르시오.

1 The siren (tasted / sounded) noisy.

2 I felt (health / healthy) this morning.

3 The actor became (famous / famously) last year.

4 That shadow (looks / looks like) a rabbit.

B <보기>의 동사와 괄호 안의 말을 한 번씩만 활용하여 문장을 완성하시오. (단, 현재형으로 쓰시오.)

<보기>	look	sound	smell	taste

1 The pants _____ on you. (tight)

2 This curry _____. (spicy)

3 Your shampoo _____. (cherries)

4 This song _____ to me. (familiar)

C 우리말과 같도록 괄호 안의 말을 알맞게 배열하시오.

1 이 초콜릿은 박하 같은 맛이 난다. (tastes, mint, like, this chocolate)
= _____.

2 숲은 여름에 푸르게 변한다. (green, turns, the forest)
= _____ in summer.

3 프라이드치킨은 항상 맛있는 냄새가 난다. (smells, fried chicken, delicious)
= _____ all the time.

4 저 양은 솜사탕처럼 보인다. (like, looks, cotton candy, that sheep)
= _____.

D 우리말과 같도록 괄호 안의 말을 활용하여 문장을 완성하시오.

1 그녀는 그녀의 집에서 편안하게 느낀다. (comfortable)
= She _____ in her house.

2 저 도서관은 오래된 장소 같은 냄새가 났다. (an old place)
= That library _____.

3 나의 부모님은 이 사진에서 어리게 보이신다. (young)
= My parents _____ in this picture.

두 개의 목적어가 필요한 동사

Answers p.24

A 괄호 안에서 알맞은 것을 고르시오.

1 Chris will send the information (me / to me) soon.

2 We cooked tomato pasta (to / for) our parents.

3 She will bring (the menu us / us the menu).

4 Dad (found / showed) the bicycle for my sister.

5 Emma will lend (to Todd a pen / a pen to Todd).

B 괄호 안의 말을 활용하여 빈칸에 쓰시오.

1 I gave _____ _____ _____ _____ . (him, a watch)

2 She made _____ _____ _____ . (Alice, some biscuits)

3 They bought _____ _____ _____ _____ _____ . (their mom, a ring)

4 He asked _____ _____ _____ _____ _____ . (his brother, a favor)

C 다음 두 문장의 의미가 같도록 문장을 완성하시오.

1 I taught the alphabet to my cousin.

→ I _____ .

2 The man built his family a small garden.

→ The man _____ .

3 She wrote an e-mail to her boss this morning.

→ She _____ this morning.

4 My aunt read me a fairy tale yesterday.

→ My aunt _____ yesterday.

D 우리말과 같도록 괄호 안의 말을 활용하여 빈칸에 쓰시오.

1 그 마술사는 우리에게 마술을 보여줬다. (show, a trick)

= The magician _____ _____ _____ _____ .

2 Eric의 누나는 그에게 수건을 건네줬다. (pass, the towel)

= Eric's sister _____ _____ _____ _____ .

3 Ava는 그들에게 진실을 말해주지 않을 것이다. (tell, the truth)

= Ava will not _____ _____ _____ .

4 그는 그녀에게 특별한 음식을 요리해줬다. (cook, a special dish)

= He _____ _____ _____ _____ .

UNIT 03 목적격 보어가 필요한 동사

A 괄호 안에서 알맞은 것을 고르시오.

1 His choice made him (poor / poorly).

2 The staff allowed us (entering / to enter) the building.

3 Helen (found / allowed) the board game fun.

4 The teacher wanted the students (to pass / pass) the exam.

B 다음 빈칸에 알맞은 말을 <보기>에서 한 번씩만 골라 쓰시오.

<보기>	darling	warm	to run	to read

1 The coach ordered the players _____ fast.

2 You should keep your body _____.

3 My dad always calls my mom _____.

4 The librarian advised them _____ novels.

C <보기>의 동사와 괄호 안의 말을 한 번씩만 활용하여 대화를 완성하시오.

<보기>	make	find	ask

1 A: Amanda is talking too loudly.
B: I will _____ quiet. (her, be)

2 A: Did you enjoy the meal at the Italian restaurant?
B: Yes. I _____. (eggplants, delicious)

3 A: That movie _____ in 2017. (him, a famous director)
B: I was so proud of him.

D 우리말과 같도록 괄호 안의 말을 활용하여 문장을 완성하시오.

1 Baker씨는 그의 아들에게 많은 물을 마시라고 말했다. (tell, drink)
= Mr. Baker _____ much water.

2 엄마는 내가 빨래를 하기를 원하셨다. (want, do)
= Mom _____ the laundry.

3 Dave는 파티에서 Kate가 예쁘다고 생각했다. (find, pretty)
= Dave _____ at the party.

[1-2] 다음 빈칸에 들어갈 알맞은 것을 고르시오.

1

Joey _____ the salt to his father.

① found　　　② passed　　　③ made
④ asked　　　⑤ bought

2

They expected the store _____ in the morning.

① open　　　② opening　　　③ opens
④ to open　　　⑤ will open

3 다음 빈칸에 들어갈 말이 나머지 넷과 <u>다른</u> 것은?

① Did you cook lunch _____ them?
② You should get a present _____ him.
③ I will send the package _____ Ryan.
④ We found a pretty dress _____ Lisa.
⑤ She's building a snowman _____ the children.

4 다음 (A)~(C)에 들어갈 말이 바르게 짝지어진 것은?

• Mr. Grant __(A)__ a doctor.
• Can you __(B)__ me the dance?
• Hot chocolate tastes __(C)__ on a cold day.

	(A)	(B)	(C)
①	became	show	great
②	sounded	show	great
③	became	show	greatly
④	sounded	advise	greatly
⑤	became	advise	great

5 다음 빈칸에 공통으로 들어갈 알맞은 것은?

• Donna _____ me a sweater.
• The exercise _____ Paul tired.

① gave　　　② advised　　　③ called
④ made　　　⑤ sent

6 다음 중 자연스럽지 <u>않은</u> 대화는?

① A: What do you think about my sofa?
　　B: It looks very comfortable.
② A: Could you lend me your phone?
　　B: Sure.
③ A: Did he write you a letter?
　　B: No. He wrote a letter to Sophie.
④ A: Mom told me to throw out the pizza.
　　B: Right. We ordered it two weeks ago.
⑤ A: The statue looks a turtle.
　　B: Really? That's interesting.

7 다음 중 어법상 <u>어색한</u> 것은?

① Matt gave me his old clothes.
② Can you read me the poem?
③ Did you tell Josh the secret?
④ Gary brought a map his friend.
⑤ Ashley bought some cookies for you.

서술형
8 다음 빈칸에 공통으로 들어갈 알맞은 말을 쓰시오.

• The teacher asked the students _____ finish the test on time.
• Sam told a lie _____ me.

9 다음 우리말을 알맞게 영작한 것을 <u>모두</u> 고르시오.

> 그 직원은 나에게 잃어버린 가방을 찾아줬다.

① The staff found me the lost bag.
② The staff found me to the lost bag.
③ The staff found the lost bag me.
④ The staff found the lost bag of me.
⑤ The staff found the lost bag for me.

10 다음 중 주어진 문장과 문장의 형태가 같은 것은?

> Dan's sister gave him the laptop.

① They want me to become a scientist.
② We bought the candles for Rebecca.
③ The sky is getting dark.
④ Ms. Wilson teaches us history.
⑤ People call him an artist.

11 다음 중 밑줄 친 부분의 쓰임이 나머지 넷과 <u>다른</u> 것은?

① Ted <u>made</u> the kids hamburgers.
② Ginny <u>made</u> her mother a birthday card.
③ My uncle <u>made</u> me a tree house.
④ Ms. Robinson <u>made</u> us colorful socks.
⑤ The soccer team <u>made</u> him a captain.

서술형

12 다음 문장에서 어법상 <u>어색한</u> 부분을 찾아 쓰고 바르게 고쳐 쓰시오.

> Seat belts keep drivers safely.

_____ → _____

서술형

[13-14] 다음 두 문장의 의미가 같도록 알맞은 전치사를 이용하여 문장을 완성하시오.

13

> Mr. Clemens sent them the message.
> → Mr. Clemens sent _____.

14

> The news reporter asked Sarah some questions.
> → The news reporter asked _____
> _____.

서술형 고난도

15 다음 글에서 어법상 <u>어색한</u> 부분을 찾아 쓰고 바르게 고쳐 쓰시오.

> Yesterday, George found his old sneakers in the drawer. They smelled really bad, so his mother told him wash them.

_____ → _____

16 다음 중 어법상 바른 것을 <u>모두</u> 고르시오.

① They call Martin a genius.
② The apple turned brown after five minutes.
③ Brian sounded angrily last night.
④ We taught some tricks the dog.
⑤ The judge ordered her pay $500.

서술형

[17-18] 우리말과 같도록 괄호 안의 말을 활용하여 문장을 완성하시오.

17
> 이 핫도그는 맛있는 냄새가 난다. (delicious)

= This hot dog _____ .

18
> 그는 나에게 침대를 정리할 것을 요청했다. (ask, make the bed)

= He _____ .

서술형 **고난도**

19 다음 대화의 밑줄 친 ⓐ~ⓔ 중 어법상 어색한 것을 찾아 기호를 쓰고 바르게 고쳐 쓰시오.

> A: I feel ⓐthirsty.
> B: I can make some lemonade ⓑto you.
> A: Great! I want it ⓒbe very sour.
> B: Then I'll put less sugar in it. Sugar will make it ⓓsweet.
> A: Thanks. And please ⓔteach me the recipe.
> B: Sure.

(1) _____ → _____

(2) _____ → _____

서술형

[20-21] 우리말과 같도록 괄호 안의 말을 알맞게 배열하시오.

20
> Eric은 우리에게 그의 그림을 보여줬다. (his painting, showed, Eric, us)

= _____ .

21
> 창문을 열어놓아 주겠니? (the window, keep, you, open, can)

= _____ ?

서술형 **고난도**

[22-23] 우리말과 같도록 주어진 <조건>에 맞게 영작하시오.

22
> 나의 여동생은 그들에게 파스타를 요리해줬다.

> <조건>
> 1. my sister, cook, pasta를 활용하시오.
> 2. 6단어로 쓰시오.

= _____ .

23
> 엄마는 내가 게임을 하는 것을 허락하셨다.

> <조건>
> 1. mom, allow, play, games를 활용하시오.
> 2. 6단어로 쓰시오.

= _____ .

고난도

24 다음 중 어법상 어색한 것끼리 묶인 것은?

> ⓐ Mr. Hall gave a necklace to his wife.
> ⓑ The news made them sadly.
> ⓒ James bought a cupcake Irene.
> ⓓ The doctor advised me to take a break.
> ⓔ The air smells differently on rainy days.

① ⓐ, ⓑ, ⓒ   ② ⓐ, ⓑ, ⓓ   ③ ⓐ, ⓓ, ⓔ
④ ⓑ, ⓒ, ⓔ   ⑤ ⓒ, ⓓ, ⓔ

UNIT 01   명령문, 청유문, 감탄문

Answers p.25

A   괄호 안에서 알맞은 것을 고르시오.

1 Don't (leave / leaving) a baby alone.

2 How excellent (the concert was / was the concert)!

3 Drink milk, (or / and) your bones will get strong.

4 (What / How) pretty butterflies they are!

5 (Not let's / Let's not) make the same mistake.

B   다음 문장을 괄호 안의 지시대로 바꿔 쓰시오.

1 You should take a taxi. (명령문으로)   → _____ .

2 It is a very colorful sunset. (감탄문으로)   → _____ !

3 You shouldn't break the rules. (명령문으로)   → _____ .

4 My neighbors are very friendly. (감탄문으로)   → _____ !

C   우리말과 같도록 괄호 안의 말을 알맞게 배열하시오.

1 그 발표에 대해 걱정하지 말자. (worry, let's, not)

= _____ about the presentation.

2 Linda는 정말 똑똑한 소녀구나! (a, what, girl, is, smart, Linda)

= _____ !

3 스마트폰을 오랫동안 사용하지 마라. (use, not, a smartphone, do)

= _____ for a long time.

D   우리말과 같도록 괄호 안의 말을 활용하여 문장을 완성하시오.

1 그 발레리나는 정말 훌륭하게 공연했구나! (wonderfully)

= _____ the ballerina performed!

2 오후 6시 전에 우리의 숙제를 끝내자. (finish our homework)

= _____ before 6 P.M.

3 빠르게 운전해주세요, 그렇지 않으면 저는 늦을 거예요. (drive fast)

= _____ , _____ I will be late.

A　괄호 안에서 알맞은 것을 고르시오.

1 Is Julia's birthday in May (or / and) in July?

2 (Wasn't / Didn't) that truck in the garage?

3 You gave flowers to the teacher, (don't / didn't) you?

4 A: Didn't he bring an umbrella?
　　B: No, he (did / didn't).

B　다음 빈칸에 알맞은 말을 넣어 부가의문문과 그에 대한 대답을 완성하시오.

1 A: They heard the news, ＿＿＿＿＿ ＿＿＿＿＿?　B: No, ＿＿＿＿＿ ＿＿＿＿＿.

2 A: Reina can't understand English, ＿＿＿＿＿ ＿＿＿＿＿?　B: Yes, ＿＿＿＿＿ ＿＿＿＿＿.

3 A: You and your sister were at church, ＿＿＿＿＿ ＿＿＿＿＿?　B: No, ＿＿＿＿＿ ＿＿＿＿＿.

C　우리말과 같도록 괄호 안의 동사를 활용하여 빈칸에 쓰시오.

1 Annie는 어제 파티에 오지 않았니? (come)
　= ＿＿＿＿＿ ＿＿＿＿＿ ＿＿＿＿＿ to the party yesterday?

2 너는 영화를 볼 거니, 아니면 뮤지컬을 볼 거니? (watch)
　= ＿＿＿＿＿ ＿＿＿＿＿ ＿＿＿＿＿ a movie ＿＿＿＿＿ a musical?

3 그는 정원에 꽃을 심고 있지 않니? (plant)
　= ＿＿＿＿＿ ＿＿＿＿＿ ＿＿＿＿＿ flowers in the garden?

4 Albert는 고기와 채소 중 어느 것을 더 좋아하니? (like)
　= ＿＿＿＿＿ ＿＿＿＿＿ ＿＿＿＿＿ ＿＿＿＿＿ better, meat ＿＿＿＿＿ vegetables?

D　우리말과 같도록 괄호 안의 말을 알맞게 배열하시오.

1 오늘 밤에는 운동하지 말자, 어떠니? (we, exercise, let's, shall, not)
　= ＿＿＿＿＿＿＿＿＿＿ tonight, ＿＿＿＿＿＿＿＿＿＿?

2 경찰관들은 너의 집을 방문하지 않았어, 그렇지? (didn't, your house, did, police officers, visit, they)
　= ＿＿＿＿＿＿＿＿＿＿, ＿＿＿＿＿＿＿＿＿＿?

3 너는 야구와 농구 중 어느 것을 더 많이 하니? (do, baseball, basketball, or, you, which, play more)
　= ＿＿＿＿＿＿＿＿＿＿, ＿＿＿＿＿＿＿＿＿＿?

[1-3] 다음 대화의 빈칸에 들어갈 알맞은 것을 고르시오.

1

> A: _____ wrote this article?
> B: Rebecca wrote it.

① Who   ② Whom   ③ Whose
④ Where   ⑤ What

2

> A: _____ visit our grandparents next weekend.
> B: Sure. I miss them so much.

① Let   ② Let's   ③ How
④ What about   ⑤ Why don't

3

> A: _____ time does the train leave?
> B: It leaves at 12 P.M.

① Who   ② When   ③ What
④ Which   ⑤ How

4 다음 빈칸에 들어갈 말이 순서대로 짝지어진 것은?

> • _____ is more expensive, the gold ring or the silver ring?
> • _____ bicycle is this?

① Which – Who   ② What – Whose
③ Which – Whom   ④ What – Who
⑤ Which – Whose

5 다음 중 어법상 어색한 것은?

① Let's join the soccer team.
② Don't you eat seafood?
③ Let's not go to the swimming pool.
④ Please not do close the windows.
⑤ Throw out the trash now, or it will smell bad.

서술형

[6-7] 다음 문장을 감탄문으로 바꿔 쓰시오.

6

> Their cat is very friendly.
> → _____ _____ their cat is!

7

> It is a really fantastic novel.
> → _____ _____ _____ _____!

8 다음 빈칸에 들어갈 알맞은 질문은?

> A: _____
> B: I watched it last night.

① How did you watch the movie?
② Where did you watch the movie?
③ When did you watch the movie?
④ How often do you watch the movie?
⑤ Why did you watch the movie?

9 다음 우리말을 알맞게 영작한 것은?

> 코끼리는 얼마나 무겁니?

① How much is an elephant?
② How far is an elephant?
③ How old is an elephant?
④ How long is an elephant?
⑤ How heavy is an elephant?

10 다음 중 어법상 바른 것을 <u>모두</u> 고르시오.

① Do not bothers your older sister.
② Not let's forget our history.
③ Be polite to everyone.
④ Get up now, and you won't have breakfast.
⑤ How did he catch the fish?

11 다음 빈칸에 들어갈 말이 나머지 넷과 <u>다른</u> 것은?

① _____ fresh the salad is!
② _____ is your mother holding?
③ _____ a lovely house it is!
④ _____ fruit do you like?
⑤ _____ expensive bags!

12 다음 중 자연스럽지 <u>않은</u> 대화는?

① A: Where do you live?
  B: I live in South Korea.
② A: How often do you meet Erica?
  B: She was watching TV five minutes ago.
③ A: Karen bought dinner, didn't she?
  B: Yes, she did. She bought dessert, too.
④ A: Was this book boring or interesting?
  B: It was so boring.
⑤ A: What are they looking for?
  B: They are looking for a frog.

[13-15] 우리말과 같도록 괄호 안의 말을 알맞게 배열하시오.

13
> 너는 무슨 악기를 좋아하니? (musical instrument, you, what, like, do)

= _____ ?

14
> 이것은 정말 어려운 퍼즐이구나! (puzzle, difficult, this, what, is, a)

= _____ !

15
> 잔디 위에서 걷지 마라. (on the grass, walk, don't)

= _____ .

[16-17] 다음 문장에서 어법상 어색한 부분을 찾아 쓰고 바르게 고쳐 쓰시오.

16
> Aaron will write in his diary tonight, isn't he?

_____ → _____

17
> Victoria didn't fight with her friend yesterday, does she?

_____ → _____

18 다음 대화에서 어법상 어색한 부분을 찾아 쓰고 바르게 고쳐 쓰시오.

> A: Don't you need a new cell phone?
> B: Yes, I don't. I bought a new one last week.

_____ → _____

[19-22] 우리말과 같도록 괄호 안의 말을 활용하여 문장을 완성하시오.

19
> 에어컨을 끄지 말자. (turn off the air conditioner)

= _____ .

20
> 그들은 그 경기를 이겼어, 그렇지 않니? (win the game)

= They _____, _____ ?

21
> 너는 이번 주말에 캠핑하러 가는 게 어때? (you, go camping)

= _____
this weekend?

22
> 우리 세계 일주를 하지 않겠니? (we, travel around the world)

= _____ ?

23 다음 중 어법상 바른 것끼리 묶인 것은?

> ⓐ How a hot the weather is!
> ⓑ Let's not stay at this hotel.
> ⓒ What small hands the baby has!
> ⓓ Be careful with the vases, will we?
> ⓔ Who sends a letter to you every day?

① ⓐ, ⓑ, ⓒ   ② ⓐ, ⓑ, ⓓ   ③ ⓐ, ⓓ, ⓔ
④ ⓑ, ⓒ, ⓔ   ⑤ ⓒ, ⓓ, ⓔ

24 다음 대화의 밑줄 친 ⓐ~ⓔ 중 어법상 어색한 것을 찾아 기호를 쓰고 바르게 고쳐 쓰시오.

> A: ⓐ How pretty flowers they are!
> B: They are beautiful, ⓑ aren't they?
> A: Yes, they are. ⓒ What flowers are they?
> B: They are roses. Please ⓓ don't touch them. They have thorns.
> A: Okay. ⓔ What do you like better, pink roses or yellow roses?
> B: I like pink ones better.

(1) _____ → _____
(2) _____ → _____

[25-26] 다음 빈칸에 공통으로 들어갈 알맞은 말을 쓰시오.

25
> • _____ fast the rabbit runs!
> • _____ tall is Mr. Brown?

26
> • Wear your coat, _____ you will be cold.
> • Are these your shoes _____ your brother's shoes?

Chapter 07 명사와 관사

UNIT 01 셀 수 있는 명사와 셀 수 없는 명사

Answers p.27

A 괄호 안에서 알맞은 것을 고르시오.

1 (Love / A love) makes us happy.

2 Tina is playing with (doll / a doll) now.

3 This rock will turn to (sand / sands) someday.

4 (Knife / Knives) are dangerous for children.

5 He is going to work in (Seoul / a Seoul).

B 밑줄 친 부분이 어법상 맞으면 O를 쓰고, 틀리면 바르게 고쳐 쓰시오.

1 I broke two dishs yesterday.   → _____

2 Paul has four pieces of paper.   → _____

3 The nurse took care of three babyes.   → _____

4 My mother bought a bottle of orange juices.   → _____

5 The zookeeper prepared ten fish for penguins.   → _____

C <보기>의 단위명사와 괄호 안의 명사를 활용하여 문장을 완성하시오.

<보기>	pair	glass	bowl	slice

1 I added a _____ on my burger. (cheese)

2 Steve gave three _____ to his cousins. (shoes)

3 She ate two _____ for breakfast. (corn soup)

4 The man served four _____. (milk)

D 우리말과 같도록 괄호 안의 말을 활용하여 문장을 완성하시오.

1 농장에 황소 아홉 마리가 있다. (be, ox)

= There _____ _____ on the farm.

2 그는 가구 네 점을 옮겼다. (move, furniture)

= He _____.

3 Gwen은 그녀의 미래에 대한 조언이 필요하다. (need, advice)

= Gwen _____ about her future.

4 그 화가는 파란색 페인트 세 캔을 사용했다. (use, blue paint)

= The painter _____.

UNIT 02 관사

Answers p.27

A 다음 빈칸에 a(n)과 the 중 알맞은 것을 쓰고, 필요하지 않으면 X를 쓰시오.

1 Brandon is practicing _____ trumpet.

2 There are seven days in _____ week.

3 She has _____ dinner at 6 P.M.

4 The students go on a field trip twice _____ year.

5 There is _____ onion in the fridge. Can you cut _____ onion in half?

B 밑줄 친 부분이 어법상 맞으면 O를 쓰고, 틀리면 바르게 고쳐 쓰시오.

1 Mr. Nelson became <u>a doctor</u> in 2010.　　　→ _____

2 <u>Table</u> in the kitchen is very old.　　　　　→ _____

3 I arrived at the airport by <u>a taxi</u>.　　　　　→ _____

4 You should not look at <u>the sun</u> directly.　　→ _____

5 She already finished her homework <u>a hour</u> ago.　→ _____

C 괄호 안의 명사를 활용하여 대화를 완성하시오.

1 A: Is Anna in her bedroom now?
　B: Yes, she is. She is studying _____ now. (science)

2 A: Where are we going to meet this weekend?
　B: Let's meet at _____. (park)

3 A: Can you send me his address by _____? (text message)
　B: Sure. Wait for a minute.

4 A: Pandas eat 14 hours _____. (day)
　B: Wow, they eat for a long time.

D 우리말과 같도록 괄호 안의 말을 활용하여 문장을 완성하시오.

1 그 문을 열어주겠니? (open, door)
　= Can you _____ ?

2 그는 작년에 엔지니어 한 명과 함께 일했다. (work with, engineer)
　= He _____ last year.

3 Isabel과 나는 주말마다 테니스를 친다. (play, tennis)
　= Isabel and I _____ every weekend.

Chapter Test +

Answers p.27

[1-2] 다음 중 명사의 복수형이 <u>잘못된</u> 것을 고르시오.

1
① party – parties　② roof – roofs
③ leaf – leaves　④ video – videoes
⑤ window – windowes

2
① woman – women　② pencil – pencils
③ watch – watches　④ tooth – tooths
⑤ piano – pianos

서술형

[3-5] 다음 빈칸에 알맞은 말을 <보기>에서 한 번씩만 골라 쓰시오. (단, X는 필요 없음을 의미함)

> <보기>　a　　the　　X

3
> There is _____ police officer at the corner.

4
> The students in this school eat _____ lunch at 12:30.

5
> I will travel _____ world on foot.

[6-7] 다음 빈칸에 들어갈 말로 <u>어색한</u> 것을 <u>모두</u> 고르시오.

6
> Kelly wants a bowl of _____ now.

① cereal　② rice
③ cake　④ cheese pizza
⑤ potato soup

7
> _____ are in the refrigerator.

① Salt　② Pumpkins
③ Chocolate milk　④ Two cans of coke
⑤ Four bottles of juice

8　다음 우리말을 알맞게 영작한 것은?

> 냄비에 물 세 잔을 넣어라.

① Put three water in the pot.
② Put three waters in the pot.
③ Put three glass of waters in the pot.
④ Put three glasses of water in the pot.
⑤ Put three glasses of waters in the pot.

서술형

9　다음 빈칸에 공통으로 들어갈 알맞은 관사를 쓰시오.

> • Can I eat _____ hamburger? You look full.
> • The orchestra will play _____ songs on the list.

10 주어진 문장의 밑줄 친 a와 쓰임이 같은 것은?

> Robert runs in a marathon once a month.

① There is a star near the moon.
② We will watch a movie after school.
③ I walk my dog twice a day.
④ Ms. Bryant is a famous designer.
⑤ The chef is cooking a chicken.

11 다음 중 밑줄 친 부분이 어법상 바른 것은?

① The man stole three loaves of breads.
② We need four slice of cheeses for the recipe.
③ Ms. Hall bought a pieces of furniture.
④ Jessica drank two glasses of milk.
⑤ The students borrowed five pair of scissors.

[12-13] 다음 중 밑줄 친 부분이 어법상 어색한 것을 고르시오.

12 ① James caught fishes at the beach.
② Seoul is a beautiful city.
③ There were five potatoes in the plastic bag.
④ Can you take some photos of me?
⑤ I had a piece of cake on my birthday.

13 ① I found a belt in the drawer.
② They went to Jejudo by ship.
③ The book about flowers was useful.
④ You should do the yoga for your health.
⑤ Ben is flying a kite.

[14-15] 괄호 안의 말을 활용하여 대화를 완성하시오.

14
> A: What will you buy?
> B: I'll buy two _____. (can, soda)

15
> A: Look at _____ in _____!
>   (airplane, sky)
> B: Wow, it is so fast!

[16-17] 다음 문장에서 어법상 어색한 부분을 찾아 쓰고 바르게 고쳐 쓰시오.

16
> My cousins and I are going to play the hockey next week.

_____ → _____

17
> You should clean the fish tank once the month.

_____ → _____

18 다음 중 밑줄 친 명사의 성격이 나머지 넷과 다른 것은?

① You should listen to my advice.
② The Golden Gate Bridge isn't in England.
③ Mr. Evans brought a frog to his science class.
④ The children made a castle with sand.
⑤ There are some sheep in the field.

서술형 **고난도**

19 다음 대화에서 어법상 어색한 부분을 찾아 쓰고 바르게 고쳐 쓰시오.

> A: Are you preparing for dinner?
> B: Yes. I'm making two bowls of soup.
> A: Great. Do you need a help?
> B: Yes. Please pass me the carrot.
> A: Here you go.

_____ → _____

서술형

[20-22] 우리말과 같도록 괄호 안의 말을 활용하여 문장을 완성하시오.

20
> 교실에 있는 아이들은 종이 한 장에 그림을 그리고 있었다. (child, paper)

= _____ in the classroom were drawing pictures on _____ .

21
> 나는 공책 한 권을 잃어버렸다. 그 공책은 새것이었다. (notebook)

= I lost _____ . _____ was new.

22
> 역사는 흥미로운 과목이다. 오늘, 우리는 서울의 역사에 대해 배웠다. (history)

= _____ is an interesting subject. Today, we learned about _____ of Seoul.

고난도

23 다음 중 밑줄 친 부분이 어법상 바른 것끼리 묶인 것은?

> ⓐ I visited the museum by <u>bus</u>.
> ⓑ Can you read <u>the sentence</u> in the textbook?
> ⓒ Jim went to <u>bed</u> early. He is sick.
> ⓓ Mr. Williams is holding <u>a empty box</u>.
> ⓔ George played <u>guitar</u> on the stage.

① ⓐ, ⓑ, ⓒ ② ⓐ, ⓒ, ⓓ ③ ⓐ, ⓓ, ⓔ
④ ⓑ, ⓒ, ⓔ ⑤ ⓑ, ⓓ, ⓔ

고난도

24 다음 중 밑줄 친 부분이 어법상 바른 것을 모두 고르시오.

> Yesterday, my friends and I went to ①café. Mike ordered a ②glass of orange juice. Jenna had three ③piece of breads. I drank two ④green teas. ⑤The café was quiet and peaceful, so we will go there again.

서술형 **고난도**

25 다음 글에서 어법상 어색한 부분을 찾아 쓰고 바르게 고쳐 쓰시오.

> Sophie and her father climbed a mountain an week ago. They brought a bottle of water, two cucumbers, and three tomatos. The weather was great, so they were happy.

(1) _____ → _____
(2) _____ → _____

UNIT 01   인칭대명사

Answers p.28

A 괄호 안에서 알맞은 것을 고르시오.

1 I wasn't looking at (you / your).

2 He hurt (he / himself) at the playground.

3 I went to the theater. (It's / Its) seats were comfortable.

4 Chris and I live in the same town. (We / They) are best friends.

5 That is not (my / mine) scarf. It is (her / hers).

B 다음 문장의 밑줄 친 부분을 알맞은 인칭대명사로 바꿔 빈칸에 쓰시오.

1 I found a box. _____ was empty.

2 Carol and I saw Nancy, but she couldn't see _____.

3 You were with a girl yesterday. Is she _____ sister?

4 Scott wrote a song about _____.

5 She bought some bananas yesterday. I ate _____ this morning.

C 우리말과 같도록 재귀대명사와 괄호 안의 말을 활용하여 문장을 완성하시오.

1 우리는 우리 자신을 잘 알아야 한다. (know)

= We should _____ well.

2 Margaret은 시험 후에 그녀 자신에게 화가 났다. (be upset with)

= Margaret _____ after the test.

3 그들은 그들 자신을 영웅이라고 불렀다. (call)

= They _____ heroes.

D 우리말과 같도록 괄호 안의 말을 알맞게 배열하시오.

1 너의 교과서는 그의 배낭 안에 있다. (backpack, in, textbook, your, is, his)

= _____.

2 나는 거울 안의 나 자신을 봤다. (myself, looked at, I)

= _____ in the mirror.

3 Amy는 그에게 그녀의 집을 보여줬다. (showed, Amy, her, him, to, house)

= _____.

A   괄호 안에서 알맞은 것을 고르시오.

1   (This / These) is my classmate.

2   Did you taste (that / those) pancakes?

3   (It / That) is February 14 this Friday.

4   His fans gave (this / these) gifts to him.

5   (This / It) will be 25℃ in the afternoon.

6   I can't see (this / that) over there.

B   밑줄 친 it의 쓰임과 같은 것을 <보기>에서 골라 그 기호를 쓰시오.

| <보기>   ⓐ It is very cloudy now.   ⓑ It is my toothbrush. |

1   It will be autumn soon.   [   ]

2   Is it your card or her card?   [   ]

3   I don't like hot sauce. It is too spicy for me.   [   ]

4   It is about five kilometers to my house.   [   ]

C   밑줄 친 부분이 어법상 맞으면 O를 쓰고, 틀리면 바르게 고쳐 쓰시오.

1   Can you see this rainbow on the mountain?   → _____

2   I will take a picture of those buildings.   → _____

3   These is Kate's name tag.   → _____

4   Is this bright inside the room?   → _____

5   My mother cleans these windows on weekends.   → _____

D   우리말과 같도록 괄호 안의 말을 활용하여 문장을 완성하시오.

1   지난주는 11월이었다. (be, November)

= _____ last week.

2   이것들은 나의 장난감들이 아니다. (be, my toys)

= _____ .

3   저 학생들은 오늘 아침에 축구를 했다. (students, play, soccer)

= _____ this morning.

UNIT 03 one, some, any

Answers p.28

A 괄호 안에서 알맞은 것을 고르시오.

1 Do you want (any / some) vanilla ice cream?

2 This small cup is cheap. That large (one / it) is expensive.

3 I bought some comic books. I will read (ones / them) tomorrow.

4 He should change the tires to new (one / ones).

5 Did you see (any / some) stars last night?

B 다음 대화의 빈칸에 알맞은 말을 <보기>에서 한 번씩만 골라 쓰시오.

<보기>	one	ones	some	any

1 *A*: Which do you prefer, sweet fruits or sour fruits? *B*: I prefer sour _____ .

2 *A*: Can you get me _____ water? *B*: Of course.

3 *A*: She couldn't solve _____ math problems. *B*: Were they difficult?

4 *A*: Our store has many types of skirts. *B*: May I try on a short _____ ?

C 밑줄 친 부분이 어법상 맞으면 O를 쓰고, 틀리면 바르게 고쳐 쓰시오.

1 Do you have any advice for me? → _____

2 He uploaded his first video yesterday. I watched one. → _____

3 Dad is making some grape juice now. → _____

4 These sneakers are too tight. Do you have bigger one? → _____

5 This café has hot drinks only. I want a cold it. → _____

D 우리말과 같도록 괄호 안의 말을 활용하여 문장을 완성하시오.

1 John은 그의 지갑에 돈을 전혀 가지고 있지 않다. (have, money)

= John _____ in his wallet.

2 나의 어머니는 수프에 약간의 소금을 추가하셨다. (add, salt)

= My mother _____ to the soup.

3 그는 3년 전에 그의 마지막 시들을 썼다. 그는 곧 새것들을 쓸 것이다. (write, new)

= He wrote his last poems three years ago. He will _____ soon.

Chapter Test +

[1-2] 다음 빈칸에 들어갈 알맞은 것을 고르시오.

1

> Josh and I visited Victoria's house last week.
> She cooked dinner for _____.

① we   ② our   ③ ours
④ us   ⑤ ourselves

2

> Those clothes are not mine. Are they
> _____?

① you   ② your   ③ yours
④ yourself   ⑤ yourselves

[3-4] 다음 빈칸에 들어갈 말이 순서대로 짝지어진 것을 고르시오.

3

> • Jason _____ built the snowman.
> • _____ man in the picture looks sad.

① his – This   ② him – This
③ him – These   ④ himself – This
⑤ himself – These

4

> • Do you want _____ tea?
> • _____ is 3 o'clock in the afternoon.

① some – This   ② some – That
③ some – It   ④ any – That
⑤ any – It

[5-6] 다음 대화의 빈칸에 들어갈 알맞은 것을 고르시오.

5

> A: Do you have a notebook?
> B: Yes. I have _____ in my bag.

① them   ② any   ③ one
④ they   ⑤ it

6

> A: Mary didn't have _____ questions
>   about the test.
> B: Really? She must know everything.

① some   ② any   ③ ones
④ it   ⑤ one

[7-8] 다음 중 밑줄 친 부분이 어법상 어색한 것을 고르시오.

7
① This story is touching.
② Will you help me with my homework?
③ You should keep that shoes in the box.
④ These flowers are roses.
⑤ My hat is yellow, but hers is red.

8
① Are there any coins in your pocket?
② Our neighbor brought us some bread.
③ I won't use any plastics.
④ Do you want some blankets?
⑤ Mr. Klaus bought any snacks yesterday.

9 다음 중 밑줄 친 it의 쓰임이 나머지 넷과 다른 것은?

① It became sunny after the rain.
② Where are you going to eat it?
③ I saw the postcard. It was on the table.
④ It was your plan, wasn't it?
⑤ Bart found a puppy on the street. It was sick.

서술형

[10-13] 우리말과 같도록 괄호 안의 말을 활용하여 문장을 완성하시오.

10

> 이 건물들은 100년이 되었다. (buildings)

= _____ are a hundred years old.

11

> 우리들은 우리 스스로를 자랑스러워 했다. (be proud of)

= We _____ .

12

> 오늘은 수요일이다. (be Wednesday)

= _____ today.

13

> 파스타에 약간의 후추를 넣어라. (pepper)

= Put _____ in the pasta.

서술형

[14-16] 다음 대화의 빈칸에 알맞은 말을 <보기>에서 한 번씩만 골라 쓰시오.

<보기>	one	ones	it

14

> A: Did you read the article about the volcano in Indonesia?
> B: Yes. _____ was so shocking.

15

> A: What color bicycle do you want?
> B: I want a black _____ .

16

> A: Do you need new socks?
> B: No. I bought new _____ last week.

17 다음 중 자연스럽지 않은 대화는?

① A: Are there any benches in your garden?
   B: Yes. There is one under the tree.
② A: Do you want some more noodles?
   B: Yes, please.
③ A: These melons taste sweet.
   B: Right. My father grew themselves.
④ A: Are those your sandwiches?
   B: No. They are David's.
⑤ A: Brenda showed me her new laptop.
   B: I saw it, too. It looked really expensive.

서술형

18 다음 빈칸에 공통으로 들어갈 알맞은 말을 쓰시오.

> · What date was _____ yesterday?
> · I won't buy this sweater. Will you buy
> _____ ?

[22-24] 다음 문장에서 어법상 <u>어색한</u> 부분을 찾아 쓰고 바르게 고쳐 쓰시오.

22
> Mandy invited us to hers birthday party.

_____ → _____

서술형 **고난도**

19 다음 대화에서 어법상 <u>어색한</u> 부분을 찾아 쓰고 바르게 고쳐 쓰시오.

> A: Did you buy a yellow raincoat?
> B: No. The store didn't have any. They only had a white it.

_____ → _____

23
> These book has 256 pages.

_____ → _____

24
> We didn't see some tigers in the jungle.

_____ → _____

20 다음 중 밑줄 친 부분을 생략할 수 있는 것은?

① I drew <u>myself</u> in the sketchbook.
② We can take care of <u>ourselves</u>.
③ You <u>yourself</u> told me the secret.
④ Judy bought a cake for <u>herself</u>.
⑤ The man was talking to <u>himself</u>.

서술형

25 우리말과 같도록 빈칸에 알맞은 말을 쓰시오.

> Hannah는 항상 그녀 자신을 천사라고 부른다.
>
> = Hannah always calls _____ an angel.

서술형 **고난도**

21 다음 대화의 밑줄 친 ⓐ~ⓔ 중 어법상 <u>어색한</u> 것을 찾아 기호를 쓰고 바르게 고쳐 쓰시오.

> A: There are ⓐ<u>any</u> pears and apples in the refrigerator.
> B: They are ⓑ<u>mine</u>. I bought ⓒ<u>it</u> at the farmer's market. Do you want ⓓ<u>some</u>?
> A: Thanks, but I don't like those fruits. I like soft ⓔ<u>ones</u> like strawberries.

(1) _____ → _____
(2) _____ → _____

고난도

26 다음 중 어법상 바른 것끼리 묶인 것은?

> ⓐ The reporter is interviewing some people.
> ⓑ Paul didn't eat any vegetables.
> ⓒ Mr. Graham met her at the art museum.
> ⓓ This is 500 meters from here to my house.
> ⓔ There aren't some people in the hall.

① ⓐ, ⓑ, ⓒ　　② ⓐ, ⓒ, ⓓ　　③ ⓐ, ⓓ, ⓔ
④ ⓑ, ⓒ, ⓔ　　⑤ ⓑ, ⓓ, ⓔ

형용사/부사와 비교구문

UNIT 01 　형용사

Answers p.29

A 　괄호 안에서 알맞은 것을 고르시오.

1 There were (a few / a little) cars in the parking lot.

2 These shoes feel (tight / tightly) to me.

3 Mark doesn't want (many / much) cheese on his pizza.

4 Do you know (smart anyone / anyone smart) in your class?

5 (Much / Lots of) people visited the museum.

B 　밑줄 친 부분이 어법상 맞으면 O를 쓰고, 틀리면 바르게 고쳐 쓰시오.

1 Kelly showed me pictures <u>interesting</u>.　　→ _____

2 Some climbers made this forest <u>dirty</u>.　　→ _____

3 Mr. Franklin is always <u>nicely</u> and friendly.　　→ _____

4 I smelled <u>something bad</u> in the kitchen.　　→ _____

C 　<보기>와 괄호 안의 말을 한 번씩만 활용하여 질문에 대한 대답을 완성하시오.

<보기>　　many　　much　　a few　　little

1 A: Why do you look so tired?　　B: Because I had _____ today. (work)

2 A: Can you lend me some money?　　B: Sorry. I only have _____. (coins)

3 A: Did you buy the ticket easily?　　B: Yes. There were _____. (empty seats)

4 A: Was the book helpful?　　B: No. I got _____. (information)

D 　우리말과 같도록 괄호 안의 말을 알맞게 배열하시오.

1 그들은 나에게 그 놀라운 소식을 말해줬다. (they, the, told, news, surprising)

= _____ to me.

2 Thomas는 어제 약간의 실수를 했다. (a, mistakes, made, Thomas, few)

= _____ yesterday.

3 Wilson씨는 부지런한 누군가를 좋아한다. (someone, Ms. Wilson, diligent, likes)

= _____.

4 많은 학생들이 도서관에서 공부하고 있다. (lot, students, a, of, are studying)

= _____ in the library.

A 괄호 안에서 알맞은 것을 고르시오.

1 Oliver rides a bicycle very (good / well).

2 Don't sleep (late / lately) in the morning.

3 She (often goes / goes often) to the flea market.

4 (Interesting / Interestingly), this train doesn't have wheels.

B 다음 빈칸에 알맞은 부사를 <보기>에서 한 번씩만 골라 쓰시오.

<보기>	hard	high	hardly	highly

1 They didn't try _____, so they couldn't win the contest.

2 Mr. Martin is my role model. I _____ respect him.

3 Kathy raised her hand _____ and asked a question.

4 He spoke so quietly. I could _____ hear his speech.

C 우리말과 같도록 알맞은 빈도부사와 괄호 안의 말을 활용하여 문장을 완성하시오.

1 나의 누나는 거의 음식을 남기지 않는다. (leave)

= My sister _____ food.

2 요즘, 하늘은 보통 맑다. (be)

= These days, the sky _____ clear.

3 Sam은 결코 그의 의견을 바꾸지 않을 것이다. (change)

= Sam _____ his opinion.

D 우리말과 같도록 괄호 안의 말을 알맞게 배열하시오.

1 이 베개는 아주 부드럽게 느껴진다. (soft, this pillow, really, feels)

= _____.

2 그의 삼촌은 밤에 매우 조심스럽게 운전하신다. (drives, carefully, his uncle, very)

= _____ at night.

3 그들은 때때로 해외에서 휴가를 즐긴다. (a vacation, they, enjoy, sometimes)

= _____ abroad.

A 괄호 안에서 알맞은 것을 고르시오.

1 His bag is as (big / bigger) as my bag.

2 Mia spoke (wisely / more wisely) than Noah.

3 Hot chocolate is (much / more) sweeter than green tea.

4 Mr. Doris is the (most nice / nicest) teacher in school.

B 괄호 안의 말을 활용하여 다음 두 문장을 한 문장으로 연결하시오.

1 It was 32°C yesterday. It is 32°C today, too.
→ Today is ＿＿＿＿＿＿＿＿＿＿＿＿ yesterday. (hot)

2 Jake runs 5 kilometers an hour. Karl runs 7 kilometers an hour.
→ Jake runs ＿＿＿＿＿＿＿＿＿＿＿＿ Karl. (slowly)

3 My test score is 90 points. Jenny's test score is 80 points.
→ My test score is ＿＿＿＿＿＿＿＿＿＿＿＿ Jenny's test score. (high)

C 괄호 안의 말을 활용하여 문장을 완성하시오.

1 *The Avengers* was the ＿＿＿＿＿＿＿＿＿＿＿＿ movie of 2012. (good)

2 Pizza is ＿＿＿＿＿＿＿＿＿＿＿＿ than a hamburger to me. (tasty)

3 The Amazon Rainforest is the ＿＿＿＿＿＿＿＿＿＿＿＿ jungle in the world. (dangerous)

4 Nina solved the puzzle ＿＿＿＿＿＿＿＿＿＿＿＿ than Mr. Anderson. (fast)

D 우리말과 같도록 괄호 안의 말을 알맞게 배열하시오.

1 그 음악은 그의 목소리보다 훨씬 더 크다. (than, is, his voice, louder, the music, much)
= ＿＿＿＿＿＿＿＿＿＿＿＿＿＿＿＿＿＿＿＿＿＿ .

2 이 수프는 바닷물만큼 짠 냄새가 난다. (salty, as, seawater, as, smells, this soup)
= ＿＿＿＿＿＿＿＿＿＿＿＿＿＿＿＿＿＿＿＿＿＿ .

3 Susan은 우리의 팀에서 가장 중요한 선수이다. (most, player, the, Susan, important, is)
= ＿＿＿＿＿＿＿＿＿＿＿＿＿＿＿＿＿＿＿＿＿＿ on our team.

Chapter Test +

Chapter 09
형용사/부사와 비교구문
Hackers Grammar Smart Level 1

1 다음 중 형용사와 부사의 형태가 잘못된 것은?

① gentle – gently ② honest – honestly

③ early – early ④ easy – easly

⑤ real – really

2 다음 중 원급, 비교급, 최상급 형태가 잘못된 것은?

① lazy – lazier – laziest

② helpful – helpfuler – helpfulest

③ kind – kinder – kindest

④ little – less – least

⑤ expensive – more expensive – most expensive

[3-5] 다음 빈칸에 들어갈 말로 어색한 것을 고르시오.

3

> French is a _____ language.

① useful ② difficult ③ beautifully

④ popular ⑤ lovely

4

> The cook is boiling _____ tomatoes.

① a lot of ② lots of ③ a few

④ a little ⑤ many

5

> This peach is _____ harder than that.

① even ② much ③ very

④ far ⑤ a lot

서술형

[6-7] 우리말과 같도록 괄호 안의 말을 알맞게 배열하시오.

6

> 아프리카는 유럽보다 훨씬 더 덥다. (than, Africa, much, is, hotter, Europe)

= _____ .

7

> 우리는 밤에 종종 별들을 볼 수 있다. (the stars, often, can, we, see)

= _____ at night.

서술형

[8-10] 우리말과 같도록 괄호 안의 말을 활용하여 문장을 완성하시오.

8

> 농구는 야구보다 더 흥미롭다. (interesting)

= Basketball is _____ baseball.

9

> 오늘은 나의 삶에서 가장 행복한 날이었다. (happy)

= Today was _____ day of my life.

10

> 너의 생일에 특별한 무언가를 하자. (special, something)

= Let's do _____ on your birthday.

Chapter 09 형용사/부사와 비교구문 **51**

11 다음 중 밑줄 친 부분이 어법상 바른 것은?

① Luke can swim really good.
② She always wears a watch.
③ Eric drank a few water after soccer practice.
④ Surprising, he already did his homework.
⑤ You should not come home lately.

12 다음 중 어법상 어색한 것은?

① Lots of customers are waiting in line.
② Lake Baikal is the deepest lake on the earth.
③ The singer sang as softly as a bird.
④ Chloe spoke too loudly in the library.
⑤ Few snow fell in Korea this winter.

13 다음 빈칸에 공통으로 들어갈 알맞은 것은?

• The violinist practiced very _____ .
• The math test was so _____ .

① hard   ② hardly   ③ harder
④ hardest   ⑤ the hardest

14 다음 빈칸에 들어갈 말이 순서대로 짝지어진 것은?

• The woman _____ showed us the way
  to the hospital.
• Mr. Johnson _____ looked at the
  diamond.

① kind – close   ② kind – closely
③ kind – closer   ④ kindly – close
⑤ kindly – closely

[15-16] 다음 우리말을 알맞게 영작한 것을 고르시오.

15

이것은 나의 옷장에서 가장 큰 셔츠이다.

① This is large shirt in my closet.
② This is larger shirt in my closet.
③ This is largest shirt in my closet.
④ This is the most large shirt in my closet.
⑤ This is the largest shirt in my closet.

16

그녀는 나보다 훨씬 더 빠르게 달릴 수 있다.

① She can run much fast than me.
② I can run the fastest than her.
③ She can run more faster than me.
④ She can run much faster than me.
⑤ I can run much faster than her.

서술형 고난도

[17-18] 다음 글을 읽고 글에 나온 표현을 활용하여 문장을 완성하시오.

17

Hangang is 494 kilometers long. Geumgang is 401 kilometers long. Nakdonggang is 504 kilometers long. Nakdonggang is _____ of the three.

18

Bill is 15 years old. Jeremy and Kate are 15 years old, too. Jeremy and Kate are _____ Bill.

[19-20] 다음 중 괄호 안의 말이 들어갈 가장 알맞은 위치를 고르시오.

19

> ① The ② sun ③ rises ④ in ⑤ the east.
> (always)

20

> Did ① you ② notice ③ something ④ about
> Mr. Ford ⑤? (mysterious)

서술형

[21-22] 다음 문장에서 어법상 어색한 부분을 찾아 쓰고 바르게 고쳐 쓰시오.

21

> My idea sounds bad than your idea.

_____ → _____

22

> The balloon was floating highly in the sky.

_____ → _____

23 다음 중 어법상 바른 것은?

① Jejudo is more warm than Seoul.
② Molly is the most funny student in my class.
③ The teacher gave much advice to the students.
④ That lamp is as brighter as this lamp.
⑤ A little books were on the shelf.

서술형

[24-25] 다음 대화에서 어법상 어색한 부분을 찾아 쓰고 바르게 고쳐 쓰시오.

24

> A: Who is your favorite hero?
> B: For me, Batman is the better hero of all
> the heroes.

_____ → _____

25

> A: This suitcase is too heavy. I can't lift it.
> B: Carry my suitcase. It is much light than
> yours.

_____ → _____

고난도

26 다음 중 어법상 바른 것끼리 묶인 것은?

> ⓐ Paul made his father sadly.
> ⓑ Jane and her brother are always calm.
> ⓒ How much pencils do you have?
> ⓓ Is there anything new in the shop?
> ⓔ I spent a little money on the ticket.

① ⓐ, ⓑ, ⓒ　　② ⓐ, ⓑ, ⓓ　　③ ⓐ, ⓒ, ⓔ
④ ⓑ, ⓓ, ⓔ　　⑤ ⓒ, ⓓ, ⓔ

서술형 고난도

27 다음 글의 밑줄 친 ⓐ~ⓔ 중 어법상 어색한 것을 찾아 기호를 쓰고 바르게 고쳐 쓰시오.

> There are ⓐmany strong animals in the
> world. You may think that tigers or lions are
> ⓑthe strongest of all. They look ⓒstrongly,
> but African elephants are much ⓓstronger
> than them. African elephants can carry 7
> tons of water. It is ⓔeven heavier than 130
> people!

_____ → _____

UNIT 01 to부정사의 명사적 용법

Answers p.30

A 괄호 안에서 알맞은 것을 고르시오.

1 My wish is (take / to take) a picture with that singer.

2 It is interesting (to see / see) fireworks.

3 She promised (to lie not / not to lie) again.

4 To learn musical instruments (is / are) difficult.

B 밑줄 친 to부정사의 쓰임을 <보기>에서 골라 그 기호를 쓰시오.

<보기> ⓐ 주어 ⓑ 목적어 ⓒ 보어

1 The snowman starts to melt. [   ]

2 My plan was to buy new clothes. [   ]

3 It is hard to make something creative. [   ]

4 Mr. Benet needs to bring an umbrella. [   ]

C 우리말과 같도록 괄호 안의 말을 알맞게 배열하시오.

1 여기에 머무르는 것은 위험하다. (stay, it, dangerous, to, is)

= _____ here.

2 나는 크리스마스에 무엇을 할지 계획하고 있다. (planning, to, what, I'm, do)

= _____ on Christmas.

3 Josh는 프랑스 식당에서 일하고 싶어 했다. (wanted, work, Josh, to)

= _____ at a French restaurant.

D 우리말과 같도록 괄호 안의 말을 활용하여 문장을 완성하시오.

1 그녀는 만점을 받기를 바란다. (hope, get, a perfect score)

= She _____ .

2 말을 타는 것은 재미있다. (be exciting, ride, a horse)

= It _____ .

3 그는 그의 고향을 떠나기로 결정했다. (decide, leave, his hometown)

= He _____ .

4 Anna의 목표는 가난한 아이들을 돕는 것이다. (be, help, poor children)

= Anna's goal _____ .

to부정사의 형용사적/부사적 용법

Answers p.30

A 밑줄 친 부분이 어법상 맞으면 O를 쓰고, 틀리면 바르게 고쳐 쓰시오.

1 My nephew was happy <u>see</u> the rainbow.　　　→ ＿＿＿＿＿＿＿＿

2 He exercised hard <u>to become</u> healthy.　　　→ ＿＿＿＿＿＿＿＿

3 Sarah goes home early in order <u>do</u> yoga.　　　→ ＿＿＿＿＿＿＿＿

4 They have something important <u>to tell</u> you.　　　→ ＿＿＿＿＿＿＿＿

B 괄호 안의 말을 활용하여 문장을 완성하시오.

1 James went to Germany ＿＿＿＿＿＿＿＿＿＿＿. (study, music)

2 I borrowed ＿＿＿＿＿＿＿＿＿＿. (read, some magazines)

3 David grew up ＿＿＿＿＿＿＿＿＿＿. (be, a soccer player)

4 She was so pleased ＿＿＿＿＿＿＿＿＿＿. (receive, the gift)

C to부정사를 이용하여 다음 두 문장을 한 문장으로 연결하시오.

1 He saved money. He traveled around the world.
　→ He saved money ＿＿＿＿＿＿＿＿＿＿.

2 Lisa saw her brother on TV. She was surprised.
　→ Lisa was surprised ＿＿＿＿＿＿＿＿＿＿.

3 The baseball players were sad. They lost the game.
　→ The baseball players were sad ＿＿＿＿＿＿＿＿＿＿.

4 Dennis called Shirley. He apologized to her.
　→ Dennis called Shirley ＿＿＿＿＿＿＿＿＿＿.

D 우리말과 같도록 괄호 안의 말을 알맞게 배열하시오.

1 Susie는 일등상을 타서 신이 난다. (win, is, first prize, excited, to)
　= Susie ＿＿＿＿＿＿＿＿＿＿.

2 Tony는 함께 일할 누군가가 필요하다. (needs, work with, to, someone)
　= Tony ＿＿＿＿＿＿＿＿＿＿.

3 이 글자들은 읽기에 너무 작다. (read, too, are, to, small)
　= These letters ＿＿＿＿＿＿＿＿＿＿.

UNIT 03　동명사의 쓰임

A 　괄호 안에서 알맞은 것을 고르시오.

1 Drawing animals (is / are) my hobby.

2 She cares about (get / getting) a good grade.

3 Mr. Hooper finished (to fix / fixing) the computer.

B 　<보기>의 동사를 한 번씩만 활용하여 문장을 완성하세요.

<보기>	upload	write	check	grow

1 Ella started _____ a poem yesterday.

2 He enjoys _____ photos on his blog.

3 My dream is _____ tropical plants.

4 _____ your answers twice is a good habit.

C 　괄호 안의 말을 활용하여 대화를 완성하시오.

1 A: Durians smell terrible.
　 B: Yes. But they _____ _____ _____. (be worth, try)

2 A: Gerald should _____ _____ choices too quickly. (avoid, make)
　 B: Right. He never thinks carefully.

3 A: What is your goal this year?
　 B: My goal is _____ _____ _____ late in the mornings. (not, get up)

4 A: _____ _____ on the phone. The movie will start soon. (stop, talk)
　 B: I'm sorry. I didn't know that.

D 　우리말과 같도록 괄호 안의 말을 활용하여 문장을 완성하시오.

1 나는 너의 생일 파티에 나를 초대한 것에 대해 너에게 감사하다. (thank, invite)
　 = _____ me to your birthday party.

2 Bob의 소원은 백만장자가 되는 것이다. (Bob's wish, be, become)
　 = _____ a millionaire.

3 에너지를 절약하는 것은 중요하다. (save energy, be)
　 = _____ important.

Chapter Test ✛

[1-2] 다음 빈칸에 들어갈 알맞은 것을 고르시오.

1

> Do you mind _____ for me?

① wait   ② waits   ③ waited

④ to wait   ⑤ waiting

2

> We decided _____ dinner together.

① eat   ② eats   ③ ate

④ to eat   ⑤ eating

[3-4] 다음 중 밑줄 친 부분의 쓰임이 나머지 넷과 다른 것을 고르시오.

3 ① David likes <u>watching</u> funny movies.

② The bird finished <u>building</u> the nest.

③ She gave up <u>reading</u> the thick book.

④ My plan is <u>taking</u> a shower before 8 P.M.

⑤ You should stop <u>talking</u> loudly in the library.

4 ① They hoped <u>to find</u> some gold.

② I promised <u>to do</u> the laundry.

③ Ms. Brown started <u>to play</u> the flute.

④ She needs <u>to visit</u> the bank in the afternoon.

⑤ It is hard <u>to remember</u> your phone number.

[5-7] 다음 빈칸에 들어갈 말이 순서대로 짝지어진 것을 고르시오.

5

> • I really want _____ you soon.
> • Anna will tell you _____ to meet Bart.

① see – where   ② to see – what

③ to see – where   ④ seeing – what

⑤ seeing – where

6

> • Chris was thinking about _____ Mexican food.
> • You should avoid _____ coffee.

① to have – to drink   ② having – to drink

③ to have – drinking   ④ having – drinking

⑤ have – to drink

7

> • It is not safe _____ a bicycle without a helmet.
> • I can keep _____ in the pool all day.

① ride – swimming   ② ride – to swim

③ to riding – swimming   ④ to ride – to swim

⑤ to ride – swimming

[8-9] 주어진 문장의 밑줄 친 to부정사와 용법이 같은 것을 고르시오.

8

> Larry turned off the light to go to sleep.

① Joyce wants to change her clothes.
② April 5 is the day to plant trees.
③ It is boring to stay home all day.
④ I jog to become healthy.
⑤ There wasn't anything to use in the box.

9

> There is a rope to tie the boat.

① It was helpful to learn about different cultures.
② Charlie's dream is to buy a sports car.
③ We need a lot of time to rest.
④ I went outside to enjoy the sunshine.
⑤ The ants started to move the branch.

서술형

[10-12] 다음 문장에서 어법상 어색한 부분을 찾아 쓰고 바르게 고쳐 쓰시오.

10

> Mom bought some flowers plant in the garden.

_____ → _____

11

> You should finish eat your hamburger.

_____ → _____

12

> This is important to recycle plastics.

_____ → _____

13 다음 중 밑줄 친 부분이 어법상 바른 것은?

① Is there to watch anything interesting on TV?
② They know when to leave for the airport.
③ Rachel goes to the gym to loses weight.
④ Matt wasn't tall enough reach the shelf.
⑤ Eric's hobby is to playing chess.

서술형

[14-17] 우리말과 같도록 괄호 안의 말을 활용하여 문장을 완성하시오.

14

> Smith씨는 그녀를 도와줄 성실한 누군가가 필요했다. (diligent, someone, help)

= Ms. Smith needed _____ her.

15

> 나는 나의 개와 함께 시간을 보내는 것을 좋아한다. (love, spend)

= I _____ time with my dog.

16

> 우리는 다양한 나라들을 여행해서 행복했다. (happy, travel)

= We were _____ to various countries.

17

> Robert는 진정하기에 너무 화가 났다. (angry, calm down)

= Robert is _____.

18 다음 중 어법상 <u>어색한</u> 것은?

① The roller coaster wasn't worth riding.

② Stop bothering your sister.

③ Jake decided what wear with the shoes.

④ I don't feel like drinking tea now.

⑤ This book is too difficult to read.

서술형 고난도

19 주어진 <조건>에 맞게 다음 두 문장을 한 문장으로 연결하시오.

> • He was busy.
> • He was fixing his chair.

> <조건> 1. 동명사를 이용하시오.
>   2. 6단어로 쓰시오.

→ _____ .

서술형

[20-22] 우리말과 같도록 괄호 안의 말을 알맞게 배열하시오.

20

> 불을 가지고 장난하는 것은 위험하다. (play, to, is, dangerous, it)

= _____ with fire.

21

> 나는 그 프로젝트를 위해 무엇을 준비해야 할지 모른다. (what, don't, prepare, I, know, to)

= _____ for the project.

22

> 나는 나의 지갑을 찾아준 것에 대해 그에게 감사해했다. (for, thanked, I, finding, him)

= _____ my wallet.

고난도

23 다음 중 어법상 바른 것끼리 묶인 것은?

> ⓐ Do you mind to bring me a glass of juice?
> ⓑ I forgot how to get to city hall.
> ⓒ Sam hopes to become a pilot.
> ⓓ Talking with the movie directors were interesting.
> ⓔ He opened the window in order to get some fresh air.

① ⓐ, ⓑ, ⓒ   ② ⓐ, ⓑ, ⓓ   ③ ⓐ, ⓓ, ⓔ
④ ⓑ, ⓒ, ⓔ   ⑤ ⓒ, ⓓ, ⓔ

서술형

24 다음 대화에서 어법상 <u>어색한</u> 부분을 찾아 쓰고 바르게 고쳐 쓰시오.

> A: Did you decide where to travel in July?
> B: Not yet. I want going hiking, but Chris hopes to go camping.

_____ → _____

서술형 고난도

25 다음 글의 밑줄 친 ⓐ~ⓔ 중 어법상 <u>어색한</u> 것을 찾아 기호를 쓰고 바르게 고쳐 쓰시오.

> Thomas loved ⓐdancing, so he dreamed of ⓑbecoming a ballerino. However, he grew up ⓒbe a teacher. But he didn't give up ⓓto dance and practiced ⓔdancing as a hobby.

(1) _____ → _____

(2) _____ → _____

UNIT 01 장소를 나타내는 전치사

Answers p.32

A 다음 빈칸에 at, on, in 중 알맞은 것을 쓰시오.

1 Her grandparents live _____ Hawaii now.

2 There is a big frame _____ the wall.

3 Kevin and I had fun _____ the party.

B 다음 빈칸에 알맞은 전치사를 <보기>에서 한 번씩만 골라 쓰시오.

<보기>   on   in   over   in front of

1 Angela threw a ball _____ my head.

2 The bookstore is _____ the second floor.

3 He will play a computer game _____ his room.

4 The K-pop band sang _____ many people.

C 우리말과 같도록 괄호 안의 말을 활용하여 문장을 완성하시오.

1 그들은 그 강 맞은편에 집을 지었다. (a house, the river)
= They built _____.

2 코알라들은 주머니 안에 그들의 새끼들을 데리고 다닌다. (their babies, a pouch)
= Koalas carry _____.

3 나는 의자 아래에서 그 열쇠를 찾았다. (the key, the chair)
= I found _____.

D 우리말과 같도록 괄호 안의 말을 알맞게 배열하시오.

1 Tom은 학교에서 농구를 했다. (at, basketball, school, played)
= Tom _____.

2 산 근처에서 화재가 있었다. (a fire, was, the mountain, near)
= There _____.

3 그 약국은 병원 옆에 있다. (to, next, the hospital, is)
= The pharmacy _____.

시간을 나타내는 전치사

Answers p.32

A 다음 빈칸에 at, on, in 중 알맞은 것을 쓰시오.

1 The car accident happened _____ noon.

2 There were many wars _____ the 20th century.

3 It snowed a lot _____ Christmas Eve.

4 Shadows become longer _____ the evening.

B 다음 빈칸에 알맞은 전치사를 괄호 안에서 골라 쓰시오.

1 (for / during)

① Some students made noise _____ class.

② Michael can hold his breath _____ seven minutes.

2 (by / until)

① Please return the books _____ Thursday.

② The guests will stay at this hotel _____ June.

C 우리말과 같도록 괄호 안의 말을 활용하여 문장을 완성하시오.

1 '기생충'은 2020년에 많은 상을 탔다. (2020)

= *Parasite* won many awards _____.

2 그 소포는 4시쯤에 도착할 것이다. (4 o'clock)

= The package will arrive _____.

3 Heather는 저녁 식사 후에 아무것도 먹지 않을 것이다. (dinner)

= Heather won't eat anything _____.

D 우리말과 같도록 괄호 안의 말을 알맞게 배열하시오.

1 개들은 보통 하루에 14시간 동안 잔다. (14 hours, for, sleep)

= Dogs usually _____ a day.

2 나는 3월 1일에 국기를 걸 것이다. (hang, March 1, on, the national flag)

= I will _____.

3 그 경비원은 일출 전에 문을 연다. (the door, opens, sunrise, before)

= The guard _____.

A 괄호 안에서 알맞은 것을 고르시오.

1 I gave some advice (from / to) Richard last night.

2 Grace always writes memos (for / with) her smartphone.

3 He is sitting (between / to) Emily and Mary.

B 다음 빈칸에 알맞은 전치사를 <보기>에서 한 번씩만 골라 쓰시오.

<보기>	about	by	for	with

1 Aaron donated a little money _____ poor people.

2 We went to the small island _____ boat.

3 The man shook hands _____ the winners.

4 Ms. Howard heard the news _____ her town.

C 우리말과 같도록 괄호 안의 말을 활용하여 문장을 완성하시오.

1 그는 관광객들에게 아름다운 풍경을 보여줬다. (the tourists)
= He showed beautiful scenery _____.

2 나는 종이를 이용해서 이 큰 비행기를 만들었다. (paper)
= I made this big airplane _____.

3 Nicole은 대기 오염에 대한 기사를 읽었다. (air pollution)
= Nicole read an article _____.

D 우리말과 같도록 괄호 안의 말을 알맞게 배열하시오.

1 그들은 도서관에서 오전 9시부터 오후 3시까지 공부했다. (to, from, 3 P.M., studied, 9 A.M.)
= They _____ at the library.

2 Reed씨는 팩스로 그 서류를 보냈다. (sent, by, the document, fax)
= Mr. Reed _____.

3 그녀는 웅변 대회를 위해 열심히 연습했다. (hard, the speech contest, for, practiced)
= She _____.

[1-4] 다음 빈칸에 들어갈 말이 순서대로 짝지어진 것을 고르시오.

1

| • Claire was standing _____ the corner of the street. |
| • You have to boil it _____ 30 minutes. |

① in – for   ② in – during   ③ at – for

④ at – during   ⑤ to – for

2

| • My uncle is sleeping _____ the sofa. |
| • There is a slice of ham _____ the bread and cheese. |

① at – from   ② on – from   ③ in – over

④ in – between   ⑤ on – between

3

| • We talked _____ our plans. |
| • Dave and I met again _____ LA. |

① about – in   ② about – on   ③ with – in

④ to – at   ⑤ to – on

4

| • You can travel to Jejudo _____ ship. |
| • The store is open _____ midnight. |

① by – for   ② with – for   ③ by – in

④ with – until   ⑤ by – until

5 다음 빈칸에 들어갈 말이 나머지 넷과 <u>다른</u> 것은?

① The Korean war ended _____ 1953.

② We saw fireworks _____ New Year's eve.

③ There are some grapes _____ the plastic bag.

④ You should be quiet _____ this room.

⑤ The new semester will begin _____ fall.

서술형

[6-8] 우리말과 같도록 빈칸에 알맞은 전치사를 쓰시오.

6

| Joe는 그의 어머니를 위해 부엌을 청소했다. |

= Joe cleaned the kitchen _____ his mother.

7

| 4시쯤에 나에게 전화해. 그때 Jenny와 함께 너의 집에 갈게. |

= Call me _____ 4 o'clock. I will go to your house _____ Jenny then.

8

| 그녀는 일요일에 백화점 앞에서 그녀의 친구를 기다리고 있었다. |

= She was waiting for her friend _____ the department store _____ Sunday.

[9-10] 다음 빈칸에 공통으로 들어갈 알맞은 것을 고르시오.

9

> • Why were you _____ the police station?
> • The concert will start _____ noon.

① by　　　　② on　　　　③ at
④ to　　　　⑤ for

10

> • I will make the poster _____ next week.
> • Dorothy ordered pizza _____ phone.

① in　　　　② for　　　　③ at
④ by　　　　⑤ from

서술형

[11-13] 우리말과 같도록 괄호 안의 말을 알맞게 배열하시오.

11

> 그들은 그들의 집에서 강까지 조깅했다. (to, their house, jogged, the river, from)

= They _____.

12

> 나무와 식탁 사이에 의자가 있다. (and, a chair, is, the tree, the table, between)

= There _____.

13

> 내가 네 옆에 앉아도 되니? (you, to, sit, next)

= May I _____?

서술형

[14-15] 다음 문장에서 어법상 어색한 부분을 찾아 쓰고 바르게 고쳐 쓰시오.

14

> Rebecca received lots of presents in her birthday.

_____ → _____

15

> Don't move your body during three minutes.

_____ → _____

[16-17] 다음 중 밑줄 친 부분이 어법상 어색한 것을 고르시오.

16 ① There is a rainbow <u>over</u> the mountain.
　　② Kelly is sitting <u>behind</u> Jason.
　　③ The bookstore is <u>next to</u> the tall building.
　　④ My dad parked his truck <u>near</u> the beach.
　　⑤ I exercise at the gym <u>across</u> the bakery.

17 ① Mr. Williams went to church <u>on</u> Sunday.
　　② You should wash your hands <u>before</u> breakfast.
　　③ Ryan broke his leg <u>during</u> the soccer game.
　　④ Thomas Edison invented the light bulb <u>at</u> 1879.
　　⑤ The airmail will arrive <u>around</u> May 13.

서술형 **고난도**

[18-19] 다음 글의 빈칸에 알맞은 전치사를 쓰시오.

18

Christina and I live in the same apartment building. I live on the first floor, and she lives on the second floor. My apartment is _____ hers.

19

My family will have dinner at 7. The movie *Little Women* will start at 8:30. We are going to watch the movie _____ dinner.

20 다음 중 어법상 바른 것을 <u>모두</u> 고르시오.

① Ms. Jenkins ran from her home to the hospital.
② Matt cut the paper about a pair of scissors.
③ Lenny lent his blanket to me.
④ They built a playground by children.
⑤ We didn't hear the rumor for her.

고난도

21 다음 중 어법상 바른 것끼리 묶인 것은?

ⓐ We wake up early in the morning.
ⓑ I must make the decision by 2 P.M.
ⓒ Let's cross the bridge under the river.
ⓓ They practiced the dance for a week.
ⓔ Ruby lived at China last year.

① ⓐ, ⓑ, ⓒ   ② ⓐ, ⓑ, ⓓ   ③ ⓐ, ⓒ, ⓔ
④ ⓑ, ⓒ, ⓓ   ⑤ ⓒ, ⓓ, ⓔ

서술형

[22-24] 다음은 Barney's 사과 축제에 대한 안내문이다. 빈칸에 알맞은 전치사를 쓰시오.

Barney's Apple Festival
Date: November 10-12
Place: Barney Park

Library	Bus Stop ●	Fire Station
★ Barney Park		Molly's Supermarket

22

Barney's Apple Festival is _____ November 10 _____ November 12.

23

Barney Park is _____ _____ the library.

24

You can go to the festival _____ bus. The bus stop is _____ the library _____ the fire station.

서술형

25 다음 대화에서 어법상 <u>어색한</u> 부분을 찾아 쓰고 바르게 고쳐 쓰시오.

A: What time do you go to school?
B: I leave at 7:30. I go to school about Hanna every day.

_____ → _____

UNIT 01 and, but, or, so

Answers p.33

A 괄호 안에서 가장 알맞은 것을 고르시오.

1 I didn't turn on the heater, (but / so) I caught a cold.

2 His younger brother can read (so / and) write.

3 Lily found him (kind / kindly) and gentle.

4 He made a mistake, (or / but) he didn't apologize to us.

B 다음 빈칸에 가장 알맞은 말을 <보기>에서 한 번씩만 골라 쓰시오.

<보기>	and went jogging	but Adam likes it
	a fork or chopsticks	so I gave it some water

1 Science is difficult, _____.

2 The cat looked thirsty, _____.

3 You can eat with _____.

4 They woke up early _____.

C 우리말과 같도록 괄호 안의 말을 활용하여 빈칸에 쓰시오.

1 Judy는 최선을 다했지만, 시험에 떨어졌다. (fail the exam)

= Judy tried her best, _____ _____ _____ _____ _____.

2 Watson씨는 의사니, 아니면 간호사니? (a doctor, a nurse)

= Is Ms. Watson _____ _____ _____ _____ _____ ?

3 사슴은 긴 다리를 가지고 있어서 빠르게 달릴 수 있다. (can run fast)

= A deer has long legs, _____ _____ _____ _____ _____.

D 우리말과 같도록 괄호 안의 말을 알맞게 배열하시오.

1 나는 허리를 다쳐서 잘 걸을 수 없었다. (couldn't, I, so, well, walk)

= I hurt my waist, _____.

2 Kyle은 영어와 스페인어 둘 다 말할 수 있다. (and, English, both, Spanish)

= Kyle can speak _____.

3 그들은 금요일이나 토요일 둘 중 하루에 스키를 타러 갈 것이다. (Friday, either, Saturday, or)

= They will go skiing on _____.

UNIT 02 when, while, before, after

A 괄호 안에서 가장 알맞은 것을 고르시오.

1 (When / Before) the dog saw me, it barked at me.

2 Tracy will be tired after she (will finish / finishes) the training.

3 They ordered hamburgers (after / before) the restaurant closed.

4 I met my teacher (after / while) I was going to school.

B 다음은 Emily의 어제 일정표이다. 빈칸에 when, before, after 중 알맞은 것을 쓰시오.

8 A.M.	12 P.M.	2 P.M.	3 P.M.
have breakfast	meet friends at the shopping center	ride a bicycle	take a shower

1 _____ Emily met her friends, she had breakfast.

2 Emily was at the shopping center _____ she met her friends.

3 Emily took a shower _____ she rode a bicycle.

C 괄호 안의 접속사를 활용하여 다음 두 문장을 한 문장으로 연결하시오.

1 I was sleeping. Tyler sent me a text message. (while)

→ _____, Tyler sent me a text message.

2 He drinks juice. He uses paper straws. (when)

→ He uses paper straws _____.

3 She fell down the stairs. She went to the hospital. (after)

→ _____, she went to the hospital.

D 우리말과 같도록 괄호 안의 말을 활용하여 문장을 완성하시오.

1 그는 3개월 동안 운동한 후에 건강해졌다. (exercise)

= He became healthy _____ for three months.

2 Sarah는 그녀의 아빠가 도착하시기 전에 집을 청소해야 한다. (her dad, arrive)

= Sarah has to clean the house _____.

3 Harris씨는 대학생이었을 때 프랑스에서 공부했다. (be, a university student)

= Mr. Harris studied in France _____.

UNIT 03   because, if, that

Answers p.33

A   괄호 안에서 가장 알맞은 것을 고르시오.

1 It is surprising (that / if) he didn't give up.

2 She ate an early dinner (if / because) she was hungry.

3 We will cancel the picnic if he (is / will be) busy tomorrow.

4 I believe (because / that) I can change my habit.

5 (That / If) the drama is fun, let's watch the next episode as well.

B   자연스러운 문장이 되도록 알맞게 연결하시오.

1 Jason hopes   ·   · ⓐ because the water is very deep.

2 Ronnie got a good grade   ·   · ⓑ because he studied hard.

3 You should not swim here   ·   · ⓒ that he will become a lawyer.

4 He will take a picture with the singer ·   · ⓓ if he meets her.

C   우리말과 같도록 괄호 안의 말을 활용하여 문장을 완성하시오.

1 나는 사람들이 이 노래를 좋아할 것이라고 생각한다. (people, love, this song)
   = I think _____ .

2 그의 어머니가 그녀의 지갑을 잃어버리셨기 때문에, 그는 새것을 사드렸다. (his mother, lose, her wallet)
   = _____ , he bought a new one.

3 만약 내일 날씨가 좋다면, 그들은 부산에 갈 것이다. (the weather, be, nice)
   = _____ tomorrow, they will go to Busan.

D   우리말과 같도록 괄호 안의 말을 알맞게 배열하시오.

1 만약 네가 두통이 있다면 잠시 휴식을 취해라. (a headache, you, if, have)
   = Take a break _____ .

2 그는 Amy가 그를 싫어한다는 것을 알고 있다. (Amy, him, hates, that)
   = He knows _____ .

3 나는 그것의 디자인이 마음에 들었기 때문에 이 가방을 샀다. (I, its design, because, liked)
   = _____ , I bought this bag.

4 만약 그가 말썽을 부리지 않는다면, 나는 그에게 유튜브 영상들을 보여줄 것이다. (doesn't, he, make, if, trouble)
   = _____ , I will show him YouTube videos.

Chapter Test +

Answers p.33

[1-3] 다음 빈칸에 들어갈 말이 순서대로 짝지어진 것을 고르시오.

1

> • Megan ate eggs _____ bacon for breakfast.
> • Do you want to go camping _____ go fishing?

① and – but   ② and – or
③ or – but   ④ but – or
⑤ but – and

2

> • _____ I was young, I lived with my grandmother.
> • Allen took a nap _____ he was too sleepy.

① If – because   ② If – so
③ That – because   ④ When – so
⑤ When – because

3

> • That bicycle looks nice, _____ I don't want it.
> • _____ you take a taxi, you won't be late.

① or – If   ② but – If
③ but – That   ④ and – That
⑤ and – While

4 다음 중 어법상 어색한 것은?

① My grandfather was 25 years old when the war ended.
② Annie sang loudly and beautifully.
③ The cucumbers were fresh, so I bought some.
④ The fact is that Bill isn't good at chess.
⑤ You can borrow my money if you will return it tomorrow.

[5-6] 다음 빈칸에 들어갈 말이 나머지 넷과 다른 것을 고르시오.

5
① Sam wore a warm jacket, _____ he wasn't cold.
② I love mint chocolate, _____ my sister hates it.
③ The question was difficult, _____ Kendra couldn't answer it.
④ It will rain soon, _____ bring an umbrella.
⑤ The vase was empty, _____ I put some flowers in it.

6
① It is amazing _____ parrots can speak.
② Jerry believes _____ the news is true.
③ Let's stop by the store _____ we have some time.
④ My opinion is _____ we shouldn't pollute the earth.
⑤ I hope _____ the concert will be exciting.

[7-8] 다음 대화의 빈칸에 가장 알맞은 접속사를 <보기>에서 골라 쓰시오.

<보기> so   after   because

7

A: When should I put the noodles in the pot?
B: Put them in _____ the water boils.

8

A: Why was Danny absent today?
B: He had a cold, _____ he stayed home.

9 다음 중 어법상 바른 것을 <u>모두</u> 고르시오.

① You can buy either the black shirt and the white shirt.
② The soda was cool because it was in the refrigerator.
③ Lock the door before you leave.
④ Our teacher will get angry if we will be late again.
⑤ It is sad that Mr. Evans lost his job.

10 다음 밑줄 친 부분을 바르게 고치지 <u>못한</u> 것은?

① You should dry your hair <u>while</u> you wash it.
   (→ before)
② We didn't have any food, <u>or</u> we went to the supermarket. (→ so)
③ The tour guide was friendly and <u>interestingly</u>.
   (→ interesting)
④ Josh wanted chicken, <u>and</u> his sister ordered pizza. (→ but)
⑤ Dad will be sad if you <u>will forget</u> his birthday.
   (→ forget)

[11-12] 다음 빈칸에 공통으로 들어갈 가장 알맞은 접속사를 고르시오.

11

• I saw some fish _____ I was swimming in the ocean.
• Brandon listened to the radio _____ he cleaned his room.

① if   ② while   ③ because
④ but   ⑤ that

12

• The good news is _____ we can get a special discount.
• Jake said _____ the children were crossing the road.

① if   ② because   ③ so
④ that   ⑤ before

13 주어진 <조건>에 맞게 다음 두 문장을 한 문장으로 연결하시오.

• He will ride a bike.
• He will wear a helmet.

<조건>   1. 접속사 when을 문장 맨 앞에 쓰시오.
        2. 문장 부호에 주의하시오.

= _____ .

서술형

[14-17] 우리말과 같도록 괄호 안의 말을 활용하여 문장을 완성하시오.

14

> 그녀는 비행기를 타기 전에 나에게 전화할 것이다.
> (get on the plane)

= She will call me _____ .

15

> 나는 열심히 공부했지만, 나의 시험 점수는 나빴다.
> (my test score, be bad)

= I studied hard, _____ .

16

> 만약 내일 눈이 온다면, 우리는 놀이공원에 갈 수 없다.
> (it, snow)

= _____ tomorrow, we can't go to the amusement park.

17

> 나는 돌고래가 한 쪽 눈을 뜬 채로 잔다는 것을 들었다.
> (hear)

= _____ dolphins sleep with one eye open.

18 다음 우리말을 알맞게 영작한 것은?

> 나는 종종 걷기나 달리기 둘 중 하나로 운동한다.

① I often exercise by either walking but running.
② I often exercise by both walking or running.
③ I often exercise by either walking or running.
④ I often exercise by either walking and running.
⑤ I often exercise by both walking and running.

고난도

19 다음 중 밑줄 친 부분이 어법상 바른 것끼리 묶인 것은?

> ⓐ The problem is <u>if</u> the storm is coming.
> ⓑ You must wait for ten minutes <u>after</u> you turn on the oven.
> ⓒ <u>When</u> you borrow a book, you should show your student ID card.
> ⓓ Jenny has to walk home <u>that</u> she misses the bus.
> ⓔ The train will leave soon, <u>so</u> I need to hurry.

① ⓐ, ⓑ, ⓓ   ② ⓐ, ⓑ, ⓔ   ③ ⓐ, ⓒ, ⓓ
④ ⓑ, ⓒ, ⓔ   ⑤ ⓒ, ⓓ, ⓔ

서술형 **고난도**

20 다음 대화에서 문맥상 어색한 부분을 찾아 쓰고 바르게 고쳐 쓰시오.

> *A*: Are you ready for the speech contest?
> *B*: No. I was very nervous, so I couldn't sleep well last night. Now, I'm tired or worried.
> *A*: I think that you will win. Don't worry!

_____ → _____

서술형 **고난도**

21 다음 글의 밑줄 친 ⓐ~ⓔ 중 어법상 어색한 것을 찾아 기호를 쓰고 바르게 고쳐 쓰시오.

> Yesterday, I went to the park for a walk ⓐ<u>before</u> it got dark. ⓑ<u>While</u> I was walking, I saw a girl next to a tree. She looked like my friend Betty, ⓒ<u>so</u> I wanted to say hi. ⓓ<u>When</u> I came near her, I knew ⓔ<u>if</u> she wasn't my friend.

_____ → _____

MEMO

HACKERS
GRAMMAR
SMART

1

LEVEL 1

WORKBOOK

해커스 그래머 스마트가 특별한 이유!

[Completely master English grammar]

1 누구나 쉽게 이해할 수 있는 **간결한 문법 설명**

2 실생활에서 그대로 사용할 수 있는 **유용한 표현과 예문**

3 '개념 확인' → '연습 문제' → '작문 연습' → '단원 마무리'로 이어지는 **4단계 문제풀이**

[Effectively prepare for middle school English exams]

1 학교 시험 기출경향을 완벽 반영한 문제로 **서술형 포함 내신 완벽 대비**

2 풍부한 문제의 Workbook과 다양한 부가 학습 자료로 **학습효과 Up Up!**